THE ACCIDENTAL GANGSTER

From Insurance Salesman to Hollywood Fixer

ORI SPADO

all my Love & Respect

Ori Spado

Visit the author's website site at:
www.theaccidentalgangster.com

How do you mark time? Some people count the gray hairs on their heads or the lines in their faces. For others, it is the number of children and grandchildren. To many others, it is the joy of growing old with a special loved one, or the accumulation of material wealth or objects they collect, such as art.

My marker of time is the people I have kept alive. Thanks to the grace of God and some behind the scenes moving and shaking by me, they are still above ground, walking, talking and breathing. Who am I? My name is Orlando "Ori" Spado, and they call me "The Mob Boss of Hollywood."

TABLE OF CONTENTS

I dedicate this book to my children,
Gina, Ori and Anthony.
Because of your love and support,
you made this possible.
I am proud of each of you,
and I love you.

ACKNOWLEDGMENTS

Being in prison was a wakeup call for me in many respects. It taught me that the life I had chosen was the wrong one, and the people I had thought were my friends weren't there for me when the chips were down. This experience has made me even more appreciative of those who did stick by me.

I would like to begin by thanking my children, Orlando, Anthony and Gina, the most important people in my life. I learned a very important thing from my children upon my release—gratitude. After I came out of prison, you showed me the right way, and then everything changed for the better. I am more grateful than you will ever know, and I love you.

I would like to thank those from across the media spectrum who have given me the opportunity to share my story, and I would like to send my love and respect to my friends on social media. Thank you for your loyalty, reading my words, and listening to me daily.

Lastly, to all the young men and women who have either read my book or listened to me and turned their lives around. I'll always be here for you.

Ori Spado
Beverly Hills, California

PROLOGUE

In my forty plus years in Hollywood, I have met a lot of people, many of whom I've forgotten and many more who are long gone. Imagine a boy from a small town in upstate New York watching television as a youngster and then meeting those actors and actresses in person as an adult. I knew Frank Sinatra, Dean Martin, Jerry Lewis, Don Rickles, Red Skelton, Connie Stevens, and many more. I ended up doing favors for some of them and sometimes spoke to other people on their behalf.

I sometimes ask myself why I can't just be a normal person and live a normal life. But at the end of the day, I know I would not trade my life. I am what I was born to be.

* * *

When I read that I was being referred to as the Mob Boss of Hollywood, I wondered, who are these people we call "they" who say a lot of things they really know nothing about? I've been searching for them, but I have not found them. If you find them, please let me know.

For nearly forty years I was a personal friend and associate of the famed underboss of the Colombo crime family, John "Sonny" Franzese. Sometimes I was referred to by Sonny and other New York mobsters as "our man in Hollywood." When I entered the federal prison in Lompoc, California, in 2010, a guard announced over the loudspeaker that I was "The Mob Boss of Hollywood."

The truth is I wasn't a *made* member of any crime family.

I had the opportunity to become *made*, but not the desire. I didn't want anyone to be able to "claim" me, as they say in *the life*. Besides Sonny, I was close to other well-known gangsters, including Jimmy Caci, who was from Buffalo but relocated to California, and England's Joey Pyle. I also met and was friends with Meyer Lansky, Carlo Marcello, and several others throughout the country.

I associated with lesser-known criminals as well who were con men, thieves, robbers and killers. Please understand that the criminal-types I associated with weren't all bad, though. Many of them had good hearts and were true friends—I was proud to know them.

I made money—lots of it—through various scams, burglaries and armed robberies. I even earned by working as sort of a debt collector, recouping money for people who, for one reason or another, couldn't go through normal channels to get their money back.

I also had a talent as a negotiator and intervened to resolve disputes between competitors before any blood was shed. And using that talent here in Hollywood, I built a reputation as a person who handled problems for celebrities, studio executives and others, quickly, fairly, and most importantly, confidentially. I did things such as getting celebrities into drug rehabs, resolving money issues between stars and their agents or studios, and straightening out overzealous fans or stalkers. Not a single client's name ever appeared in the newspapers or on TV. And I will take their stories to my grave. My motto was to keep it simple, and that all problems can be resolved when each party is treated with honor and respect.

Yet, in spite of my lengthy criminal career, I can honestly say that as a kid growing up in a small city in upstate New

York, I never had any thoughts of becoming a gangster. I believe I came to the attention of the FBI because of my personal relationship with Sonny, not because of my own activities. I spent a lot of time with him, and he was one of their priority targets, putting me in their sights as well. As far as I'm concerned, my initial reputation as an organized crime figure was primarily an accident. In the end, though, how or why they came across me didn't matter. Once you're on the FBI's radar, and if they want to get you badly enough, it's just a matter of time.

In the pages ahead, I'll tell you all about my life. There will be a lot of crime stuff and some legitimate deals that took place in locations such as New York, Los Angeles, Beverly Hills, San Francisco, Las Vegas, Florida and even in England. I think you'll find them interesting, and in some cases, humorous. I sincerely hope you enjoy the read.

There is something else that I want to convey through this book. I'm addressing the following paragraphs to those who are considering following my path to what they think will be a life of easy money, nice clothes, fast cars and even faster women. I'm going to say it here, and you'll see it again as you make your way through the book, DON'T!

That's right, I said don't do it. Sure, for a while you'd probably experience all that stuff—maybe even enjoy the lifestyle for many years, as I did. The trouble is, someday it will all come to an end, and you'll be held accountable by somebody. It might be the law, or it could be at the hands of another criminal. If it's the law, you'll spend a lot of time—maybe the rest of your life—locked up like a fucking animal with a bunch of guys who, in some cases, *are* animals, and your money, clothes, cars and women will be long gone.

As bad as that is, at least you'll still be breathing, if not really living. If a rival takes you out, though, your body will be found in the trunk of an abandoned car making music as the gases escape out of it, or you might simply disappear.

It isn't all about you, either. You probably have people who love you, parents, grandparents, a wife or children. Think of how what you do will affect them. I can tell you, it really hit home for me when the FBI raided my place in Beverly Hills on June 4, 2008. This can happen to you. I was pretty cocky when they put me in cuffs and shackles and took me out. I even boasted that I'd be back at home before dinner—that was 62 months later.

And then I saw they'd cuffed my son Anthony, too. They removed the cuffs later, but the look on his face as the FBI car I was in pulled away from the curb made me want to die. The next five years were hell for me and my children. I was in federal prison on RICO (Racketeer Influenced and Corrupt Organizations Act) charges, and their father was a convicted felon. I would have given anything to spare them the pain, but it was too late.

I was first incarcerated in the Metropolitan Detention Center (MDC) in Brooklyn, and later in the Bureau of Prisons facility in Lompoc. While locked up, I learned the hard reality that many of the people you thought were your friends aren't. There are informants and snitches that will turn on you in a heartbeat in return for a benefit such as reduced charges or a lighter sentence. This became very clear when Chris and I listened to the recordings at our discovery, and I heard all these people discussing how I lived and what I drove and how everyone knew me in Beverly Hills. Some of them will wear a wire on you, as several did on me—Johnny Franzese, Guy Fatato and Nick Besnik. Others are willing to provide a proffer or sworn testimony on the witness stand to say whatever the government needs in order to convict you, and the truth doesn't really matter.

I can say that I did my time and never ratted on anybody. Today, when I look at myself in the mirror, I don't have to be ashamed.

I'll close with this advice. You may be smart, but you're not smarter than the FBI, and you don't have the resources they have. If they want to get you, they will. They have a long memory, too. An FBI agent told me in 1997 that they were going to take me down. It took eleven years, but that same agent was there the day they arrested me. You can't outspend them, you can't outsmart them, and you can't outlast them.

Regarding prosecution, I believe the RICO statutes are the most powerful weapon in the government's arsenal, and I think they are illegal. RICO charges are almost impossible to beat at trial, and if you reject a plea bargain and lose in court, you'll get hammered at sentencing. It's my opinion that mandatory minimum sentences are too harsh in some cases and should be abolished. My feelings aside, that's the system you'll have to deal with, so think long and hard before you start down a road where there may be no turning back.

Ori Spado
Beverly Hills, California

PART

Taking The Wrong Path

Sentencing Day

Metropolitan Detention Center
Brooklyn, New York
September 7, 2010

The door to my cell was opened early—about 4:00 a.m. A guard, dressed in his neatly pressed uniform, stepped inside to wake me. I was already awake, though, and had been for hours, wondering if I'd made a mistake. Later in the morning I'd be in a federal courtroom, where a judge would pass sentence on me—a term from 97 to 110 months in a federal prison. I agreed to that amount of time in a plea deal, but now, I was having second thoughts. If I'd gone to trial, could I have beaten the charges? Could I have walked out of court a totally free man? As I sat on my bunk staring at the cell wall,

I began to think maybe I could have.

Knock it off, I told myself. *What's done is done.*

They charged me under RICO, the federal government's most effective weapon against organized crime. If you fought and lost, which most defendants did, they threw the fucking book at you. That point was driven home to me by my friend and fellow inmate, Anthony "Tico" Antico, while we were in the courthouse bullpen area the day before I accepted the government's offer.

"Spado, take the plea and you'll see daylight soon. You've already been in here thirty months. After you get the good time credit you got coming, you'll be out quick. If you go to trial, they'll shut your lights out."

As I recalled that conversation, my confidence returned—I'd made the right move.

After showering and dressing in my olive-colored jumpsuit, I grabbed my cup, went down to the first floor of my tier, and fixed myself a coffee (I bought instant coffee from the commissary and just had to add hot water). After that, I was taken downstairs, where I swapped my jumpsuit for my court apparel, a blue shirt and tan pants. And then the shackles were put on. The first time I'd been shackled after being arrested it really bothered me, and so did the first time I was put in a cell and the door clanged shut. If I didn't already know I'd lost my freedom, I sure as hell knew it then. But that was years ago. By now, I'd been transported back and forth to court so many times, and heard that cell door so often, the effect was gone.

Securely chained, the marshals put me and the other inmates going to court on the prison bus for the trip to the federal courthouse in Brooklyn. Once there, we were placed in large holding cells under the courthouse called bullpens, where our shackles were removed. Now, it was just a matter of waiting to be called upstairs to face Judge Bryan Cogan.

My mind wandered back to my plea and what would happen in the courtroom. Doubts lingered. I kept asking myself, will the prosecutors try any of their last-minute tricks to get me more time? What kind of guy is Judge Cogan? Will he give me a fair shake, or is he in bed with the government? Am I really going to see daylight soon, as Tico said? Or will there be an unexpected snag that puts everything down the toilet? Those questions and more spun around my head as I waited, but the answers were yet to come.

With my stress level rising, I knew I needed to stop thinking about all the "what ifs." To keep my mind occupied I asked myself a question: *How in the fuck did I end up here?*

Go figure.

Growing Up

When I think about my childhood, I have no recollection of wanting to be a gangster when I grew up. In fact, I think my early years were pretty normal. I was born on December 17, 1944, in Rome, New York, a small city situated in the center of New York State. At that time, the population was around 44,000. It had a large Air Force base, Griffiss, which employed a lot of civilians from the area. It was also known as The Copper City because of its many factories that made copper wire and other copper products. My memory is that it was a safe city to live in, with very little serious crime.

There were complications with my delivery that kept my mother and me in the hospital until Christmas Day. I was told later that when I was brought home, our house was packed. My father, aunts and uncles, grandparents, older brother and sister, and some of my father's close friends were all there. They put me under the Christmas tree to take a picture, and when they did, the tree fell over. I understand it was quite a day and everyone enjoyed themselves.

We lived in a duplex home at 215 West Liberty Street. It was a working-class neighborhood with mostly older homes, but the residents were all terrific. On one corner was a Texaco gas station, and I can remember them selling gas for twenty-three cents a gallon. Two more gas stations and a small store that sold candy, cigarettes, soda, and stuff like that were on the other corners. I used to go there and buy Kit Kat caramels when they were two for a penny.

St Mary's School, the rectory, the convent, and the church were right across the street from our house. Before I started school myself, I used to look out my front window and watch the school buses pull up and let the kids out. I would watch them until they were all inside. The way they dressed, and the fact they could afford to attend St. Mary's, told me those kids came from money. They thought they were something special, and their mannerism and attitude showed that they thought they were above everyone else. However, I did not think that way. They were marks for me, and I would take their lunch money from them, and they did nothing but give it to me.

My parents, my brother, sister and I lived on one side of the house. Later, the family grew when my mother had a set of twins, and after that, my baby sister. On the other side were my mother's mother and father,

an aunt, and a few uncles who had just returned from
World War II.

My father, Joseph, worked at Revere Copper and
Brass. It was a hard job physically, and I remember he
had the biggest and strongest arms I'd ever seen. He
earned $35 a week, which had to pay all the bills and put
food on the table. I don't know how he did it, but he did.

My mother, Livia, had to figure ways to feed
everyone—a total of thirteen—on the limited food she
was able to buy and what my grandparents and uncles
provided. She was the best cook in the world, though,
and could put food together like nobody else. The table
was always full of food. To supplement what came from
the store, we had a garden where we planted tomatoes
and peppers. My mother canned them, and we ate them
year-round. So even with a crowded dinner table, she
was able to do a lot with a little and we ate well. Her
pasta and meatballs were the best, Gnocchi that was my
favorite. They were heavy, and I would eat a dish and
run around the house and come back and eat more pasta.

Fagioli was another of my favorites we had often, as
it was not expensive to make. And her chocolate chip
cookies, which she had to hide on us (but I always found
them), they were out of this world.

At dinner, I always sat next to my father on one side,
and my grandfather always sat next to him on the other.
My mother and one of my uncles sat at the end of the
table, close to the coal-burning stove.

We had three bedrooms on our side. Mom and dad
had their own bedroom, and my older brother had his.
In the other bedroom there were two beds. My other
brother and I slept in one, and my two younger sisters

in the other. There was one more little room, not much bigger than a closet, where my older sister slept in a small bed. Our one bathroom was very small and had a bathtub, but no shower.

The pants I wore were hand-me-downs from my uncle to my older brother, and then on to me. By the time I got them, the crotch had usually been sewn so many times that when I started school, I kept my legs together so the other kids wouldn't notice.

But despite the lack of money, I had a great childhood, one that I wouldn't trade for anything in the world. I had love and I had a family, and that was all I needed.

* * *

At the age of five it was my turn to go to school, and believe me, I did not want to go. My kindergarten was at Barringer, a public school located on the next block from my house. My mother brought me the first day, and when we got to the school, there were these huge double doors with windows, and the principal was standing behind them. While looking through the window at the principal, I put a hand on each of the handles and my feet on the doors so they couldn't open them. It was quite a scene, but my mother and the principal finally convinced me to cooperate, and I went inside. My teacher was Miss Garrison, and she was beautiful. At five years old, I fell in love with a woman for the first time.

I adapted to school fairly quickly, except for one thing. It seemed I was always getting into fights while defending kids that couldn't defend themselves. That meant I usually tangled with bullies, and it was a trend that lasted through my school years and beyond. I'm not sure why, but in most cases, after we fought, we'd become friends. All through my life, tough guys ended up becoming part of my circle of friends. In school, that made me a go-to guy for other kids who were having problems with my buddies and wanted me to intervene.

When I was around ten, it was common for kids my age to go to the movie theater on Sunday afternoons. Admission was only a quarter for a double feature, and if you were lucky enough to have a girl, you could do a little making out at the same time.

One Sunday I went to the rest room and one of my friends was in there smoking a cigarette—it was a Lucky Strike. I'd never smoked before, and when he offered me a drag, I took it. I coughed my brains out, but for some odd reason I liked it and got hooked on cigarettes. I think that was when I started doing my first bad kid stuff. I began stealing quarters from around the house to support my habit. I'd take the quarter to one of the corner gas stations and buy a pack of smokes from their machine. The cigarettes would come out along with two cents change.

So, before I was a teen, I knew I liked girls and smoking. I'd picked up another habit, too. I liked to read. I loved biographies of famous people. Reading their stories took me all around the country and the world. And they planted the seed in my mind: *Do I want Rome, New York, to be the extent of my world?*

After a couple more years passed, I became convinced I didn't want to live my life in such a small town. My father even told me one time that Rome was not for me. Even back then, factories in Rome and other parts of the northeast were moving their operations to warmer climates with cheaper labor, or shutting down outright. My father and I saw it, but to my mother, Rome was still the best place in the world.

I made friends with a kid named Joe from New York City (the City), whose family had moved to Rome for a short time and then moved to Greenport, Long Island. When I was twelve, he invited me to come visit him for a week during the summer. My parents gave me permission to go, and Joe's father drove up in his Hudson to get me. I'll never forget that drive and how exciting it was. I'd never been so far from Rome before, and when we passed through the City, I was in awe. The size of the buildings, and all the stores and crowded streets were amazing to me. I'd dreamed about scenes like this while reading books, and now it was real.

When we got to Greenport, I was amazed again. If you walked out the front door of Joe's house, beaches and the Atlantic Ocean were only a block away. I'd never seen the ocean before, and I loved it. I knew right then that when I was old enough, I was going to move to a big city near an ocean. I wanted to be able to enjoy the sandy beaches and the beautiful girls that hung out there.

My week with Joe ended up becoming a whole month. We went to the beach every day and got clams; then we went to Joe's house and ate them. And we met girls—lots of them. I went for the older girls (14 or 15) because I figured they were more experienced. In the evenings we went to the girls' houses and just had fun. Then there was the night we were at Joe's friend's house, and the older sister and I were on the front porch smoking and talking. She kept asking me if I trusted her. Every time

I answered "yes," she pulled my zipper down a little more. Like I said, it was a great month.

I really didn't want to go home, but I had no choice. My mother and father visited the City every summer to see a Broadway play—that was their vacation. So, when they were going to be there next, Joe's dad took me in to meet with them, and we rode the train back to Rome together.

My time in Greenport and the day I spent in the City with my parents will live in my memory forever. They were not only fun, they cemented my future move out of Rome.

* * *

In 1955, my father bought his first car. It was a new Buick Special, blue with a white top and whitewall tires. It was a beautiful car. I'll never forget walking into my parents' bedroom after they made the deal. They were counting their war bonds to take to the dealership, Bill Smythe Buick, to pay the twenty-three hundred dollars for the car. Smythe later moved to San Jose, California, and became one of the largest car dealers in the country.

My parents were savers and lived on a tight budget, something I never learned how to do. It wasn't that they didn't try to tell me—they did. But I never listened. And I'm still unable to save money. It seems to burn a hole in my pocket, as they say. I have made more money than most others, and I made it quickly, but I spent it quicker.

At thirteen, I got my first job delivering newspapers and collecting the forty cents per week from customers. At the same age, I started hanging around a small neighborhood store run by an ex-Marine named Tom Arcuri. He taught me the importance of always being alert—to know what is going on around you, to know when something or someone might be a threat, or when something just isn't right. I always remember to observe everything around me—I'm always looking behind every tree, every car and building. His words have served me well. I believe they helped to save my life more than once. You'd be surprised where people can hide. It especially came in handy when the LAPD (Los Angeles Police Department) organized guys to follow me. I remember another thing that Tom taught me well. When walking down a street, it is very easy for someone to wait for you behind a tree, and as you walk past the tree, the person can then move around and come up behind you. To this day I still watch for this.

I also played poker with the older kids that hung around Tom's store. I won sometimes, but not often. And when I lost, I would go and collect money from my newspaper customers, particularly the ones who paid five weeks in advance and were a little lax in their record keeping. Sometimes, if I was on a run of bad luck, I'd collect from them every week by convincing them it had been five weeks since their last payment. That was how I covered my poker losses. Eventually, I came to the conclusion that kind of gambling was for suckers.

I learned how to play pool and found it was much better to bet on my own skill and not have to rely on luck to any great degree. I hung out at the local pool rooms and hustled a few dollars every week to supplement my income. At sixteen, I gave up my newspaper job, but given I'd used the money I collected to pay for my gambling, my account fell behind, and I hadn't made it up. They wouldn't let me quit until I was paid in full. So, I borrowed the money from my father and then turned the route over to my younger brother. Unlike me, he took after our parents and saved the money he earned. I wouldn't doubt but that he's still got some of it stashed somewhere.

My next job was at a grocery store stocking shelves and bagging groceries. Even though I didn't handle money very well, from the time I was a kid, I always worked and hustled to make a buck. That's why, years later when an informant testified that I'd never worked a day in my life, I took offense.

* * *

I was thrown out of school so many times I lost count. Mainly I got bounced for skipping classes and going to the pool room, or sometimes for fighting or mouthing off to a teacher. I admit I wasn't a good student, but I didn't get in trouble for anything criminal. One time when I got suspended my mother had to meet with the principal, Mr. Page, before they'd let me back in. He showed her my attendance record and all the written excuses I turned in saying I'd been out due to illness. She said she didn't remember writing so many of them. She was right, she didn't. I had a friend of mine write them, so they'd all be in the same handwriting. Even when I was really sick and my mother wrote an excuse, I threw hers out and turned in the one my friend wrote.

Another time, I got tossed for drinking and having booze at the Valentine Day dance. I wasn't the only one with booze that night. You have to remember that the legal drinking age in New York was eighteen in those days. It wasn't hard to find somebody who was eighteen, or at least could pass for eighteen, to us buy booze.

The guy that bought it that night was named Andy, and I'll never forget him. When word got out to the chaperones that there was alcohol in the building, the adults went nuts. They started searching lockers and rounding up the usual suspects. When they pressured Andy, he ratted us out—all seventeen of us. Having a parent meet with the principal wasn't enough this time. We had to see the Superintendent of Schools. That meant my mother was on the hook once again. She didn't want to upset my father, so she was always the one who went to these meetings with me and never told my father I'd been suspended. We had to pretend everything was normal, so she made me a lunch every day and I got up every morning as though I were going to school. It wasn't much of a vacation.

Anyway, my mother and I went to the superintendent's office where he read me the riot act. My mother and I were sitting in front of his desk next to each other. I just listened and nodded my head. When we left, my mother took me downtown and bought me a milk shake and some other things. I still don't know why she did it, but it was sure nice.

All of us who were thrown out of school over that deal were really pissed at Andy. We planned to give him a good beating, but his father was a high-ranking cop, so everyone else chickened out. I was determined to get some payback, though. One day when we were riding the bus to the Steven's Field Park, I pulled the emergency cord.

When the bus stopped, I threw Andy out and beat him up. I did not like rats then, and I hate them now.

In spite of my lack of enthusiasm for school, my grades were surprisingly good, and I passed from grade-to-grade. I credit that in large part to my love of reading.

* * *

When I went to the pool room one evening in February of 1963, three of my buddies were there. They told me they had joined the Army and would be leaving for basic training in a couple of days. Two of the guys were eighteen, but the other was only seventeen, and his parents had to sign for him. He asked me if I'd take a ride to the recruiter's office in Utica (about fifteen miles from Rome) with him the next day to turn his papers in. When we got there, the recruiter asked me if I was interested in enlisting, too.

At first, I passed on his offer because I planned to join the Marines sometime in the future. Yet, as I sat there looking out the window at the snow and the flag fluttering in the cold wind, I thought about it some more. I told the recruiter, "If I can go with my friends to a place that's warm for training, and you can guarantee me I'll receive computer training, I'll sign up."

"You've got it," he said. "You'll have to go to Albany tomorrow morning for your physical and some other tests. I'll pick you up at 8:00 a.m., just bring your toothbrush and not over forty dollars in cash."

That was it. I was eighteen and able to make my own decisions, so I signed the papers and left.

When we got to Rome, I got off at my school, Rome

Free Academy, I went inside and told my homeroom teacher I was quitting school. She was shocked, and she sent me to see the principal, Mr. Page. I told him the same thing. He tried to talk me out of it, of course, but I told him my mind was made up. I emptied-out my locker and headed home to break the news to my mother. In all my years in school, it was probably the first time I ever took books home with me.

When I told my mother, she got so upset she started yelling at me. I'd never seen her like that before and didn't know what to say, so I kept my mouth shut. My aunt Helen was also there, and my mother yelled and threw my books at me. Then my father got home from work, and she told him what was going on. He was upset, but not like her. He calmed her down a little, and then he talked to me for a while. Next, he called my American History teacher, Mr. Kan. He was a former pilot in WWII and a great guy. His was my favorite class. He convinced my father that perhaps going into the Army would be best for me. My father gave his approval, and he gave my mother forty dollars to give to me.

The next morning when I was ready to leave, I found my mother was sitting in a chair near the window just staring blankly straight ahead—no emotion at all with the forty dollars in her hand. She wouldn't speak to me, and I actually had to pull the money out of her hand. I was hurt, as she did not even kiss me or hug me.

The recruiter pulled up in front and I left. A few minutes later, Rome faded from sight.

Go figure.

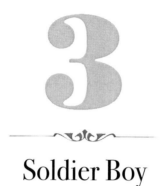

Soldier Boy

During the drive to Albany and the start of my new life, lyrics from the Shirelles' 1962 hit *Soldier Boy*, played in my head. The other guys didn't have to report for another few days, so it was only the recruiter and me. In kind of an odd twist, I was the last of the four of us to sign up, but the first to go, so I was a week ahead of them all the way through training.

I figured when I got to Albany, I'd take the required test and physical and then be put up in a hotel for the night, but that did not happen. Instead, right after the exams, all the recruits were taken to the airport and put on a plane for Fort Jackson, South Carolina. This was my first time on an airplane, and at first it was a little scary, but before long I was enjoying the flight.

When we got to the base, we were taken to the mess

hall to fill out a bunch of forms. One of them asked, "Are you interested in Airborne?" Well, I was, so I checked the box for Airborne Training. Another form asked where you wanted to be assigned and allowed three choices. I picked Germany because I'd heard the girls there were great, followed by Italy and France. If none of them were available, I chose Hawaii as an alternative. As soon as I was allowed a phone call, I got hold of my buddies in Rome and told them about the paperwork and my choices. They said they'd put in for the same things I had.

After completing the paperwork, we were taken to our barracks. It was around 4:00 a.m., and they wouldn't put the lights on. We had to find a bunk in the dark, and it seemed like we'd just got to bed when they woke some of us up to go to the mess hall for duty as Kitchen Police—commonly known as KP. The cook showed us some big boxes containing old fatigues and told us to put them on over our civilian clothes and get to work. My job was scrubbing garbage cans.

When we got to work that afternoon, the sergeant told a few of us to report to the company headquarters for an additional assignment. We were sent to the medical clinic and had to scrub it down using toothbrushes. We finished around 2:00 a.m., and after that, it was back to the barracks for a few hours of sleep, then more KP. This time I was a food server, which was an improvement over cleaning garbage cans. Things improved even more when my buddies checked in later that week. A couple of days after that we were all transferred to Fort Gordon, Georgia, for Airborne Training.

It was rigorous training, harder than what other recruits went through. One of the things we were required to do was to run everywhere we went. It didn't matter if it was to the mess hall, dental clinic or barracks—if you moved, you ran. We were up at 4:00 a.m. running around the base while everybody else was still sleeping. And if you didn't run, you were taken out of Airborne and transferred to a regular unit. I made it through and came out in the best physical shape of my life. They instilled a spirit in me, and sometimes I still sing some of the songs we sang while we ran.

I was in quite a few fights at Fort Gordon, usually helping guys I'd become friends with who were doing battle with other recruits. But one time it was strictly personal. I woke up and had to go to the bathroom. As I was at the urinal, another trainee, who was an acting sergeant, called me a "mother fucker." That was a term I wasn't familiar with, and I considered it an insult directed at my mother. By the time I finished my business at the urinal, the guy had gone into the shower room. He was alone. I walked in and asked him what he'd said to me. When he repeated it, I grabbed him and banged his head against the water pipes. When his blood started spurting all over the place, I let him go. He never reported me, nor did he ever say another word to me. I know different now, but at the time, I thought I was defending my mother's honor.

There were a lot of blacks in my unit, and I was friends with many of them. One kid, whose last name was Walker, was one of the nicest guys you would ever want to meet. In the seventh week of training, we got our first pass to go into town. It was just for four hours, but since we were only getting $74.50 a month, we probably couldn't have afforded much more time off the base anyway.

A few of us decided to go into Augusta to have dinner, and Walker went with us. We found a restaurant, and when we started to walk in, we were told that Walker couldn't sit with us because blacks could not be in the same side of the restaurant as whites. The black and white sides of the room were separated by ropes and there was even a separate entrance for blacks.

The white guys found a table next to the dividing rope, and Walker sat at a table on the other side of the rope—the black side. We were close enough that we were pretty much together, but still in compliance with the house rules. Fifty-two years later, I still remember that incident, but can't comprehend it. Walker was in a U.S. Army uniform, ready to fight for our country and go wherever he was asked to take up arms. Yet, he couldn't use the same door or sit at the same table as the rest of us.

Finally, basic training was over, and I got my two-week pass to go home before I went to Fort Sill, Oklahoma, for advanced training. It was really nice seeing my whole family and all my relatives and friends. It was prom week when I got to Rome, but I did not go because I didn't feel I belonged. My mother was speaking to me again, but she was depressed over the recent death of her father. Of course, I had already known from my phone call that he passed away, but it hit my Mother very hard. My mom always had a difficult time with this sort of thing, especially with her parents. As for me, although death hurts, it is something I accept, as it will happen to all of us. It was great seeing my brothers and sisters, and there were parties with all my aunts, uncles and cousins. They all treated me with respect for serving my country honorably.

Things got more upbeat the following week when the guys I enlisted with got into town on leave before they, too, went to Fort Sill. We spent some time at the pool room, of course, met some girls from Utica, and had some good times. All too soon, my leave was over.

* * *

Because I was the first to leave for Fort Sill, it was my duty to report to the other guys what they could expect. Traveling in uniform, I flew into Lawton, Oklahoma, on a Sunday and spent the night in a hotel before checking into the base on Monday. I'll never forget Oscar, the bellhop who showed me to my room. After dropping my bags, he said, "If you need anything else, anything at all, just pick up that phone and ask for Oscar."

I changed into my civvies (civilian clothes) and went out to do the town. I found out fast that Oklahoma was a "dry state," and if you want to do any drinking, you have to be a member of a bottle club. Disappointed, I went back to my hotel room. As I sat there, I thought about what Oscar had said and grabbed the phone.

"What can I do for you?" Oscar asked.

"I need a girl."

"Sure, Mr. Spado. It won't be long."

A half-hour later there was a knock at my door, and standing there was this beautiful girl dressed like a school teacher. I invited her to come in, and we talked. She asked me what I wanted—did I want to go around the world or half way around the world? It made sense to me to go around the world. She gave me a price, which

I imagine included something for Oscar. I paid her and then the clothes came off. I got my money's worth.

I sent a letter to the guys back in Rome and told them about the hotel, Oscar and the girl. When they showed up the following week, they did the same thing with the same girl. They couldn't thank me enough for doing such a good job of recon.

* * *

At Fort Sill we received artillery training, which I found very boring, and I never got the computer training I'd been promised by the recruiter. After the eight-week course, everyone got orders for their next assignment. Not me, though. My orders hadn't been cut for some reason. A week later my three buddies finished up, and they were all assigned to Germany, which was our first choice on the form we filled out when we started training. It was over a month before a sergeant told me I was going to a place where it was hot and with a jungle. The U. S. involvement in Vietnam was just starting, and some guys were being sent there. I figured I was going to be one of them, and then the sergeant smiled and said, "This is your lucky day, Spado. You're going to Hawaii." The following Sunday a bunch of us were put on a train to Oakland, California, and it turned out to be the best train ride ever. There were a lot of girls traveling on that train and I had a ball. At Oakland, I was put on a troop transport and we sailed to Hawaii.

It took seven days to cross the Pacific Ocean. The morning we approached the Island of Oahu, we were all on the top deck. It was overcast and clouds hung low over the island, but by the time we docked at Pearl Harbor, the sun was out, and it was the most spectacular day I had ever seen. Imagine coming from upstate New York, where the sun only shines four or five months a year, to a place where it shines every day.

In awe, I stood by the railing and thought, *Here I am, eighteen-years-old and doing something my parents were never able to do. They would have loved to be in Hawaii, and I'm the one that got to go. How fortunate am I?*

After getting off the ship we were bused to Schofield Barracks, which would be my home for the next thirty-two months. Schofield Barracks is where the Japanese planes came through Kolekole Pass on their way to bomb Pearl Harbor on December 7, 1941.

I was placed in C (Charlie) Company of the 13th Field Artillery Regiment, 25th Infantry Division, and assigned to quarters on the third floor of the barracks. I was issued a mattress, and I had to carry it and my duffle bag up the three flights of stairs. As I did, I was thankful for all that running I'd done in basic training. I'm sure it made getting up those steps with that load a lot easier.

That day, I started using the first name of "Ori" instead of Orlando. I had thought about it while crossing the Pacific, thinking it would limit people asking a lot of questions about the origin of the name Orlando, or thinking I was from Orlando, Florida. I also dropped telling people that I was from Rome, New York, to simply New York. Everybody has heard of New York, but how many people knew Rome was an upstate city? Starting that day, whenever I was asked my name and where I was from, my answer was, "Ori from New York."

I was initially put into what was called the Survey Section. In the event of a war, we'd be among the first to go to the frontlines to plot targets for the artillery. I guess you could call it a high-risk occupation.

A few months later I was transferred to B (Bravo) Company. I had issues with the First Sergeant, primarily because of my hair. I kept it regulation length, but he liked it shorter. When I refused to get scalped, it really pissed him off. Other than that, it was okay duty.

And then I was made an offer I probably shouldn't have refused, but I did. One day, I was ordered to report to the lieutenant's office. He had the results of the tests I'd taken when I was first enlisted and in basic training. "The Army can select five hundred qualified enlisted men to attend West Point," he said. "Your test scores are sufficient for you to be considered. If you become a candidate, you'll first be sent to Fort Belvoir, Virginia, for six-months of training. If you complete that training successfully, you'll be assigned to the Academy."

Ori Spado in West Point? Me, an officer and a gentleman? I couldn't believe it, but that's what the lieutenant said was possible. I was flattered and excited. However, as I heard more, my enthusiasm cooled. If I made it into the Academy and graduated in four years, I'd have to commit to another five years on active duty. That idea didn't appeal to me.

Instead of giving an answer right then, I said I wanted to take some leave and go home to talk things over with my father, which I did. He agreed it was a great opportunity, and so did Mr. Kan, my American History teacher in high school. The final decision was mine, though, and the thought of staying in the Army until I was at least twenty-nine was a deal- breaker for me. I thought of that as being an old man, and that my life would all be behind me. I returned to Schofield and turned down the offer to apply for the program. You're probably thinking it and I've said it to myself a hundred times over the years—I was an idiot.

Go figure.

4

A Lesson Learned

One day a friend told me about a guy he knew in the outfit that was getting freebies at a brothel in Wahiawa. The deal was that he was more or less a pimp, referring customers to the brothel. When they showed up and paid, he was rewarded with free time with the girls.

I gave it some thought and came up with a plan. I told my friend we should make a move on the brothel and take a part of their action. I was not interested in freebies with the girls. After all, this was in Hawaii and there was no shortage of women. We agreed to give it a try, and I would be the lead on it.

I got the phone number of the brothel, called and talked with the boss. I told him I knew his place was doing a lot of business, and I had a plan that would bring in even more customers and money for everyone.

I asked if we could meet so I could explain it to him. He wouldn't commit to seeing me at first, but after a few calls he agreed to meet the following Saturday.

I borrowed a car and drove to the brothel to pick him up. When I arrived, he had some of the girls on the porch try to lure me inside, but I wouldn't go. He finally came out and got into the car. We drove around for a while, making small talk, and then I told him my plan. He told me he knew a quiet place we could talk. He directed me to a sugar cane field and told me where to pull off the road. I drove quite a way into the field, stopped when he told me to, and shut the car off. We got out, and when we walked to the front of the car, he pulled a handgun from under his shirt and put it to my head.

"You have no idea who you're fucking with," he said. "I work for other people, and they operate several houses. You try to shake them down and you're dead in a heartbeat."

I don't know if he would have shot me, or if the gun was just for show. Either way, I was scared but tried not to show it. I talked calmly and tried to make him think I was part of something bigger—that I had people behind me. I told him if he killed me, within two days my friends would find him and cut him into pieces. I concluded with, "There's no need for either of us to die."

There wasn't really anyone else behind me, of course, but my words must have been convincing because he stared at me for a few seconds and then put the gun away. "Let's go get something to eat," he said.

We got back in the car, and I drove to a restaurant. While we were there, he called his boss. He told him about this crazy guy he met, and how I might be able to help them boost their business. The boss said he wanted to meet me at his home in Diamond Head the following week. What could have gone very badly for me ended up on a positive note.

This was the first time a gun had been put to my head (it wouldn't be the last) and it taught me something that came in handy over the years. People who use guns to scare you usually do not have the guts to actually do what they threaten. They are not the people you need to worry about.

When I got back to Schofield, my two partners were waiting for me. I told them the whole story and their faces turned white as chalk. They were so scared I thought they were going to piss their pants. They both backed out of the deal on the spot, and there was no way I was going to go any further by myself. When I didn't go to the meeting in Diamond Head, the brothel guy started calling the barracks in the evenings looking for me. After a few of those calls. I told the CQ (Charge of Quarters) to say I'd been transferred back to the mainland, and that ended it. Nobody got hurt, and it was a great lesson.

* * *

I hooked up with another guy from my unit, who was on the same floor. We both loved the beach and the girls, so we decided to rent an apartment in Waikiki for a hundred-fifty dollars a month. Getting an apartment was cool, as we now had our own place to bring the girls we met. It was located just two blocks from Waikiki Beach. Keep in mind that my monthly military pay didn't even cover my half of the rent. Obviously, I had to hustle to earn my spending money. Whether it was playing pool or some other scam, I kept busy and was good at what I did. Although I was keeping my head above water, a pay raise from the Army would have been welcome and taken some of the financial pressure off me.

In the Army, it is supposed to be automatic to be promoted to Private First Class (PFC) after eight months. Unfortunately for me, my First Sergeant in Bravo Company held up my promotion because we were feuding over the length of my hair. So, I stayed at the same pay grade for my first eighteen months.

Then, one day a lieutenant came around looking for guys who could type. I'd taken a typing class—I think I failed it, but they did not know that—and I volunteered. I was sent to headquarters to type after-action reports for some majors who had just returned from Vietnam. While there, I got to know some of the officers and a sergeant assigned to Personnel. The sergeant liked me and said his unit needed a clerk. He asked if I was interested. Yeah, I wanted to get the hell away from First Sergeant "Hairdo" in Bravo.

The first thing I was told to do was type up my transfer papers, which I then took to Hairdo. He was pissed, but there was nothing he could do about it. When I got back to headquarters, I was given my second order—type up the paperwork promoting me to PFC. I finally got my pay raise. My new office was also where newly arrived officers checked in. One of my duties was to help them with their housing assignments and furniture needs. That put me in a position of influence over who lived where and the quality of their furnishings. The officers who wanted better locations and top-of-the-line furniture showed their appreciation for my services in the form of cash commissions, which were instrumental to supporting my lifestyle. After all, living in Waikiki and going out almost every night to Dukes in the International Market Place (where I had front row seats at The Don Ho show) or the Hilton Hawaiian wasn't cheap.

The expense of hanging out at those places and other piano bars on the beach was worth it, though, and I was having the time of my life. Girls from California vacationed there regularly and every week I had a different one. In fact, I learned the flight schedules and knew when the current batch of girls would be leaving and a new group coming in.

Although I had good luck meeting girls in the bars, Waikiki Beach was where I had my best success. After all, I was young, in shape and had all my hair. The only trouble was trying to keep track of what line I fed the broads I met. For example, one Sunday I was catching some sun when I saw this very beautiful girl in a bikini reclining on a towel. On a scale of one to ten, she was a twelve. She was with an older woman who turned out to be her mother, and when her mother went for a walk, I went over to her and introduced myself. I have no idea why, but I gave her a real load of bullshit, that I owned several restaurants in New York. I didn't tell her I was in the Army and made out like I came from money, myself. The lies flowed freely. We hit it off, and I made a date with her for dinner the next night.

However, when Monday came, I knew I couldn't keep the date because I couldn't remember exactly what I'd told her about myself. Rather than get into an embarrassing situation, I just stood her up.

Later that day, I was walking near the International Market Place when I saw my dream girl and her mother across the street. I wanted to hide, and when I turned to walk away, I bumped into a guy in a Navy uniform. It was a friend of mine from Rome named Dennis "Denny" Griffin. What a surprise that was, running into somebody I'd gone to school with while walking on a street in Waikiki. Not only had he been a classmate, he was one of the kids that, thanks to that rat Andy, got thrown out of school with me for having booze at a dance. Denny was stationed at Barber's Point Naval Air Station on the island. We had a drink and shot the breeze for a while, and then went our separate ways.

A few months later, I had to go to Tripler Army Hospital for a regular physical. When I finished my business, I wanted to kill time and roamed through the halls looking around. I looked into one of the patient rooms and saw somebody in the bed with his head all bandaged up like a mummy. I didn't know who it was, but he called my name. It was Denny. He'd been in a bad car accident and was pretty banged up. His right hand was in a cast, and he couldn't write. He asked me to call his mother for him and tell her what had happened, which I did. I did not see or hear from Denny after that for fifty years.

And then one day I was on the phone talking with my cousin back in Rome. While we were talking, an old friend of mine from high school stopped at my cousin's house. He got on the line with me, and we did a little catching up on our lives since school. I told him I was writing a book and he asked me if I remembered Denny Griffin. He said Denny was now an author and he might be able to help me with my book. After the call I went to the computer and looked Denny up. Not only was he an author, but one who writes organized crime stuff.

Had I not lied to the girl on Waikiki Beach and been trying to avoid her, I would not have been at the International Market Place that night and bumped into Denny.

* * *

Then it happened. I fell in love with a girl who was vacationing from Beverly Hills. She was beautiful and came from a very wealthy family. Things got serious fast, and in almost no time we decided to get married when I got out of the Army. My discharge date was rapidly approaching. I lined up a job with Pan American Airlines in Los Angeles and was excited about the future, but I needed to earn more money before then, so I'd have a couple of bucks in my pocket when I became a civilian again.

The days of skipping school and hanging out at the pool rooms in Rome paid off for me in a big way. I became known as one of the better players on the island, and I teamed up with another kid from New York who shot a good stick. Some weekends we would go to A'ala Park in Honolulu and hustle nine-ball games. We earned pretty good, and I made enough money to buy my first suit, one that I'd wear when I got to California.

Finally, my enlistment was just about up, and I got my discharge orders. I was twenty-one and had a girl and a job waiting for me. The Army made an attempt to get me to stay. Colonel James Taylor called me into his office and made the pitch. Vietnam was heating up and the Division was going to be deployed. He asked me to extend my tour of duty. This was a major decision for me. I was a gung-ho soldier and believed in defending my country, but I wasn't sure we should be involved in Vietnam. I had wedding plans and was anxious to start the next phase of my life. After plenty of thought, I looked at him, respectfully declined and stated my reasons. He was disappointed but accepted my decision.

So, around February 20, 1966, I boarded another troop ship for Oakland, where I was discharged on February 26. I left with only my few civilian clothes and a dress uniform, and I flew to Los Angeles. I got a room at the Hilton, my girlfriend came, and we made love. It was beautiful, but then the roof caved.

She started to cry and told me her father would disown her if she married me because she was Jewish, and I wasn't. She said she still wanted to marry me, but I knew it wouldn't work out without her father's blessing, especially if he withdrew his financial support. I told her to go back home because there was no way I could provide her with the lifestyle she was accustomed to.

That night, I called a girl from West Covina I'd met in Hawaii. She came to my hotel where we had dinner, and then went to my room. She fell asleep after our lovemaking, but I was too keyed up to sleep. I thought about my father and made a decision. I got up, put my uniform on, and packed my things. When she woke up and asked what I was doing, I said I was going back to New York. I kissed her goodbye and headed for the airport.

Go figure.

5

Back to Rome

I flew from Los Angeles to New York City, then took the train upstate to Rome. I was allowed to wear my uniform to return home after discharge, so I was able to get the airline ticket for a hundred bucks. When I got off the train in Rome, I spotted Richard, my younger brother, on the platform looking for me. He looked right at me, didn't recognize me, and went downstairs into the station where our father was waiting. Thinking I wasn't on the train, they headed outside to the car. I ran out and caught them before they pulled away.

I said to Richard, "Why didn't you wait for me?"

Looking sheepish, he said, "I saw the uniform, but thought you were a janitor and didn't look at your face."

We had a good laugh over that.

When we got to the house, it was packed. My mother,

siblings, aunts, uncles, cousins and some friends were all there to welcome me back. After things settled down, my father and I found a quiet spot where we sat down and talked. The first thing he asked was, "Son, why did you come back to Rome? There is nothing here for you; you should have stayed in California where you have opportunity."

"Dad, I was worried about you and your health. I wanted to see you. But I know you're right, I can't stay here forever. I'll tell you what, can you get me a job at Revere (Copper and Brass) for a few months so I can save some money and then go back to California?"

He smiled and nodded. "You're making sense, son. I'll set it up for you."

My father was one of the original founders of the union at Revere and was highly respected. When I was young, sometimes he had to attend meetings in cities like Chicago and even in Canada. He was gaining clout when something happened regarding the union that caused a problem between him and one of his friends. Dad left the union and took a position in management for a while, then went back into the work force as a laborer.

Dad was very proud of his Italian heritage. When I was a kid, one time at a local high school football game, a rooter for the other team who was sitting behind us called the referee a WOP (without papers). Dad slugged him once, and the guy ended up in the hospital. Another time, someone called Dad a Guinea, and he knocked him out with one punch. too. He instilled that same pride in me.

Dad was also a die-hard Democrat. One of the first things he did after I got out of the Army was to make sure I registered and voted Democrat. I had no idea who the hell

I was voting for or why, but I always did what he asked of me. Things changed, though, and I've been registered different for the last thirty years. My poor father is probably turning over in his grave because of that. Sorry Dad, but I believe what I believe, just as you did.

Anyway, he had to get me in for the required screening tests at Revere right away. I passed the aptitude test but failed the mechanical. However, my father pulled some strings and I was hired. I took the graveyard shift and really hated it. My days were upside down, and I was totally disoriented. At night I'd wake up thinking it was morning and time for breakfast, and then I'd smell my mother cooking pasta and realize it was actually dinner time. How weird is that?

When I got my first paycheck from Revere, I gave my parents a few dollars. They never asked for money. It was just something we did in those days. Nothing like today, where kids think their parents owe them and are responsible for them their whole lives.

I took the rest of the money and went to a strip club owned by a friend of mine. I picked up a good-looking waitress, went to a hotel, and spent the weekend with her. By Monday I was broke. After three weeks of work and three checks, I hadn't saved a dime. I gave my foreman the required two-week notice that I was leaving. He knew I hated the job and the hours, so he said, "Spado, don't worry. I know your father, and if you want, you can leave tonight, and I'll take care of the records for you." I took him up on his offer and never went back after that night.

My next job, which I also got through my father's influence, was at Kelsey Hayes in Utica, where they made parts for airplanes. I wasn't in love with the job, but at least it was a day shift and I lasted there a few months.

* * *

One Sunday evening I was in the Club Martin in Rome, when I noticed three girls come in. I went over to them and struck up a conversation. The three were cousins from Frankfort, a village about twenty-five miles away. The one I was attracted to was Antoinette, who had recently graduated from college in Buffalo and was working as a school teacher. She went by Toni. I learned later my feeling toward her weren't mutual at first—she thought I was arrogant and conceited. But she did agree to go out with me, and we began to date. She lived with her parents and introduced me to them. Before long, I was going to their house most Friday nights for dinner and to play four-handed pinochle.

Toni's parents were great people. Her father, Frank, was a farmer and owned most of the property on both sides of Route 5S in Frankfort. He grew strawberries in the summer and had greenhouses. He loved the farm and was an avid hunter. He seemed to know about everyone in town, and they all loved him. Susie, Toni's mother, was a housewife and a sweetheart, too. It was a very loving family and I was fortunate to have been accepted by them.

It wasn't long before I came to the conclusion that Toni was the girl I wanted to spend my life with, and my marriage proposal followed.

* * *

I had my stag party at the Grand Hotel in Rome. It was well-attended by my male relatives and friends. It was a great party, but what I cherish the most is the time I spent with my father after the party ended. We went to the San Carlo restaurant on James Street, which was owned by my friend Frank Russo and his brothers. We got to talk at length, just him and me. I believe our conversation had a major impact on my future life.

My father was the best man I've ever known. He was quiet and strong. Yet, in spite of that strength, he cried easily. To him, family was the most important thing. I know he loved my mother deeply, even though I think her stubborn ways sometimes interfered with his plans and dreams. That evening at the San Carlo I learned a great deal about my father and his father, who died before I was born.

I knew my mother's parents hadn't approved of her marrying my father, but never knew why until then. My father told me it was because his father and brother had been part of the Mafia. In Calabria (Italy) the organization is known as the Ndrangheta. In Rome (New York), Frank Russo's dad was a boss, as was Calabria native Frank Costello in New York City. Frank Russo later confirmed this was true. He said his father hosted meetings of the top Ndrangheta guys at their house every Saturday, and that he was the one who opened the cellar door to admit the guests. My grandfather was always in attendance. That's why my maternal grandparents initially opposed their daughter marrying my father. Over the years their attitude changed, and they came to love my dad.

He told me how during the depression he and his father would travel from city-to-city and state-to-state looking for work. Because they thought being Italian hurt their chances of getting hired, they used American-sounding names. Still, the jobs they landed were short-term, often for only a day.

On one trip they ended up in Riverside, California, and my father was able to get a job at the Revere plant there. My mother refused to move to California, though, so it was back to Rome.

Dad also made frequent trips to Pittsfield, Massachusetts, which was the Ndrangheta stronghold in the east. He developed contacts and was given various tasks that involved illegal activity, including managing a whorehouse for the boys. He didn't take those jobs because he wanted to, but because he had a family and had to put food on the table. However, to my mother, Rome was the best place on earth. She wouldn't even consider moving where the opportunities were, so Dad always ended up going back there.

My father told me that his uncle Gregory died in prison while serving time for killing a man at my grandfather's home on Palmer Avenue in Rome. The guy wanted a job at Revere and got mad at my grandfather when he arranged for someone else to get it. The guy, who was a *made* man, went to my grandfather's home in a rage. He put hands on my grandmother, and Gregory shot him for that. Gregory supposedly hung himself in prison, but I don't necessarily believe that is what happened. Knowing what I know now, I think he was murdered as punishment for killing a *made* man without permission. That's a violation of Mafia rules that carries a death sentence.

Whenever I think of the time I spent with my father that night, I believe the information he shared with me influenced many of the decisions I made later in life. It may even account for why I'm so different from my brothers, sisters and cousins.

I believe a *real* man is someone who thinks on his own, stands for what he believes is right and will fight for it. A man defends his family at all costs. Not every male in this book meets that definition.

My father was a MAN and I am a MAN. I thank him for that, and I know he'd be proud that my two boys are MEN, also.

Go figure.

Married Life

Toni and I got married on July 8, 1967, at St. Mary's Catholic Church in Frankfort. My brother, Joe, was my best man, and he stayed with me the night before the wedding. The next morning, he left for the church while I was still getting dressed. Suddenly alone, I started getting cold feet and seriously considered running away as a friend of mine had done on his wedding day. That wedding was to be at the same church as mine, but at the last minute, he had a panic attack and left for California while his bride-to-be and their families and friends waited for him at the church. But I came to my senses, drove to Frankfort, and married the best woman in the world.

We had a giant wedding, with a luncheon for the wedding party paid for by my parents, and the reception—which was, as I recall, attended by four to five hundred guests—was paid for by Toni's father. After the reception, we left for Puerto Rico for our honeymoon, paid for by our cash wedding gifts.

Upon our return, we lived in my apartment in Rome. Toni continued teaching school, and I started work as a salesman for the Prudential Insurance Company. Selling came easy for me and I was good at it. I was making about five hundred dollars a week, and that was in the late 1960s. Later I became a member of the Million Dollar Round Table and went to all their conventions. I enjoyed what I was doing, and the long hours never bothered me. Although I was gone a lot, Toni never complained about me not being home. She never whined, but of course there were times she got pissed off, especially when I stayed out all night and get home just in time to shower and go to work. I did that quite often, and she had every right to be upset.

* * *

In September 1969 my father passed away, and a month later, on October 10, my daughter Gina was born. Toni's mother and mine helped us out a lot with the new baby, but they couldn't be there all the time.

I was taking a course on Friday nights in Syracuse (about thirty miles from Rome) with my cousin, Jimmy DeMare, who was in the real estate business. On a Friday, about a week after Gina was born, Toni asked me to come home right after school to help with the baby so she could get some rest. I had good intentions, but after Jimmy and I got back to Rome that night, he suggested we stop at a lounge my cousin Bucky owned for a quick drink. At that time, my drink of choice was Chivas Regal on the rocks, with a splash of water and a twist of lemon. Jimmy and I met up for a few drinks almost every night, and he knew I could drink a whole bottle of that stuff over an evening.

Anyway, Jimmy started taking bets that I could drink a whole bottle of Chivas. I knew I didn't have a much time to do it, though, because I had to get home to Toni and Gina. So with the bet money on the bar, I told the bartender to pour the bottle in a big mixer with some ice, water and lemon and mix it up. When he finished, I took the pitcher and chugged it all down at once. It took two guys to get me home. I could have died and probably should have.

That was the one time I can remember Toni getting really upset, and who can blame her? Now, she not only had the baby to take care of, but me, too. And it took me two weeks to recover. I was never that sick, and I was vomiting all over the house, and I fell and hit my chin on the living room table and was bleeding also.

* * *

On a cold winter day in 1971, I decided I couldn't handle living in Rome any longer and told Toni we were moving to California. I drove out to Sherman Oaks where my cousin Steve and his family lived, along with another friend from Rome named Orlando Fortini. Orlando was married to Steve's sister. I rented an apartment, then sent for Toni and Gina. I got a sales job with John Hancock and then went back to Prudential, working out of their office on Sunset Boulevard. My territory was Hollywood.

One day at the Prudential office I saw a guy I recognized from my apartment complex, who was also working there. I introduced myself and we soon became friends. His name was Dan Gold. Dan was a sharp guy, and we started making extra money pulling some small scams and doing a little bookmaking.

Back then, the credit card companies did not have the technology they have now, and it was fairly easy to commit credit card fraud. For example, I had an American Express card that Dan and I decided to bang-out. We went to various businesses and made purchases using my card and Dan's signature. When the bill came in, I would call American Express and say these were not my transactions, and that someone had stolen my card. I'd get a new card, and American Express ate the charges. One time my wife opened the American Express bill and went berserk when she saw how much was on it and started yelling at me. I denied everything and used the stolen card explanation on her, too, and it worked.

Also during those days, if the charges on a card were under fifty dollars, there were virtually never any questions asked. So we'd take orders for cases of whiskey, drive to Ventura Boulevard and buy three bottles in every liquor store on the street, keeping the amount per store under fifty bucks. Let's say the total for a case from the stores was a hundred and twenty dollars. We'd sell it to our customer for sixty, and because it actually cost us nothing, we made sixty dollars and our customers were happy as hell. I remember having booze stashed all around my apartment—in the closets and even under the beds.

Another thing we made money on was airline tickets. We'd call the airline and order a first-class ticket using a fraudulent card. After it was approved, we could stop in any of the airline offices around the city and pick up the ticket. Let's say a round trip from L.A. to New York cost six hundred. We'd sell it for four, which was all profit. But we had to give the credit card stuff up because of a fluke.

One day Dan went into an American Airline office that was located at Hollywood and Vine to get a ticket. I was waiting in the car, and all of a sudden, he came running out of the building and said to get away fast. It turned out that Dan had called in on the same day for two different tickets. Incredibly, he spoke with the same ticket agent on both calls. She remembered the earlier transaction and put an alert on both tickets. As soon as he got to the counter for the pick-up, he sensed something was wrong and ran out. We never got arrested for the credit card stuff, or even questioned. But that near miss was close enough to make us quit the credit card scams.

During that same time, we started taking football bets, too. A guy who worked in our office had connections in Vegas, and for a few bucks, was able to get us the betting line ahead of everybody else. We got most of our customers through bartenders in Beverly Hills, where Dan and I were well-known. It was nice money, but we had to shut it down when one of the bartenders told me that an established bookie, one with the local cops on the pad, was getting pissed off at us for working his turf. So some of the guys in blue visited the bars and put out the word—stop doing business with us, or else. And that was the end of that. Although it didn't last long, my first real foray into fast money convinced me I had a knack for it. It was something I'd put to use again later.

Weekends were fun times. Toni, Gina and I would go out to Orlando Fortini's house. Gina, Orlando and me, we would hang-out by the pool while Toni and Orlando's wife did the cooking. Orlando's niece was married to an organized crime guy, Tommy Gambino, the nephew of Carlo Gambino—a real nice guy and he had class. They stayed with Orlando when they were passing through town on their way to Vegas, or after landing at L.A. while returning from a trip somewhere. This was my first exposure to people in "the life," and I must say I liked them and found them to be good people. Still, I had no particular desire to take on that lifestyle.

* * *

Unfortunately, the good life in California had to come to an end. Jimmy DeMare and I owned a lot of real estate back in Rome, and we owed the banks there a lot of money. I felt I had no choice but to go back and tend to business. Jimmy arranged a home for me and my family to move into, and Toni's father loaned us the money to ship our furniture. Toni and Gina flew back. I drove and took my time, spending a couple of weeks in Palm Springs and a couple more in Vegas. By the time I pulled into Rome, I was broke and needed to start making money quick just to cover basic necessities.

I was in a diner and met a guy that told me about a life insurance company, Combined Life, where you could

Taking The Wrong Path | Married Life

take your commissions daily and make a hundred a day, no problem. I was used to working for companies that didn't pay a commission until the customer's physical exam was completed and the policy went into effect. That could take thirty days or longer. I didn't have that kind of time to wait, so this job got my attention.

At that time, Combined Life was owned by W. Clement Stone out of Chicago. He was considered a genius by many in the business world because of how he started with nothing and built the empire he had, as well as written a few success books. I loved the concept he'd put together for his company's life insurance policies.

I applied for a sales job and was hired. After two weeks of paid training in Boston, I was out in the field and made some decent money, enough to keep a roof over our heads, food on the table, and pay our other bills. Even though I did pretty well and didn't mind doing cold sales calls door to door, it just wasn't my cup of tea. I felt I would be happier and make more money running my own insurance agency. My last week at Combined was what they called W. Clement Stone Week. This was when the company tried to break the sales record from the previous year. I worked Cooperstown (home of the Baseball Hall of Fame), and we smashed the record. Before I left the company, I attended a convention in New York City where I got an award from W. Clement Stone.

* * *

George Grogan, president of Franklyn United Life Insurance Company in Garden City, New York, approved me for my own general insurance agency, and I came to think of Mr. Grogan as one of the best and smartest individuals I ever met. I went to the company's headquarters for two weeks of schooling, with my salary and expenses paid for by Franklyn. When I successfully completed the training, Mr. Grogan loaned me five thousand dollars to open my office.

My territory was Oneida, Onondaga and Herkimer counties, and that is when I was introduced to credit life and health insurance on loans. My clients would be auto dealers, and I'd get paid for every car they financed through their dealership and put insurance on. I felt this could be serious money, and I started a training course for auto sales people on how to get more of their customers to add the insurances to their car loans. That meant more commission money for them, and more money for my agency.

As time went by, things were working out very well, but my territory was limited to a few counties, and I wanted the whole state of New York. I wanted to expand. I talked to George Grogan, but due to his agreement with other agencies, he couldn't increase my area. He said he appreciated my ambition and suggested I find another company to represent, even though that would mean I could no longer be an agent for Franklyn.

I found Federal Home Life Insurance Company, located in Battle Creek, Michigan, and applied. They accepted me and gave me all of New York State as my territory for selling credit life and health insurance to auto dealers. In addition, unlike Franklyn, I could represent other companies as well, so I became a general agent for Sentry Life Insurance too, but things were pretty rocky financially at first.

I'd given up my office, and I was working out of my cellar with my desk next to the washer and dryer. My car had been repossessed because I was broke and just beginning a new business, so I was a few months late with my payments. I had to drive my wife's 1965 Chevrolet. It wasn't what I considered to be the kind of car that would create the image of a successful businessman. Being short on money, if I had to do any traveling, I'd go to the bank where a friend of mine, Bob Egger, was vice president. I'd write a check, which he'd give me the money for, but not actually cash. When I returned, I'd pay him back, and he'd give me back my check. So our transactions were more or less loans, with my checks as collateral.

* * *

One day while returning home from a business meeting in New York City, I stopped off at the Holiday Inn in Kingston for coffee. The waitress provided me with a phone book, and I checked the yellow pages for auto dealers. There was a full-page ad for Ron Prince Chevrolet. I got directions and went there, parking a block away so nobody would see what I was driving. I made my pitch to the receptionist and immediately got meeting with Ron Prince. I told him he could make a lot of money for his sales people and his dealership if he used my agency for their loan insurance on the vehicles they financed.

I will never forget him pulling a gun out of his desk drawer and saying, "You'd better be telling me the truth." I assured him I was.

He not only signed on with me, he called other dealers in nearby Poughkeepsie and greased it for me to stop by their dealerships and talk with them as well. I drove there (always parking a distance away), and signed dealer after dealer.

I frequently think that my ability as a salesman helped make me successful in later endeavors, such as settling disputes and collecting money from people who didn't want to pay. That, along with my appearance, voice, and the way I use words, let me do it all without ever having a gun.

Go figure.

Success &
The Road to Divorce

I was signing car dealers as fast as I could and started making good money.

Toni and I wanted to have more children, but we had a difficult time conceiving and thought there might be a problem. Finally, we were successful, though, and on the night of July 10, 1975, she woke me up to tell me her water had broken. She was wrong. It wasn't her water—our bed was full of blood, and I feared the worst. I got Toni to the car, went back inside to get Gina, and then rushed the ten miles to the hospital. I dropped Toni off at the emergency room door and then took Gina to my mother, who only lived a block away. By the time I got back to the hospital, my son Orlando Joseph had been born. Boy was I was happy. Did I go get drunk? Of course, but nothing like the time I drank the bottle of Chivas Regal when Gina was an infant. That would never happen again.

* * *

I bought a small one-story abandoned former school building and converted it into two offices. One was for my company, the Ori Agency, and I rented the other office out. The insurance company regularly sent their auditors, Dick Leamy or Bob Bushke, to audit me. They allowed me to show them records that were always a month behind. The ability to use dated information was very important in being able to grow my business. In addition to Dick and Bob, the company president, Dick Sikora, knew about the arrangement, and they were willing to go along with it when they found a hard-working agent like me.

During one audit, Bob Bushke told me about a paint sealant company called Polyglycoat. I remembered the name because they'd bought a full-page ad in *Automotive News*, which went out to auto dealers all over the country. On paper it appeared the company owned a giant office building in Manhattan, but in reality, they were headquartered in the village of Scarsdale, New York, in Westchester County. I called and made an appointment to catch an early morning flight into White Plains and meet with Walter Fiveson, the founder and president. In addition to the print ads, Walter was all over the TV doing commercials as well. Walter picked me up at the airport. He was tall, had a beard and was casually dressed. I'd been impressed by his TV ads, and was even more impressed meeting him in person. There was no doubt in my mind that he was a great salesman. He started calling me "Kid."

Walter drove me to his beautiful home. His wife and partner, Gloria, were working the phones, and their maid cooked us a wonderful breakfast. Afterward, Gloria pitched me on becoming a distributor for all of upstate New York, from the Tappan Zee Bridge to Niagara Falls. As she talked, I heard Walter on the phone. When he hung up, he said, "Kid, that was Audiovox Radio out of New Jersey. He's signing up, too. This is going to be huge—don't miss out."

I promised him I'd consider it. And then he and Gloria drove me into the City to the Warwick New York Hotel on West 54th Street. I loved that place, and for over thirty-five years, I stayed there whenever I had business in the City. Everyone knew me and treated great. They always gave me super good rates for a suite, plus the location was convenient for everything.

When I got to my room, I called the guy at Audiovox and asked him about his conversation with Walter. He had no idea what I was talking about. He didn't know Walter, and hadn't spoken with him that day or any other time. I hung up and chuckled at the con Walter tried to pull on me. I had to give him credit for it. I said to myself, *this product is going to be a winner because this guy is good.* So I called Walter and said to draw up the contract and meet me at the Warwick the following Monday. I'd have my lawyer, Frank Russo, review it, and if everything was okay, I'd sign and give him my buy-in check. The next Monday, I signed and became a distributor for Polyglycoat. It was the start of a beautiful friendship between Walter and me that lasted until he passed away in 2002.

* * *

Frank Russo was older than me, as were most of my associates, but he was one of my best friends. We were both Calabrese. In the old days, his father was considered the "boss" of Rome, and my grandfather was very close to him. Back then, our family name was Spada, but somewhere along the line it got changed to Spado.

Frank had been a good friend to New York City mobster Frank Costello and his brother Eddie prior to Costello's death in 1973. Through Frank Russo, I was introduced to so many people I can't begin to remember them all, but how could I forget meeting Russell Bufalino—mob boss of Northeastern Pennsylvania and Western New York— and entertainers such as Vic Damone, Tony Bennett, Frank Sinatra and Dean Martin?

With Frank being a lawyer and having all those connections, he was able to intervene when asked to save people from beatings or possibly being killed. It was something I really admired about him, and it had a great influence on me. I saw Frank's skill at work many times and have one example I want to share with you.

One of Frank's friends was a multi-millionaire named Henry Panasci. Henry ran a string of drugstores in the northeast, and Frank handled the legal work for him when Henry began with the first few stores. He never charging him a penny. But Henry had a bad habit—he thought he could have any girl he wanted, and more times than I can count, he went after the girlfriend of a respected wise guy. On those occasions, Frank came to the rescue and saved him from the wrath of the pissed-off boyfriend. Most of the guys Frank helped appreciated it and did right by him in return, but not Henry. But Frank was always there for Henry, and therefore Henry never had a problem.

I talked with Henry shortly after Frank suffered a heart attack. He said, "Frank doesn't have any worries while he's laid up. I'll take care of everything."

He didn't lift a finger to help Frank, though, and later on I told him what I thought. "You never did anything for Frank except have him save your ass from all your egotistical screw-ups."

He didn't like it, but I told him like it was.

Anyway, meeting so many stars through Frank began my love for Hollywood. Later, when I moved there, I became known to many more celebrities. Behind the scenes, they would call on me for help when they had problems because I had ways to handle them in a quiet manner. I became what you could call a "fixer." Whenever I did a favor, I never talked about it to others. That's how I preferred it and my discretion was appreciated.

My rule was if it took me more than fifteen minutes to convince someone to do the right thing, I wasn't getting the job done. I don't recall ever taking that long. I'd say what I had to say, get a confirmation, and then leave. It was forgotten and never discussed again. Most disputes are easy to settle when you eliminate ego, greed and jealously, and the message is delivered in a respectful manner.

* * *

I'd hired Bob Egger from the bank, and a guy named Gary Katz to train automobile salesmen in financing.

As I became a pioneer in other aspects of after-sale products, I had them include that training as well. Our salesmen learned how to earn more money selling those products than they made on selling the car itself. I became a "golden boy" for the insurance company, as they received millions of dollars a year through my agency. I'd be flown to their headquarters in Battle Creek to receive awards and stay in their condo. The awards had envelopes taped to the back with cash in them. Yes, the insurance company was happy and growing, and I was growing with them. I bought a big new home in the best part of Rome for fifty-five thousand dollars, and I put twenty thousand down on it. There were only three other houses on the block.

My family was getting larger, too. Toni was pregnant again, and on March 4, 1977, my son Anthony was born. I had a loving wife, three beautiful children, and an expanding business. What more could a man ask for?

* * *

My business was doing so well that I had several employees, both sales and in-house staff. With plenty of money coming in, I was able to help my relatives and friends out if they fell on tough times. And because of my dislike for cold weather, I bought a condo in Pompano Beach, Florida, right on the beach at 2000 South Ocean Boulevard.

In the meantime, I was doing a lot of traveling to the west coast—Los Angeles and Las Vegas. Frank Russo went with me several times and introduced me to big time film makers Ralph Serpe and Dino De Laurentiis.

He had become connected to Dino when Dino wanted to film one of his movies in Harlem and needed to get the appropriate permissions from the wise guys whose turf the filming would take place on. Frank made the arrangements, and Dino was very appreciative. He and Frank became friends.

Frank told them what I was doing with my business, and that I was thinking about going national. They were interested in financing me. Later, we flew to Boston where Ralph was filming *The Brink's Job*. We had dinner at Jimmy's Harborside with Ralph, actors John Cassavetes and Peter Falk (who played Tony Pino in the film), and with Jazz Maffie, one of the men who actually did the Brinks robbery. Before we left Boston, Ralph said he'd try to set us up to meet with Dino in Los Angeles.

* * *

My plan to take my concept national wasn't cheap—it required at least twelve million dollars, and probably more. Between running my business and trying to line up investors, it seemed I was always on the go. I was on airplanes so often that my friends started calling me Howard Hughes.

In my suite at the Warwick in New York City, Frank Russo introduced me to Lou Perry, the casting agent known for his discovery of Dean Martin and Jerry Lewis. And while at the Warwick, I met a very nice gentlemen and his dog. It turned out the guy was Meyer Lansky, commonly known as the "Mob's Accountant," and he also stayed at the Warwick when he came to New York. In the evening, I'd walk with him and his dog. We talked politics and general things. I really enjoyed the time we spent together. At the time, I was attending fundraisers for the United Jewish Appeal and Brandeis University, and donating money. Meyer really liked that, given I was an Italian and still doing this. I found him to be very intelligent and exceptionally street savvy.

* * *

On one of my trips to Vegas, I was sitting in the lounge at the Las Vegas Hilton in the afternoon when a stunningly beautiful girl walked in. I like women who are sexy, sensual, classy, elegant and beautiful—and this girl had it all. She walked over to a table a few feet away from me where two gentlemen were seated and joined them. I tried to put her out of my mind because of the rule I live by—never go after another man's woman, it's not the right thing to do.

Later that night, I was standing at the bar of the club in the Hilton watching the long line of people waiting to get in. The last person in the line was the girl of my dreams I'd seen that afternoon, and she was by herself. I went to the doorman and asked him to get her from the end of the line and seat her at a table right in front of the band. I gave her a chance to order a drink and then went over to her table. "Is it okay if I sit down?" I asked.

She shook her head. "I just want to be by myself."

"I just want to be by myself, too. So why don't we be by ourselves together?" I replied.

She smiled and I sat down. We made some small talk and had a couple of glasses of wine. She said her name was Rosemary; she lived in San Francisco and worked for a lawyer there. She'd come to Vegas with a guy she knew to take in the Lou Rawls show. She emphasized the guy was a friend and nothing more than that. After the show he went to his room and went to bed, and she decided to come to the bar and kill some time.

From the club, I took her to the baccarat table where I played a little. Every time I won, I gave her half. Then we hit the blackjack table, and then we went to the coffee shop for a bite to eat. By that time, it was around 6:00 a.m. and we both had to catch early flights—her to San Francisco and me to New York. We said good-bye and rushed to our respective rooms to pack. As I was checking out, I heard my name over the PA system. I went to the house phone and it was Rosemary calling from another house phone. She asked me for my address, and I gave her my office address.

The next day when I got to my office there were a dozen red roses delivered for me from Rosemary. I was totally blown away and started making some really stupid decisions. Thinking back later, I remembered what Walter Fiveson used to tell me, "Kid, when you think with your Jewish head and not your Italian head, you make money and always make the right decision." You can guess which head I was thinking with when it came to Rosemary.

The following weekend I flew to San Francisco to meet Rosemary. It seemed like a pretty safe thing because Toni, the kids and my mother were all at the condo in Florida for the winter. She met me at the airport, and we went to a restaurant and had dinner. After that she took me to the hot tubs, which were big at the time, and we had a ball. From there we went to her apartment, where we stayed in bed all weekend. On Sunday she drove me to the airport, and on the flight back, I couldn't get her out of my mind. I was hooked and our coast-to-coast relationship began.

The next week I called her and told her that when she got off work on Friday, to go right to the airport, and there would be a ticket to New York waiting for her at the TWA counter. A car would pick her up at Kennedy and bring her to the Warwick, where I'd be waiting. That was our pattern. I'd go to San Francisco, she'd come to New York, or we'd meet in Vegas. I was in a passionate affair that could end in nothing but trouble.

* * *

We had an appointment with Dino De Laurentiis in Beverly Hills. Frank and I flew out of Kennedy first-class (everything was first-class for me back then). We landed and checked into the Beverly Hills Hotel.

The next morning, Ralph Serpe picked us up at our hotel and brought us to Dino's office, which at the time was on Canon Drive. They listened attentively as I explained my idea to them.

I said that in order to sell insurance, you had to be licensed in each state you wanted to do business in, and many of the states also had a residency requirement. When I first thought about going national, that was a stumbling block. How could I possibly legally reside in all fifty states?

I told them about the day Jimmy DeMare came to my office and asked me to review a contract he was considering signing to become a Century 21 real estate agent. I did, and then I realized what I needed to do—have resident agents in each state that I would train in what I called the Ori Concept. I copied Jimmy's contract and adapted it to the Ori Agency. I laid out the details of how we'd make money. In those days, when an auto dealer sold a car and financed it, they put it through the bank or finance company. The dealer got paid from the financial institution for the financing, but not the insurance. With my program, they got paid for both the financing and the insurance. I'd also place a finance manager in the dealership to increase the number of cars that were financed through them. I figured by doing it that way, I could take a dealer that was selling a hundred cars a month and financing thirty percent of them, and increase that number to fifty percent. That would generate big money for everybody.

But I had one more thing in mind that I was sure would keep me way ahead of any competition. I'd pay monthly cash bonuses to the largest dealers in return for their business, and that would be an offer hardly anybody would refuse. It would be tricky, but I was sure I'd be able to pull it off.

In addition, I knew that supplying women to the dealers would endear me to them and almost guarantee me a lock on getting and keeping them on board. Having met several famous madams in New York City, getting girls wouldn't be a problem.

Once I got up and running, I would have training sessions in different cities. The dealers would send half their salesmen in the morning, and the other half in the afternoon. In the evening, I'd host a cocktail party for the owners and general managers. I'd bring in a couple of high-class hookers from the City (who at the time were getting a thousand dollars a trick plus expenses). These girls were sharp and mingled with the guests as though they were employees of the Ori Agency. They'd each hook up with a dealer and take care of them, making the dealers feel like a million bucks.

I'd also hire a local girl to service the general managers. Local talent worked much cheaper, usually around a hundred fifty per roll in the hay.

The local girl might take care of ten general managers in a night, while the City girls would only focus on one dealer. But the dealers were the ones that really mattered, and they got the best care.

The madams and their girls were stand up women, too. Later, when I was under investigation, the law interviewed some of them. Not a single one admitted knowing me, even though I had lines of credit with them.

I concluded my presentation by announcing that my only competition was a company called Pat Ryan and Associates, out of Chicago. According to Dick Leamy, who had worked for Ryan, he began just like I did. But because of my bonus plan and other incentives, I knew Ryan wouldn't be able to keep up with me.

I told Ralph and Dino that in order to fully implement my plan, I'd need a total of twenty million in investments. I then offered to show them the program in operation.

We left Dino's office and drove to a large dealership in downtown Los Angeles, where I'd already made arrangements to demonstrate the operation. I walked them through the program step-by-step. Everyone was impressed, and Dino said he was in. His ability to raise large amounts of money was well known, and his investors always got a return.

With that, I felt sure I was on my way. All my business endeavors were making money. I had a great staff and sales force, and now getting investment money had been resolved. The best part was I wouldn't have to take any money out of the Ori Agency.

That evening, Ralph had us all up to his home on Angelo Drive, and his lovely wife Jane put out a fantastic dinner. Ralph had also invited the head of the studio that had just released *Saturday Night Fever*, starring John Travolta. As the evening passed, I learned a lot about Hollywood and the movie business. It was a great night, and the beginning of me meeting many more movie executives and celebrities.

When I got back to my hotel room, I was ecstatic. My plans to go national were on track. My current businesses were successful, and I had a wife, kids and a girlfriend. Who had it better than me?

* * *

Ralph Serpe and I became close friends after this. After the place on Angelo Drive, he purchased a home in Bel Air on Bellagio road, another beautiful home with a beautiful view and a pool. Every Christmas I was invited to his home for their big party, and it was always a fun time with everyone in the entertainment business.

I never will forget the one time I had a couple dozen lobsters left over from our business, International Seafood Distributors. The lobsters were still in the crate, and when I parked my car, I let them out all over his front yard. Then I went inside to the party. I looked for Ralph and I told him there were lobsters all over his front yard, and he thought I was crazy, so we went outside, and he knew immediately it was me who put them there. The next thing he did was get the maids and the help, and we boiled them, and he froze them. He didn't want to serve them to his guest—he loved lobster and kept them for himself and his family.

Ralph's wife Jane was a fantastic lady and a great cook, I started to spend weekends at his home, and I must say the bed I slept in was one of the most comfortable beds I ever slept in. One morning, I got up, walk into the kitchen, and Jane was cooking breakfast. She asked if I slept good, and I said, "Great!" She then told me that she loves that bed, and that's where Sofia Loren sleeps when she comes. I said to myself—"I've slept in the same bed as the most beautiful women in the world has slept!"

Ralph and Jane were close with Carlo Ponti and his wife, Sophia Loren. Ralph's son-in-law is Greg Evigan, a very good actor and the star of *BJ and The Bear* and *My Two Dads*, as well as countless other films and TV shows. Greg had invented a lock, and we became partners on it for a short period of time. I remember one-time Greg was filming in a small town near Seattle and I flew up to have a meeting with him. We were in a small restaurant when all of a sudden, a person recognized him, and before we knew it, the whole town was lined up for autographs. When my two boys Ori and Anthony would come out for the summer, we would go to Greg's home and his kids and mine had a great time together.

At this time, I had a connection to Meyer Lansky, and I believe his grandson and was trying to put a movie together. Ralph was close friends with Jimmy Alo, aka

Jimmy Blue Eyes, a capo in the Genovese family, and also a friend of Meyer's. They were trying to do a film. In addition, there were other people like me trying to put a film about Meyer Lansky together, so obviously it got the attention of the FBI.

At this time, Ralph and Jane moved into a high rise across the street from me on the Wilshire corridor, and Ralph called me and asked me to come over. What had happened was the FBI had a visit with him, primarily about what he knew of Meyer. However, the first name they came out with was mine, and they ask him how he knew me and Jimmy Blue Eyes. They asked Ralph more and more questions about me, and they told him who I was, like he didn't know already. But it got Ralph nervous, and he said I should not be partners with Greg anymore, which I agreed with. After all, if I got pinched for something, I would not want Greg's name to come up. The lock was a great idea, and I believe we could have made good money, but oh well. Deals come and go, but friendship is more important and protecting your friends is something I always believed in.

Go figure.

Las Vegas

My first trip to Las Vegas was in the late 1960s when Jimmy DeMare, me and our wives stopped there on our way from New York to Hawaii. We stayed on the Strip at the Stardust. That was when the Mob was running things and had hidden control of several of the casinos. It was a classy town with a lot going on. When you went to a dinner or show you dressed up—no shorts or tank tops.

A friend from high school, Frank Riolo, was a dealer at the Four Queens, and we stopped to see him. I've got to tell you, Frank was a class act. He was good looking, smart, truthful, and always respectful. He introduced us to his co-workers, and we were having a great time.

We had reservations to see Elvis at the International (later the Las Vegas Hilton). Jimmy and I were playing blackjack, so we told our wives to go to the International, and we'd meet up with them. When we got there, the girls were near the end of a very long line waiting to get into the show.

I said, "What are you doing back here? Follow me."

We walked to the front of the line, and I greased the doorman's palm. We were ushered right in and seated at a table next to the stage. That's what I loved about Vegas. If you took care of the people, they took care of you.

The next time I was in Vegas was when I was moving to California. I decided to stop in Sin City for a few days, see Frank, and have a little fun.

When I walked into the Four Queens, I was astonished at the number of dealers who remembered me from Frank's introduction and said hello. They offered to comp me to a meal or show. That's how Vegas was run then—they made you feel special.

* * *

After moving back to Rome from California, I was invited on a Las Vegas junket run by Joey Mazza from Utica. When we got off the plane, Joey told me I had a five-thousand-dollar line of credit at the Dunes, the host hotel, and was approved for more if needed. I also had five grand in cash on me. On a junket, you didn't pay for food, drinks or shows, so it was all fun money.

Frank Riolo stopped in and watched me in action at the blackjack table. I was doing so bad he walked away after a few minutes, shaking his head. By the time I went home, I had lost my five grand and had to send the Dunes a check for the ten thousand I ran up on my casino credit.

By my next trip, Frank had moved from the Four Queens to the former International, which was then the Las Vegas Hilton, where he was a pit boss. I went there to see him and play some blackjack. I was gambling at a blackjack table when Frank tapped me on the shoulder.

He said, "I'm going on break, and I'd like to talk with you. Cash in and we'll take a walk."

When we got to a private area he said, "I'm not trying to tell you what to do, but you're the worst blackjack player I've ever seen. You're always watching the girls walk by and not paying attention to your cards. You don't make the right bets, and you're drinking too much. You need to change things around, or you'll continue to donate."

I knew he was right.

He then proceeded to give me some instructions on how to improve my game. I stopped drinking when I played, kept my mind on the game, and made smarter bets. Thanks to Frank, my play improved dramatically, and Vegas became even more fun. I began to visit more frequently for both business and pleasure. I had lines of credit at several casinos. I saw the biggest and best shows, ate at the best restaurants, and it never cost me a dime.

Vegas has changed a lot since then, for the worse in my opinion. Today, I can't even go there unless I get permission from my probation officer. If I did get approval, I'd have to check in with the Las Vegas police upon arriving in town. So I don't go any more, and I don't gamble.

As for Frank Riolo, he moved up the ladder in Las Vegas. When Indian casino gambling was approved in New York State, he was contacted by the Oneida Indian

Nation and offered a position at their Turning Stone Casino in Verona. He is the Chief Operating Officer and serves on the board of directors. He earned it. He is a great guy and a hard worker. God bless him!

* * *

As I mentioned earlier, I really do not care for Las Vegas anymore. It has changed a lot from the old days when the Italians were in control. In those days, it was a classy town. We dressed in those days, whether going to dinner or to a show, which I never paid for because they were always comped.

Las Vegas changed when corporate America took it over. However, Jimmy Caci and I still had reasons to go there often. Normally, I would pick up Jimmy at his home in Cathedral City, and then we'd take the back roads into Vegas. We would spend a day and come back, and if we had to stay it would be in a small motel off the strip. We would conduct our business and leave. Of course, we would spend some time gambling.

I was having lunch one day at Il Pastaio on Canon Drive in Beverly Hills when I met a beautiful young lady. She told me about her boyfriend in San Diego who was in the garbage business, and that he would like to meet me. We spoke on the phone a couple of times, and I went to see him in San Diego. After a few more calls, he invited me to Las Vegas just before New Year's. I drove in a couple days before, and he put me up at the MGM and paid for everything.

What he wanted was to get into the garbage business in Las Vegas, and after analyzing it, I felt I could do it, but it would take a considerable retainer. Yes, I always ask for a retainer, as I need to grease a lot of hands to do what is needed, especially on a job like this one. Just try to imagine what it would take to get a new guy into the garbage business in Las Vegas. But no, this wasn't what the guy had in mind.

He wanted me to be his partner, and I already knew that would be a bigger problem. I'm not one to look at your books and see if something is wrong, which can become a real headache. I always try to avoid future problem because, trust me, they will come. No, just pay me for my expenses, give me a handsome bonus, and I am happy. I left early in the morning to get home for New Year's Eve and get out of the new Vegas.

The next day, there was an article in the Las Vegas Review-Journal by an investigative reporter John Smith. Ori Spado was seen at the MGM, and it went on as to what I might have been doing in Las Vegas. Obviously, someone recognized me and could not wait to tell on me. Obviously, that deal never happened, and that guy never got into the garbage business in Las Vegas.

Go figure.

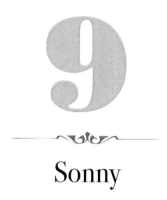

Sonny

I was not only meeting important people in the entertainment industry. I also met and became close friends with John "Sonny" Franzese of the Colombo crime family.

It happened because of my relationship with Walter Fiveson. I'd begun spending a lot of time and all my winters in Florida. One day, Walter called to tell me he had an appointment in New York City to pitch his Polyglycoat program to Victor Potamkin, owner of Potamkin Cadillac. At that time, Potamkin was the largest Caddy dealership around and would be a very profitable account. Walter asked me to meet him there. I knew who Victor was—he used the same barbers at the Warwick Hotel that I did. He was always well groomed and impeccably dressed. I told Walter I'd be there.

When I arrived at the dealership and went into Victor's office, Walter and one of Victor's employees were seated around Victor's desk. After the formal introductions, I said I needed to use the bathroom before the meeting began. Victor pointed to the bathroom door and said, "We left you something. Enjoy."

I got inside, shut the door and looked around for whatever it was I was supposed to enjoy. Not seeing anything, I stepped over to the toilet and lowered my zipper to do my business. As I stood there, I noticed it. On the top of the toilet tank were two lines of white powder. I was sure it was cocaine. I had never done cocaine and wasn't interested. I finished what I was doing, blew the powder onto the floor and left.

"Well, how did you like it?" Victor's guy asked.

"It was great. Thanks." What else could I say, right?

The meeting was successful, and Walter closed the deal. Afterward, Victor invited us all to the 21 Club for lunch. We took Victor's limo to the restaurant and were sitting around the table when Walter left to call his office. When he came back, he was as pale as a ghost. He leaned over and whispered in my ear, "Kid, I got another death threat."

I knew he had received phoned threats before, but I figured they were bullshit because a serious killer probably wouldn't give his target a warning. But this latest threat was different—it was more specific. Walter had hired his brother-in-law to work for him. Not long afterward, warranties began showing up with numbers Walter hadn't issued. He investigated and found that somebody was offering customers an inferior Polyglycoat-type product, and their warranty was being given under

Walter's business. He knew the warranty piece of the scam had to be an inside job, and putting two and two together, he figured his brother-in-law had to be the inside guy. He planned to fire him, but this latest threat said if he fired the guy, he'd be killed.

"What do you want me to do?" I asked.

"Kid, I know you're plugged in. Don't go back to Florida right away—stay here and see what you can find out. I'll cover your expenses."

I got back to the Warwick and called Frank Russo in Rome. I told him what was going on with Walter, and asked if he knew anybody who might be able to find out who was behind the threats and help straighten things out. Frank told me to call Lou Perry, the casting agent he had introduced me to previously. "Lou knows a lot of people. He'll be able to put you in touch with whoever you need to talk with," Frank said.

I called Lou and told him the story, and that I wanted to get the problem resolved. He told me he'd get back to me. It wasn't very long—probably a half hour or so—and he called me. "I'll stop by your hotel at seven. We're going to go out to dinner, and I'll introduce you to someone who can help you out."

Lou showed up on time, and we took a cab to the Trattoria Siciliana Restaurant on 2nd Avenue. I learned later that it was owned by Sonny's son-in-law, Eugene, who was married to Sonny's daughter from his first marriage, Lorraine. Eugene and I became very good friends. He ended up owning five restaurants, and this was the first of many meetings that Sonny and I would have at the Trattoria. On one of those occasions, when I arrived, Sonny was just finishing a conversation with another guy. He said to me, "Kid, say hello to John." It was John Gotti, who went on to fame as the boss of the Gambino crime family.

Anyway, on that first day the place was packed, and Lou brought me to a table and introduced me to the legendary Sonny Franzese, his wife Tina, his daughters Gia and Tina, and his son John. Sonny had me take a seat right next to him, so we'd be close enough to talk without being overheard. I thought he was a very good-looking guy, and figured he had to be pretty smart to climb the organized crime ladder the way he had.

We didn't start talking right away, so I looked around the place. I saw a few guys I suspected were part of Sonny's crew, and some more I took for the law. Sonny told me later that I was right. His boys and some FBI agents were there that night at the bar and other tables.

After a while, he leaned toward me and whispered, "Explain to me this problem your friend is having." I told him everything I knew, also in a whisper. He took both my office phone number in Rome and my Florida number. He said he'd try to find out what this could be about and get back to me.

With our business out of the way, I ordered fish. Sometimes I'm allergic to fish, depending on the waters it comes from. Well, I was allergic to this one and got very sick with vomiting and diarrhea. Sonny had two of his guys—Johnny Irish and Red Crabbe—take me to NYU Hospital. I passed out during the ride and woke up lying in a bed in a hospital room. With my eyes still closed, I heard the doctor who was treating me ask Johnny and Red, "I need to know the patient's name."

One of them answered,

"No, Doc, you don't need to know that."

"What about your names, then?"

"You don't need to know them, either."

I was released a couple of hours later, and Johnny and Red drove me to the Warwick. The next day, I flew back to Florida. Sonny and his family never forgot about me getting sick, and it became a part of the conversation whenever I was around them. Little did I know how close I would become with this entire family in the years ahead, right up to my arrest 30 years later. Michael, Johnny, Tina and Gia were all the children of Tina. Tina told me that Michael was a year and a half old when she met Sonny, and eventually Sonny legally adopted him.

Gia would eventually die of an overdose in a Motel in Florida, and Johnny would become a crack addict. Young Tina died of cancer the same week we were all indicted, and their mother died of cancer shortly after the trial. I also got to know Sonny's three other children from his first marriage, Carmine, Lorraine and Rosemary. These three children all grew up to become law abiding citizens.

* * *

Walter called me again right after I got to Florida and asked me to come back to New York City. He was having problems with those bogus warranties and given different prices to different auto dealers when he started his business. On top of that, reporter John Stossel was on Channel 2 almost every night talking about what a farce Polyglycoat was. I said I'd come back and give him a hand.

Rather than fly, Rosemary and I decided to drive to New York and make a little vacation out of it. When we got to Utica, Rosemary would fly from there back to San Francisco, and I'd go into the City to meet Walter. We took our time driving, stopping wherever we wanted, and didn't get to Utica for two weeks (I used to drive it alone in a day). Every day I called my office to check for messages (this was prior to everyone carrying a cell phone). My secretary told me some guy was calling every morning asking for me. He wouldn't leave his name or number.

We finally arrived in Utica and checked into the Ramada. The phone was ringing when I opened the door to our room. I figured it was probably for the previous guest, but the ringing didn't stop, so I answered it. The caller was my friend Tommy DeMare (Jimmy's father). He said, "Where in the hell have you been? You need to call Frank (Russo) right away."

"Okay. How did you know I was here? I didn't even know we were gonna stay here until we checked in."

"Don't worry about that. Just be glad I found you."

I called Frank. He said, "That guy (Sonny) has been trying to reach you for two weeks. He found out what you asked him to find out, and we need to meet with him in New York at ten-thirty Monday morning."

The next day Rosemary flew to San Francisco, and on Sunday night Frank and I drove to New York.

* * *

Frank and I got to The Russian Tea Room on West 57th Street a little before ten-thirty for the meeting. The place didn't open for business until noon, but Sonny was there along with Lou Perry and another guy about my age, who was his stepson Michael. I learned the first booth on the left was Sonny's whenever he was there. The first booth on the right was for Jackie Kennedy Onassis.

Walter was in the City for a Polyglycoat distributor meeting at the Hilton, and Sonny told me to get him and bring him back. I went to the Hilton and took Walter right off the stage in the middle of his presentation. Back at the Tea Room, we took our seats for the sit down. Sonny, Michael, Walter, and I were in Sonny's booth. Frank and Lou sat in chairs to my left.

When the discussion began, it came out that Walter's brother-in-law—who served as Walter's distributor in Suffolk County—was also an in-law to Michael, and the two had gone into business together. They began selling an inferior and cheaper product, representing it as Polyglycoat. To complete the scam, they stole Walter's warranties from Walter's office, taking them from the bottom of the stack and issuing them to their customers. Walter found out when claims started to rise, and the warranty numbers had never been issued.

Walter threatened to revoke his brother-in-law's distributorship, resulting in Michael calling him with death threats.

As the meeting proceeded, I felt Sonny was not grasping what had happened. I said to him, "Suppose someone tries to move in on your territory in the Bronx—" Sonny stopped me dead.

With the scariest eyes I have ever seen in my life, he looked at me and said, "Do not think for one moment that I don't understand what is going on here. Keep your mouth shut and listen." He scared the hell out of me, and I don't scare easily.

In the end, Sonny determined that Michael was wrong and ruled in Walter's favor. Michael wasn't happy about it, and he never liked me after that.

When the meeting broke up, we all went outside. Sonny grabbed me by the arm, and we walked to 57th and Broadway. He said, "Kid, I like you. You've got balls. You're with me, and if you ever have any problems, you have permission to use my name. I want you to bring your family to my home for Christmas."

Even Frank never got invited there and was shocked that I did. I didn't go, but from that day, Sonny and I became close friends.

Go figure.

The Troubles Begin

Shortly after my trip to Los Angeles to close the deal with Dino, I had to go to Las Vegas for a Polyglycoat distributor meeting. Of course, I had Rosemary fly in, but that was not enough for me. After the meeting, I decided to spend a few more days with Rosemary in San Francisco. We checked into the Fairmont Hotel. I don't want to preach, but us men think we're pretty smart. Actually, we can be a bit dumb sometimes and women are much smarter than we are. Sorry guys, but it's the truth, and I learned it the hard way. The phone in our hotel room kept ringing, but because no one but Rosemary and I knew we were there, I didn't answer it. I was wrong. My wife knew.

It's said that all good things must come to an end. I'd had it made for quite a while, but decision time was rapidly approaching, and my record for making good decisions concerning my love life wasn't very good. I caught a flight to Florida to face the music.

On my flight to Ft. Lauderdale, I started feeling guilty about what I was doing to Toni. She was a wonderful woman, a great wife and mother. She deserved much better from me. But I was as addicted to Rosemary as an alcoholic is to booze. What could I do that would be fair to her without giving up what I had with Rosemary?

The plane landed, and Toni was waiting for me in my gold Cadillac Eldorado. I put my luggage in the trunk, got in the passenger seat, and she drove away. I didn't want our ride to turn into a miles-long argument, so I didn't wait long to tell her what I wanted to do. "Toni, you're still a young and beautiful woman, and you don't deserve what I'm doing to you. The best thing is for us to get a divorce. We have the condo here and the big home in Rome. We both draw good salaries and have all the benefits we need, so money isn't an issue."

That was it. No talk about trying to work things out—I went right to the final option. In my mind, that was the perfect solution. She and the kids would be in good shape financially, and she wouldn't have to worry about where I was or who I was sleeping with. I'd be able to get rid of my guilt and still have what I wanted. Plus, my company would soon be national, and I'd be right on top in the business world. It didn't get much better than that—or so I thought.

I'm not sure what I expected her reaction to be, but I got nothing—no reaction. She drove on without a word, as though she hadn't heard me, but I was sure she had.

Things changed when we got to the condo and went

inside, though. Toni started to cry and went into the bedroom and shut the door. I went out on the patio and could see my mother and the kids playing on the beach. Under different circumstances, it would have been a beautiful scene.

Just then the phone rang. My marital situation wasn't my only problem—far from it.

* * *

My brother-in-law Frank, who worked for me as my bookkeeper at the time, delivered the bad news. "Dick Leamy is coming in to close us up. I'm not sure of the reason. Dick is at a hotel at LaGuardia (airport) and wants you to call him."

I called Dick. "What the hell's going on?"

"We've got problems. Jim Generilli knows about the deal Bob (Bushke) and I have with you to base our audits on month-old reports. He's threatening to take it to the New York State Insurance Department, tell them that you're out of trust, and that we're allowing it."

"What's in it for him? If I get closed down, he's out of a job."

"Here's the deal, Ori. He said if we ditch you and let him take over the business, no problem. If not, he'll blow the whistle to get you shut down, and probably cost us our New York license."

"A shakedown?"

"You can call it that."

Generilli was one of my salesmen. Before I hired him, his best year in the insurance business he made thirty-eight grand. With me, he was making a hundred, and I thought we were close. I'd taken him to Vegas, got him a line of credit, and introduced him to a lot of people. I found out later that Generilli had been dating my office secretary, and they sometimes double-dated with my accountant and his girl. On one of those occasions, and after a few drinks, the accountant let my arrangement with the insurance company slip. Generilli saw an opportunity and took it. "Okay, Dick. What do I need to do to resolve this?"

"It will take about three hundred thousand to get back in trust. If you don't do that, we'll have to pull the plug and maybe do business with him."

Three hundred grand was an awful lot of money in the '70s. Still, I said, "I'll come up with the money. If something happens that I can't, I'll sell the business. Generilli isn't going to get it. I'll call my lawyer and banker now and get them to meet with me and see what I can do. I'll let you know what we come up with. Will that work?"

"Sure. But don't let them stall. We've gotta get this done."

My next calls were to Bob Spears, my banker at the Bank of Utica, and Frank Russo. I told them I'd be flying in from Florida in a few hours, and we had to meet at my office as soon as I arrived. I booked a first-class ticket on Eastern and headed north.

Frank and Bob met me at my office. We were there until around four in the morning going over everything. We figured I'd need somewhere around three hundred and twenty-five thousand to get back in trust. That was more than Dick Leamy had told me. To make matters even worse, there was a recession going on, and I already owed the bank a lot of money on my real estate purchases. Bob said there was no way they could let me have the additional money I needed.

I turned to Frank, "What can happen to me over this deal? How much trouble am I in?"

"I'm not sure, but I think there's a chance it could land you in prison."

"*Prison?* You've gotta be fuckin' kidding me. I don't see where I've done anything wrong—nothing criminal, anyway."

"Look, Ori, this could be a long and complicated case, and I'm a little too old to take it on. My best advice is that you get a good criminal lawyer to handle this for you. I can make a call and hook you up with Louie Brindisi, if you want."

Louis Brindisi had an office in Utica and a reputation as a top-notch criminal attorney. At the time, he was rated the third best criminal defense lawyer in the state. "Set it up."

* * *

Frank, Bob and I met Louie at Grimaldi's Restaurant in Utica the next day. We went over the case in detail, and he said he'd represent me. He needed fifty thousand dollars up front, and told me that if I did as he said, I wouldn't have to worry. The Bank of Utica agreed to split Louie's fee with me. It was nice of them and showed that they believed in me, but it was also a good business move. I owed them a lot of money, and it was in their interests to have me stay in business.

As we talked, the realization that with all that was

going on, there was no way I could move forward with my plan to take my business national. This hit me like a sharp punch to the stomach, but I had to accept that my arrangement with Dino De Laurentiis was dead. I needed to switch my focus from expansion to survival, with the emphasis on staying out of jail. I told Louie I would sell the Ori Agency to get myself whole with the insurance company, and put my Polyglycoat and other businesses in Toni's name. He was against putting anything in her name because of the pending divorce, which he also agreed to handle for me. But I told him, "She's the mother of my children, if I can't trust her, who can I trust?" I subsequently brought him the books for my businesses. He backdated the minutes and put them in Toni's name.

After that initial meeting with Brindisi, I reached out to a guy I knew from Long Island named Bob Russell, who ran a leasing business. He had money—so I thought—and he'd previously expressed an interest in buying the Ori Agency. He thought my business would complement his and give him access to a lot of upstate customers. It turned out he was a snowbird and was in Florida, so I flew down to see him there. I told him I wanted three hundred and eighty-five thousand for my agency—that would get me even with the insurance company and leave about eighty-five thousand for me. He didn't bat an eye. We agreed to meet again at his office in Long Island, after he returned from Florida the following week.

When I got to Russell's office for the meeting, there was another guy in the room, who might have been his partner. Russell started saying something about me owing a lot of money to the boys. I stopped him and asked the other guy to leave the room; then I asked him, "Did you say I owe a lot of money to the boys, and that they're after me?"

"Well, that's what I heard."

"I think you had a phone call from Jim Generilli. What you heard couldn't be further from the truth. I don't owe the boys a penny, and I have no problem with them. Let me tell you something else. There's a guy who lives right down the road named Sonny Franzese. He's my friend. Now, do you think I have a problem?"

"No, you have no problem."

Russell's son attended college in Batavia (New York), and we agreed to a follow-up meeting there the next Saturday, when I'd have Louie with me. Back then, there was a small airport, the Oneida County Airport (between Rome and Utica), where Louie and I were going to fly out of to get to the meeting. But we had one hell of a snowstorm that day, and all flights were cancelled. I ended up hiring a private pilot who flew us there. When we got to Batavia, we needed a taxi. I'll never forget that the taxi turned out to be a farmer who came out of his field or barn to give us a ride to the Holiday Inn. We got Dick Leamy on the phone at his home in Battle Creek (Michigan), and everyone agreed to the terms.

A meeting was scheduled for the following Friday in Utica to let all parties, including Dick Leamy and Bob Bushke from the insurance company, look at my books and finalize the agreement. I agreed to kick in the additional eighty-five thousand dollars my client dealerships had sent to the Ori Agency as part of the deal. All was looking good, but things don't always work out as planned.

* * *

I was excited when Friday rolled around. I planned to fly to Florida Saturday morning, and Rosemary was coming in from San Francisco to help me celebrate the resolution of my problem. Before I went to Louie's office for the meeting, I stopped at my travel agent's office to pick up my ticket to Florida. The agent told me that Louie had called to tell me the meeting was off. I called Louie and told him I'd be right over.

"What do you mean the meeting's off?" I asked him.

"They wanted to look at your books, and I told them to go fuck themselves."

I'd had my books taken to Louie's office basement for the inspection. "That was the whole idea," I said. "They were going to look at the books today. I've got to find these guys and straighten this out. I'll call you as soon as I talk with them."

I left Louie's office and with the help of a friend, located them at the Ramada. When I got to the hotel, I found Dick and Bob, and an insurance company lawyer from Michigan was with them. I said, "Come on, Dick. Let's get this done." "I'm sorry, Ori, but I can't talk with you without our legal representative present."

I turned to the lawyer. "You're the lawyer and you're here. Let's go."

"I'm sorry, but I'm from the home office. We can't talk with you without our New York counsel present."

Something was obviously happening that wasn't good. I went to a pay phone and called Louie. After I explained what was going on, he said, "So what are you going to do now?"

"Hold on," I said.

I went back to Dick, Bob and the lawyer and said, "Hey guys, go fuck yourselves."

I then got back on the phone and told Louie what I'd done. He had played hardball by not letting them see the books, and that was a big mistake because I had nothing to hide. Now, the negotiations were over.

Not only did the insurance company pull the rug out from under me, it turned out that Bob Russell couldn't come up with the money anyway, and he was out of trust, himself, in his leasing business.

The day I had been so looking forward to turned out to be a nightmare.

* * *

On Saturday morning I flew to Florida. Rosemary was there, and Louie and his girlfriend came down. My mother, Toni, and the kids had returned to Rome, so the four of us stayed at my condo.

With the insurance company backing off and Russell not being able to come up with the purchase money, the Ori Agency was still mine. Not knowing what the future held, Louie and I agreed to take the eighty-five thousand dollars of dealership money out of the Ori Agency and deposit it at the Landmark Bank in Pompano Beach in an account in Louie's name. He said the interest rate we got was good, and the money would grow quickly. After the case was over, we'd split it up. He was right about the interest. In the four and a half years it took for the case to be settled, the money doubled.

As far as the case against me went, I got indicted

on ten counts of mail fraud and one count that had something to do with stopping payment on a check. While all this was going on, I made arrangements for a guy in Buffalo to take over my agency, and he handled the accounts for the insurance company at a reduced commission, allowing them to get back every penny I owed them.

When my case was settled, I was fined ten thousand dollars (which Louie paid from the account at Landmark Bank), ordered to pay the insurance company a hundred dollars a week for five years, and placed on probation for five years.

I went a little light on my payments to the insurance company, and on my fifty-ninth month of probation, my probation officer told me I was in danger of being in violation and sent to prison for five years. I told him the insurance company was getting paid through the reduced commission arrangement I'd worked out with the guy in Buffalo. It didn't make any difference. The order was that I pay them the hundred dollars a week, and I hadn't been doing it.

The insurance company had moved from Michigan to Florida, but Dick Sikora was still the president. I called and asked to speak with Mr. Sikora. I told the receptionist to say it was an old friend of his named Ori.

He came on the line, and I could detect the nervousness in his voice. After a little small talk I said, "Dick, I have a little problem. My probation officer wants to violate me because I haven't paid you the hundred bucks every week. That would have amounted to about to about twenty-six grand. We both know you've been paid a lot more than that through the reduced commissions, but the judge did order me to pay you. I wanted to tell you that I have some news for you. My friends in New York, and you know who they are, will put up the money to pay you off. That would be good, wouldn't it, Dick?"

"Well, yes, sure that would be good," he stammered.

"Okay. Now let me tell you the bad news. They'll put up that money under the condition that I go back into business representing another insurance company. And if that happens, guess who the car dealers are going to go with? If you want to avoid that, here's what I can do. I'll give you a thousand dollars today with a balloon payment of twenty- four thousand in five years. You'll generate a document today stating the restitution has been paid in full. What do you want to do?"

"Somebody will get right back to you."

Within two minutes I got a call, and by that afternoon, I'd paid the thousand dollars and had the paperwork stating full restitution had been made. I dropped the papers off to my probation officer. "How in the fuck did you do this?" he asked.

"Let's just say it was a lucky day."

* * *

One day while the investigation was still ongoing, I got a call from Jim Generilli. He acted like nothing was going on and didn't think I knew what he'd done. I took the high road and chatted with him like nothing was wrong. Then he started asking me questions about my friends Meyer Lansky and Sonny Franzese. I figured it was a setup. "I don't have any idea what you're talking about," I said. "I might have heard their names or read about them, but they certainly aren't friends of mine."

My suspicion was right. When my case was getting ready for trial, and Louis and I got the FBI's information on me during the discovery process, that tape was there. The FBI wanted to make an organized crime connection to what I was doing at my agency.

* * *

Regarding Toni and me, she and the kids lived at our house in Rome, and I was all over the place—California, Florida and New York City mainly. Rosemary and I saw each other as often as we could, but she never actually lived with me until we shared an apartment in Queens.

It took a couple of years for us to go from separation to divorce. During that time, Toni gave me chances to get back with her, but I rejected her every time. I caused that girl a lot of hurt for no good reason, and there was some animosity. I was supposed to pay her a hundred dollars a week, but I didn't. I provided for the kids, though.

The separation agreement was dated November 19, 1980, and the divorce was final on January 27, 1981. I'll say it again, I really fucked up.

Go figure.

Becoming Known
As A Gangster

Sonny and I had become friends, and not long after meeting him, I got an apartment on Little Neck Parkway in Little Neck, between Northern Boulevard and the Long Island Expressway. Sonny lived a short distance away in Roslyn at 47 Shrub Hollow Road. I'd often meet him and his crew on Fridays at Douglaston Manor.

We also met for breakfast several times at a restaurant in a shopping center down the street from me. Sonny would come in, take his jacket off, sit down, and place his order. Then, he would excuse himself, saying he had to go to the men's room. I thought maybe he had a health issue that required lengthy men's room visits. It wasn't until I saw an article in one of the New York papers with Sonny's picture and a caption that said, "Sonny evades the cops again," or something similar, that I understood. After reading that piece, I realized that Sonny, who was under constant law enforcement surveillance, would crawl out the men's room window, go to the other end of the shopping center, meet with his associates, and then return through the window.

Here are a couple of other Sonny stories. On Northern Boulevard in Great Neck, there was a nightclub called Strawberries. It was a great joint with chicks galore, and a ten- or fifteen-dollar cover charge to get in. I used to go there by myself a few nights a week. One day Sonny called and asked me to meet him there. I went to the club and found him sitting in a booth. "You know this place?" he asked.

"Sure. I come here all the time."

"You don't pay to come in here, do you?"

"Yeah, you have to pay, or you don't get in."

Sonny called the manager over. "How many times you been in here?" he asked me.

"Lots. Probably fifteen or twenty."

He said to the manager, "Get him his money."

The manager left and came back with all the cover charges I'd paid. When he walked away, Sonny said, "We don't pay to come in here, people pay us. I've got a piece of this place, and you'll never have to pay again."

Sonny also had a unique way of handling restaurant bills. He hardly ever picked up a check unless it was just the two of us, and then he would split it with me. Normally, there were others with us, and when the bill came, he would kick me under the table (we always sat next to each other), and he would whisper in my ear, "If you pick up that bill, I will kill you." The others always paid. He explained that the other people were there because they were telling him their problems and seeking his help. Therefore, it was their duty to cover the cost of the meals.

Sonny taught me other things, too. He said to always be on the side of the underdog, and to never call or say someone was a rat unless they were on a witness stand pointing their finger at you. He taught me other "right from wrong" lessons too. Whether you like it or not, the truth is that Sonny and others like him are really very wise and smart. Their ability to process information and make decisions is remarkable. I believe many of them are capable of running legitimate corporations, if they wanted to take that route.

He was also a magnet for women, they absolutely loved him. It wasn't just his looks and style that drove them wild. It was his charisma, as well. Besides appealing to the women, the kids admired him and wanted to be like him. I consider him to be the last of the old-time gangsters, and he's no doubt a legend in that world.

Sonny was not one to flaunt his status. I never saw him with a new car, and I remember one day he picked me up at Kennedy driving an old clunker. It quit running as we were leaving the airport, and we had to get out and push it out of traffic. He was very cautious, too, and during our conversations—unless we were talking about boxing or baseball, which he loved—we spoke in whispers. He hated telephones and rarely used one. When he did, he would never make an introduction or mention a name. If he called someone and did not hear their voice on the line, he said nothing and hung up.

In spite of his low profile, he was unquestionably a man who wielded great power. One night when we were in the Trattoria, I witnessed him giving assignments to his crew. He issued orders like a military commander, and the men accepted them without hesitation or question. It was something to watch and left no doubt as to Sonny's standing.

Another thing about Sonny was his appeal to the residents of his neighborhood. They treated him like a celebrity. People came up to him just to pay their respects. They almost always thanked him for keeping their streets safe. They loved to tell me stories about Sonny because they knew he was my friend.

I remember my friend John Connolly, an investigative journalist for *Vanity Fair* and other magazines, he always wanted to write a book about Sonny. He said if he ever did, the title would be *The Last Gangster*. Unfortunately, the book was never written.

I want to stress that in my mind, I was a friend of Sonny's, and I never considered myself to be a part of the Colombo crime family. Twice I was offered the chance to become a *made* man—once in New York and again in California. I declined both times.

I never kicked any money up to Sonny. I didn't feel I had to, because the illegal things I did in Florida and California had nothing to do with Sonny and there was no reason for me to pay him a tribute. The legal problems I had with my legitimate businesses in New York didn't involve Sonny, either.

I came to the attention of the FBI because I spent a lot of time with him, and he was one of their priority targets. As far as I'm concerned, my reputation as a gangster was due to my relationship with Sonny and not my criminal activity. Although I didn't engage in crimes with Sonny, I did discuss things with him. I remember the first time I went to him was to talk about a hit. An acquaintance of mine from Rome, who knew I was connected to Sonny, came to me with an offer of fifty thousand dollars to whack his former business partner. This guy told me that he'd gone into business with another Roman (who I also knew) in Florida, where it was fast times for Colombians and drugs in those days. His partner started using and dealing, got involved with some bad people, and screwed my friend over big time. He wanted his former partner dead.

Sonny said, "This has nothing to do with us, and we don't know the story from the other kid (the partner). And remember, if you take one dime from this guy, you have to go through with it. I don't think it's the right thing to do because we only have one half of the story."

That was the end of it for me, although I did hear later that the guy who was to be killed disappeared and has never been seen again. I don't think my acquaintance found somebody else to do the job. It's more likely that his partner screwed his drug supplier, too, and they took care of him.

* * *

Michael Franzese never liked me. In spite of what's been written by people claiming to be in the know, Michael and I had very little to do with each other and were never in business together. I never worked for him, or him for me. I always thought of him as a very smart guy, though. I believe he could have been a doctor, lawyer or anything else he wanted. Another thing I came to believe is that Michael was envious of Sonny and Sonny's friends. Understand that I have no animosity toward Michael and only wish him the best. After I moved to California and got to know Michael's mother, she called me almost every day asking about Michael and saying she needed money. I believe Michael probably did help her out sometimes, but with Tina, it was never enough.

I saw Johnny grow up, and for a while I think he may have seen me as a father figure. After he became a drug addict, I did everything I could to help him. My thanks was for him to wear a wire against me, try to entrap me, and tell lies about me on the witness stand.

Go figure.

The Sunshine State

L ouie Brindisi was a top criminal lawyer. He started coming to Florida frequently and often and stayed with me at my condo. He had already passed the bar to practice in Florida. Big drug cases were happening there every day, and Louie wanted his license, so he could get in on some of them. He had a problem, though. He was under investigation in New York about a fire that was considered suspicious in a building he owned in Utica. Florida held off issuing him a license while the investigation was still ongoing. Even with the delay in licensing, Louie ended up buying his own condo in Tiara Condominiums on Singer Island.

Louie had won a big case back in New York for a good friend of ours from Utica named Don Ritz. Don moved to Florida and opened a restaurant on Singer Island called Don's Pizza. There were a bunch of wise guys in town who claimed to have political connections that could help Louie get his Florida law license. He met with them and passed out money like it was candy. All they did was take the money, though. No favors were done.

One day Louie said he wanted to introduce me to somebody, and invited Rosemary and me to Palm Beach for dinner at an Italian restaurant. At the dinner was Louie and his wife, Don Ritz and his wife, and a guy named Joe Iannuzzi, known as Joe Dogs, and his girlfriend. Joe Dogs was affiliated with the Gambino family.

We discussed an escort business I was planning to start. I intended to use a phone number in Dade County, but wanted to set it up so the calls would actually be answered in Broward County. Joe told me he could get me connections into the major hotels on the beach, The Diplomat, Fontainebleau, etc. He also said he had a friend with a real estate office in Plantation, Florida (Broward County), and that I could probably rent space there to run my business. He promised to make arrangements for me to look at the place.

On our way home, Rosemary told me that when I'd left the table to use the restroom, Joe Dogs tried to hit on her. There is a rule in *the life* that you don't mess around with another man's woman. I knew then I couldn't trust the guy, and I warned Louie about him.

A short time later, Joe did have his friend call me to arrange a meeting. Louie and I were at my condo when the guy called. We agreed to get together at a restaurant and lounge called Stan's, located on the Intracoastal Waterway in Fort Lauderdale. The meeting was on a weekday afternoon. Normally, I would just go to valet, leave my car, and go inside. Because I was suspicious of Joe Dogs, I did things a little different, though. The guy had given me a physical description of himself, so on the day of the meeting, I parked across the street and watched the valet line. He showed up in a new car with no plates with stickers still on the windows. That made me even more suspicious. I let him get inside the restaurant, and then went in behind him. We talked a little, and then I suggested we go check out his office and the space he might rent to me.

We left the restaurant in our own cars, and I followed him out to the location, which was in a strip mall. Remember, this was supposed to be a real estate office that he owned. He unlocked the door and we went inside. There was no one else there. Each desktop was arranged in an identical manner, containing a phone, notepad and pen. I knew a little bit about real estate, and this was not a working real estate office—no way. I was sure it was a setup.

I looked at the guy and said, "I've been thinking this over and decided I'm not going to get into business here. I really like California and that's where I'm heading."

That ended it right there. When I told Louie about what happened at the meeting, he agreed the guy was probably an FBI agent. Many years later, when I was being questioned by the Secret Service in Los Angeles, they let it slip that the incident had in fact been an attempted sting.

It turned out Joe Dogs was a big FBI informant. Not long after I met with his "friend," I learned that there had been a plan to give Joe a beating in the kitchen of Don Ritz's restaurant, and then kill him. It was going to happen on a Monday, the day the restaurant was closed.

Tommy Agro (known as Tommy A), Joe's local boss, and two of his crew scooped Joe up and took him to the restaurant. They beat him with pipes and were ready to kill him when Don's wife came in unexpectedly. The murder was scrubbed, and Joe was turned loose with just the beating. Marilyn Ritz's impromptu stop at the restaurant saved Joe's life.

Joe ended up testifying for the government in major organized crime trials and helped put several New York and Florida mobsters in prison. His cooperation earned him a spot in the federal Witness Protection Program.

* * *

Another time, I had just flown back to Florida from New York, where I'd taken care of some business and had dinner with Sonny. Louie called and said he had found another guy, a bar owner, he thought could do him some good and he wanted me to meet him. I wasn't especially excited about it because of what had happened with Joe Dogs, but I agreed to the meeting anyway. Rosemary and I again drove up to Palm Beach.

Louie and his wife Rosemary, me and my Rosemary, and Don Ritz and his wife, we all went to the joint that this guy owned. I thought it was kind of a dump, and not someplace I'd hang out at. Louie spotted his new friend at the bar, went over and talked with him, and then brought him over to me and introduced us. I was talking with the guy, we were feeling each other out, when Louie blurted out that I'd had dinner with Sonny in New York the previous night. Louie had no business mentioning Sonny's name. Anyway, the guy asked me directly if I knew Sonny. I said I did. He turned white as a sheet. He told Louie that there was nothing he could do for him. If he tried, he'd probably have a problem. He was obviously trying to grab Louie for a few bucks.

We all left, and when we got outside, Louie grabbed me and kissed me on the cheek. He said, "Introduce me to Sonny—please"

Not long after that, Frank Russo, Louie and his pal Carmine Tripolone, and I, we went to the City where I made the introduction. As the ones who introduced Louie to Sonny, Frank and I were responsible for him. It turned out to be a real headache.

After meeting Sonny, it seemed that Louie started to think he was a gangster and not a lawyer. He began drinking heavily and started carrying a gun, which he sometimes waved around in nightclubs. He and Don Ritz bought a steak house on Okeechobee Road in West Palm Beach, and they started booking sports bets. That's when the problems began. They had trouble over some bets they made with the wrong guys. Don got a beating, and Louie was going to be next. That meant I had to talk with Sonny to see if he could work his magic and get the matter resolved before it went any further.

I met with Sonny at Douglaston Manor and told him what was happening. This was the third time Sonny had to intervene on Louie's behalf, and he was getting pissed. He asked me to get Louie to come to the City immediately to talk things over. I called Louie and couldn't get him to commit to the meeting. After my fourth failed attempt, Sonny told me to meet him again at Douglaston.

It turned out that while I'd been trying to pin Louie

105

down, the people who had the beef with him had come to Sonny with their side of the story.

"So what should be done?" Sonny asked.

"Squash it. He is my friend."

"Okay, Kid, but this is the last time I will do it. Louie is starting to make us look bad. Tell him to come in and talk. No more delays."

The following week Louie, Carmine and I went to meet Sonny at a joint in Brooklyn. When we got there, I was surprised that a guy I'd never seen before was waiting for me at the door. He asked my name and then told me Sonny had called. He left a message for me that he'd be late, and we should wait for him. After a while Sonny called. He told me he'd be in shortly and to keep everybody there.

I went back to the table and told Louie and Carmine we'd have to wait a little longer. They had the balls to get upset. I'd used my connections to get Louie out of trouble several times and actually saved his life. His ass was being kept above ground, and it wasn't costing him a dime. He was still walking, talking and breathing because of Sonny and me, and he had the nerve to get upset because he had to wait a little while for the meeting. I couldn't fucking believe it.

Sonny finally arrived. He told Louie, "This is the last time I will intervene for you. Never come to me again with this kind of thing."

Sonny got Louie off the hook, as promised, and it was the last time he went to bat for him. It wasn't the last time Louie screwed up, though. And he remained someone I had to deal with frequently. In spite of the dumb things he did sometimes, he seemed to walk on water and was always able to make money—lots of it.

As for me, I felt I needed a change of scenery, so I decided to move to California.

Go figure.

PART

TWO

California

13

~∘∘∘~

Pregnancy Issue
& A Wedding

The Ori Agency investigation was still ongoing when Rosemary got pregnant. So there I was, not knowing what would happen with the investigation, recently divorced, and with a pregnant girlfriend. Rosemary made it clear she wanted to have the baby. She said she hoped it was a girl and, if so, she would name her Brianna.

The pregnancy really played on my emotions. I was sure Rosemary would be a great mother, but I didn't want any more children. I didn't want my kids talking about step- brothers or sisters. I was still feeling guilty over splitting up with Toni—whom my mother, family and friends all loved, and they hated me for leaving her and the children.

Under the circumstances, I felt I had no choice but to talk Rosemary into having an abortion. She eventually agreed with me and aborted the pregnancy, but she hated me for it. A short time afterward we had a big argument, and I told her to get out. She left. I figured she would probably take a walk around the block to cool off and come back, as she had before. She didn't. A week went by, and I didn't hear from her. I called her mother in San Francisco—she wasn't there. When Rosemary lived with me in Little Neck, I introduced her to my friend Louie Lentini and his wife. They had become quite close. I thought I'd take a chance and see if Louie or his wife had heard from her. I called and could tell by Louie's voice he had information about Rosemary, but wasn't able to talk openly. He called me back later. Rosemary was staying at his place, and she and his wife had sworn him to secrecy. I told him that secrecy or no secrecy, he was to get her a plane ticket to San Francisco and get her out of New York. That cleared up one problem, at least for the time being.

* * *

I had created a Polyglycoat lotto designed to get people back into the dealership service department to sell them additional Polyglycoat-related products. It was based on the New York State Lottery. Walter Fiveson's operation was receiving a lot of bad press at the time. John Stossel was still actively condemning the products on TV, and competitors were popping up.

Walter loved my idea and arranged for me to visit all of his distributors throughout the country to introduce the lotto to them. My first stop was Houston, followed by Los Angeles, and then San Francisco on a Friday.

My friend Pat (Buddy) Caselnouvo from Orange County, California (originally from Rome), was in town at the same time, and we decided to meet at Fisherman's Wharf for dinner. Prior to leaving for the restaurant, I was still in my hotel room when it occurred to me to give Rosemary a call and invite her to join me, Pat, and his girlfriend for dinner. She accepted.

I've heard it said that absence makes the heart grow fonder. That was certainly true in my relationship with Rosemary. We had a great time that night, and the animosity she'd had toward me over the abortion seemed to be gone. We all decided to go to the wineries in Napa the next day, and we visited several. We bought wine and cheese at one and relaxed on the lawn on a blanket we brought along. Feeling pretty good from the wine, Pat said to Rosemary and me, "Why don't you guys cut the shit. It's obvious you love each other. Why don't we shoot over to Reno, and you can get married?"

Rosemary and I looked at each other.

"What do you say?" she asked.

"Let's do it," I said.

You need to understand that Walter wasn't paying me to do the tour—I was representing my own company. I had virtually no cash. I'd bet that between Pat and me, we didn't have over a hundred dollars. That didn't stop us, though. We drove to Reno, arriving at night, and found a wedding chapel that would do the service for thirty-five bucks. Within five minutes Rosemary and I were married. Then the realization hit that we didn't have enough money for hotel rooms, much less a party.

I was by no means a gambling professional, but I'd always enjoyed playing blackjack, and that night I had a good feeling. I was known as a hit and run artist, meaning when I won I took my money and ran. So I drove around Reno looking for a small casino where I could try my luck. When I found what I was looking for, I parked on the street and had Pat give me his remaining money—about fifty dollars. I told him and the girls to wait in the car, and I went inside and found a table. I was hot and rode the streak, doubling and redoubling my winnings. In a fairly short time I was five thousand dollars ahead, and cashed out. I rented a suite at a nice hotel, and we had our party.

* * *

Walter had scheduled a distributor meeting in Boca Raton, Florida, at the Boca Hotel and Country Club, a very beautiful and expensive place. My cousin, Anthony Bartolotti, known as Bucky, who was to be my partner in a new operation that Walter was developing called Polyglycoat Service Centers, met me there. I told Rosemary that I wanted to see him alone for a few minutes to break the news about our marriage. I met him at the pool.

"Great seeing you," Bucky said, giving me a big hug. "There's a lot of action here. We're gonna have a ball, believe me."

"Sorry, but I can't. I'm married now and those days are over for me."

He looked shocked. "You're bullshitting me, right?"

"No, I'm not." I nodded toward Rosemary, who was making her way toward us.

His shocked expression was replaced by what I

thought was sadness. "Okay. I never liked her, but because she's your wife I will respect her." And he did.

Bucky is the best. He has always been there for me, supporting me with his time and money when I needed it. That relationship continues. I don't have the words to adequately express my feelings toward that man.

Unfortunately, in a matter of weeks, Walter Fiveson's business had dropped off to the point he had to file for bankruptcy. With Walter's idea of Polyglycoat Service Centers now out of play, Bucky and I decided to open our own auto service center in Yorkville, New York (a suburb of Utica), called Centurion Automotive. We'd staff it with the people from the Polyglycoat business. The Carbone family operated several automobile dealerships in and around Utica, the largest auto group in the area. I was friends with Joe Carbone (the old man) and arranged to rent one of their unused buildings on Commercial Drive, a prime business location. Centurion did well, and even after I moved to California, Bucky ran it for several more years. It is still in business today under different ownership.

Go figure.

Yellow Pages

After our wedding, Rosemary and I made the decision to move to San Francisco, her hometown. I had nothing going for me businesswise—I needed work, and since sales was my strong suit, I started looking for something to sell. I answered an ad for Asian Yellow Pages advertising sales, but didn't get a response and forgot about it. Then, almost two months later, I got a call from a man named David Savin. He asked me to come into the Yellow Pages office at 680 Beech Street.

When I arrived, there was no receptionist and the room was empty, but I could hear guys talking in another room. I knocked on the door where I heard the voices. It was answered by David Savin and his partner George Zozzaro. I found it odd they seemed to have no staff, no printed material, no nothing—just an office. It was weird, yet intriguing, so I stayed, and we talked. They told me they were planning to print yellow page phone books in Chinese and Japanese—two major populations in San Francisco— and were looking for salespeople. Then they interviewed me and asked questions about my background in sales.

I was offered a salesman position, and I said I'd let them know and left. When I got home, my phone was ringing. It was David. He told me he and George felt I was very sharp. Would I take the position of sales manager? I declined, but David called the next day and asked me to meet George for lunch to discuss a business proposition. I agreed.

The gist of the proposal was that I could buy half of the business for fifteen thousand dollars. I looked at him and said, "George, I bet your phones are being shut off. You're behind on the rent, and who knows what else. Any minute I expect Dave to walk in the door to try to close the deal."

George leaned back in his chair and smiled at me. "We were right. You are pretty sharp."

As if on cue, Dave showed up and sat down with us. I said, "Your idea is fantastic, but I don't think you're the guys to pull it off. I'll tell you what. I'll give you five thousand for the whole business. That'll take you off the hook and give me something I might be able to build up."

They accepted my offer, and we met again the next day at Hippopotamus Hamburgers on Van Ness Avenue to finalize things. The only problem was I didn't have any money, not even the five-thousand-dollar purchase price. That issue was resolved the same day, though.

Across from my apartment was a call girl, and we had

become friends. She worked for the biggest agency in the city, owned by an Englishman named Frank Grace. She introduced me to him. He and his two main call girls, Margo and Ruth, agreed to put up the money—about twenty grand total—to cover the purchase price and initial operating expenses. They would own the business, and I'd run it for ten percent of the sales.

With the financing resolved, I got busy on the Asian Yellow Pages. Sales for the first issue had to close soon, and I needed to find a place to get the books printed. I decided to use a printer in Los Angeles, the largest printer of Yellow Page directories at that time. I also started hiring sales staff.

And then Frank dropped the hammer. He came to the office and said he and the girls no longer wanted me running the business. He offered me a five thousand dollar buy-out. I said I'd take ten. He said he had to talk with his partners, left and returned with a check for ten thousand. I cleaned out my desk and caught a taxi home.

When the telemarketers and sales people learned I was no longer there, they all walked off the job, leaving Frank and the girls with no employees and deadlines approaching.

Frank reached out to me several times to tell me they wanted me back, but I wouldn't talk with him. After a couple of weeks, I agreed to meet. He tried to hire me back at a lower percentage, and I said no. He finally reinstated me at the same ten percent I had originally agreed to. I knew this resolution was only a temporary fix. A legitimate business can't show a pimp and prostitutes as the owners of record. I knew there would be more battles with Frank down the road.

Upon my return, the staff came back to work, and I put on additional sales people. One of my first hires was a young man named Jimmy Stein. He was originally from Los Angeles and had worked at a circus where he guessed the height, weight and age of customers. Even though he was short on sales experience, there was something about him I liked. On his first day at work, I taught him how to make appointments on the phone. The next day I took him with me on those appointments. We sold everyone we talked to. In addition to his natural talent, Jimmy was eager to learn. He came to my apartment almost every night, and we talked about sales techniques. I really liked him, and we became quite close.

Although things were off to a good start, I still had a problem—Frank Grace.

* * *

Frank had become a real pain in the ass. He didn't know anything about the business, but wanted to flex his muscles as an owner. He came to the office nearly every day looking for something to do, or just hung around and drove me nuts.

I hadn't told him about my intention to use the printer in Los Angeles. So to get him out of my hair, I had him go to local printers to get prices for the directories, knowing that they couldn't compete with the printer in L.A. As expected, the prices he came back with were crazy. We needed to distribute about 250,000 books. The local printers wanted three dollars per book. I told him, "Frank, there's no way we can come up with that kind of money."

That was true, but unbeknown to Frank, Jimmy and I had gone to Los Angeles and made a deal to get the directories printed for sixty-four cents each. We had sold enough advertising that getting the number of directories we needed printed was doable at that price.

The next thing I had to do was get Frank and his girls out of the business. My selling point for them to give up ownership would be that money had been collected from advertisers for the directory. However, because the amount was insufficient to get the directories printed at the prices Frank had found, the paid advertisers would undoubtedly want their money back. They might even make criminal complaints that they had been defrauded. If Frank and the girls gave up their ownership to a company I set up, they would lose their initial investment, but avoid any additional civil or criminal liability. I went to a lawyer and had him prepare the documents to set up a company for Jimmy and me to take over the Asian Yellow pages. Fifty percent of the stock was in Jimmy's name. The unassigned fifty percent was mine.

When I approached Frank and the girls with my proposal, the women were all for it. They didn't want any legal problems and were ready to bail. Frank was stubborn, though. It wasn't a matter of money for him—he wasn't hurting financially. It was an ego thing. Frank wouldn't budge and got very upset with me. The situation was bad and went downhill from there. In fact, he imported a hit man from England to kill me.

* * *

Ever since I was a kid back in Rome and Tom Arcuri lectured me about being alert to my surroundings, I have been efficient at spotting potential danger. When Frank's guy started tailing me, I detected him right away. I didn't know he was working for Frank then, just that he was on me and watching my movements. I started keeping an eye on him.

I got a jolt when I realized he'd moved into the apartment building right across the street from mine. Our windows were facing, and we could actually look at each other from our respective apartments. I called the manager of his building and spoke with him. I eventually got him to tell me that the guy in that apartment was from England and was on a short-term lease. The person who had signed the lease was Frank Grace. I got the picture and knew I had to move quickly.

When I previously lived in Los Angeles, I became friends with a guy named Emilio Camera, who was my limo driver. He was a tough guy, a very tough guy. I reached out to him and asked him to come to San Francisco right away, to act as a bodyguard to Rosemary and me.

A day or so after Emilio got into town, Rosemary, Emilio and I went to the Chestnut Bar and Grill for dinner. As we waited for a table, Frank and his hit man walked in. I grabbed the guy's arm and said I wanted to introduce him to Emilio. After the introduction, Emilio said, "I've got something very important to talk with you about—in private."

They went outside, and a few minutes later, Emilio came back in alone. He whispered to me that Frank's guy had decided to return to England and caught a cab to the airport. I never saw him again after that.

There was still a piece of unfinished business, though. The girls had signed the papers to turn the business over to my new company, the Ori Advertising Agency, but Frank was still being stubborn and wouldn't sign. There was only one thing to do.

A day or two later Emilio paid a call on Frank. Before he left, Frank's signature was on all the necessary documents. I paid Emilio for his services, and he went back to Los Angeles a happy man. We remain friends and talk regularly.

I really didn't want to have to run the new company on a daily basis, so I offered Jimmy an equal partnership. He took charge and got the directory printed and distributed. I later sold him my half for twenty-five thousand dollars.

I never heard from Frank again. I understand he fled the country because the law was looking at him concerning prostitution-related charges. Ruth went to college and became a lawyer. Margo became a nurse.

I should have been celebrating my success. There was more going on in my life than the Yellow Pages, though, and not all of it was good.

Go figure.

15

Indictment

I was doing a lot of traveling between San Francisco and Los Angeles. When in L.A., I received my phone messages at a friend's hair salon on Hillhurst Avenue in West Hollywood. On a Friday, about four and a half years after the investigation of my Ori Agency began, I walked into the salon and was given a message to call Louie Brindisi. I dialed him up and got the bad news. I'd been indicted on eleven federal counts of mail fraud.

I couldn't help but think that if Louie had let the insurance company see my records when they wanted to, maybe none of this would have happened. Regardless, it was what it was, and I had to deal with it.

Louie said he'd arranged for me to surrender in Syracuse the following Wednesday, and he'd have a bail bondsman there. I flew back and turned myself in.

At arraignment, I was granted bail, and the court gave me permission to fly back and forth between California and New York to appear at necessary proceedings. After I was released, I met with Louie to discuss what had happened and what he thought would happen.

The first thing I wanted to know was how in the hell I'd been charged with mail fraud. Louie explained that because the car dealers sent me their reports through the mail, it was considered mail fraud. I thought of it as a normal way of conducting business and had trouble believing it was a crime. After all, I had a deal with the insurance company, and they were well aware of what I was doing. *How could it be illegal?*

Louie had his uncle, a former judge, and a promising twenty-six-year-old lawyer named Joey Dacquino, doing the research work on my case. Based on what they'd found and his own experience, Louie said he was sure he could work out a deal that would require me to admit to one or more of the charges. It would cost me money— probably almost everything I had—but no jail time.

As I digested Louie's words, I began to have doubts about how he had represented me so far. In spite of his stellar reputation as a lawyer, could I have done better? I told him I needed to think the plea offer over, and I'd get back to him on what I wanted to do.

Unbeknown to Louie, I decided to contact F. Lee Bailey and Melvin Belli, two of the best-known attorneys in the country, as potential replacements for him. They both told me the same thing. They could beat the case at trial, but it would cost me fifty thousand dollars up front. I knew that this fifty grand would no doubt double, triple, or more, as the case ran its course. I didn't have that kind of money and was stuck with Louie and his plan for a deal. I told him to go ahead.

On January 4th, 1983, while negotiations on my case were still in progress, two things happened. Louie's wife Jackie died in a Utica hospital following a long illness, and later that day, Joey Dacquino was murdered. Below is a portion of an article that appeared on the *Utica Observer Dispatch* website on May 9, 2009;

"Joseph Dacquino was finishing some last-minute legal work on the upstairs floor of Louis Brindisi's law office on Genesee Street in South Utica when the cleaning woman began vacuuming the carpet.

"Brindisi's wife had died from cancer earlier that day, so he was not in the office.

"As Dacquino came downstairs, he stumbled upon an unexpected visitor. While the vacuum cleaner hummed upstairs and a radio played in the background, the intruder—armed with a .38 caliber handgun—knotted Dacquino's hands and feet with rope. His eyes and mouth were also taped shut.

"The visitor then wrapped a jacket around his weapon and walked towards Dacquino. The cleaning woman upstairs would never hear the three gunshots fired into the young attorney's head.

"Just hours after his wife's death, Brindisi was forced to cope with the violent death of his legal associate. At the time, there was no easy answer to explain why.

"Perhaps someone was trying to send a message to Brindisi, who had made plenty of headlines in the previous decade representing a variety of rough characters linked to organized crime. Or maybe it was a case of mistaken identity, and the killer thought he was shooting Brindisi himself.

"The year was only four days old, but 1983 was dawning as one of the most violent in Utica's annals of organized crime. Yet, while it wouldn't yet be clear, it also marked the beginning of the end of traditional racketeering in the city.

"And it meant an important decision for Brindisi himself: Soon, he would be done handling criminal cases.

"'I always liked the practice of criminal law,' says the 74-year-old Brindisi, whose civil law firm has advertised heavily on television over the past year. "I was a good lawyer, and I did a good job for my clients. But after that incident involving Joey, I just didn't want to be involved with any criminals.'"

Louie had made some dangerous enemies over the years, and I'm convinced the killer was after him, not Joey Dacquino. In a way, even in death Jackie Brindisi (whom I'd met) saved her husband's life by keeping him away from his office when the murderer visited. It seemed obvious to me that the hit man was from out of town. Jackie's death was big news in Utica and Rome, and local talent probably would have known Louie wouldn't be in his office.

Later, a dead body was found in New York City, and it was speculated that the dead man was Joey Dacquino's killer. I don't know if that was ever verified, though.

Louie made a decision not to practice criminal law anymore, and he didn't. Instead, he became an ambulance chaser. One of his first cases was against Niagara Mohawk Power Corporation, and he got close to forty million dollars for his clients. I don't know what Louie ended up with, but it had to be a lot.

* * *

As my case got closer to trial without an agreement being reached, I made more frequent trips to New York. I flew in for one final session while on crutches due to a sprained ankle. Louie had a meeting scheduled with U.S. Attorney Paula Ryan in a last-ditch effort to get a plea deal in place before jury selection began.

I was sitting in the waiting room and getting anxious. I decided to go into the meeting room and find out what was going on. When I entered the room, there were boxes all over the floor with "Ori Agency" written on them. I knew damn well that couldn't be good.

I joined the conversation. The prosecutor offered me five years of probation, plus a fine and restitution. Still thinking I could beat the case in court, I said, "Let's go to trial," and the next day, we were in the courtroom waiting to start jury selection. Louie and Carmine Tripolone were seated on either side of me.

Carmine said to me, "Ori, take a look at the prospective jurors walking into that room. They all look like hayseeds, and we're going to have to pick some of them to hear your case."

"I know that. What about it?"

"They are all farmers. Your defense is complicated— all about insurance, contracts and agreements. Do you really think they'll understand it enough to acquit you?"

I gave his words some thought and then said, "I see your point. It's something to think about."

The case that was going on while we waited was the sentencing of a young guy who'd been convicted at trial of pulling off a fifteen-thousand-dollar scam. The judge gave him three years in prison.

I was accused of stealing three hundred and eighty-five grand. If I was found guilty, what kind of time would I get? This was getting scary.

I nudged Louie and told him, "Go see the prosecutor and see if that plea offer is still on the table. If it is, I'll take it."

The deal was made. I pled guilty to one count of mail fraud and one count having something to do with stopping payment on a check. I received probation, a fine and restitution, but no jail time.

When I left San Francisco for my date with destiny, I asked Rosemary to come with me. She refused. With one exception, I had no one backing me—no wife, family members or friends.

The only person in the courtroom to support me that day was the always reliable Bucky. When we walked out of the courthouse together, the reporters thought he was me. Bucky's picture ended up making it into all the local TV and newspaper reports.

* * *

Bucky has always been by my side. On weekends when I was living in the City, I would drive to Rome to visit my children. I stayed in the living quarters Bucky had above his restaurant. The restaurant was doing well, and every week when I got there, I found money in a drawer that he'd put aside for me. I never asked him for it, he just did it.

There aren't many Buckys around. If you find a friend or relative like him, treat that person like a rare treasure.

Go figure.

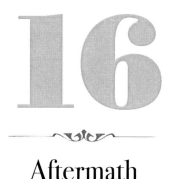

Aftermath

After leaving the courthouse, I called Toni and asked her to bring the children to my mother's house so I could see them. When I got there, Toni congratulated me for not going to jail. Then she said, "I've got some bad news. The IRS was just here and served me with papers."

Approximately forty minutes after I had made my deal in Syracuse, the fucking IRS was at my mother's in Rome serving papers to my ex-wife. In the time it took for Louie to drive me from court to my mother's home, they served the papers to Toni. They said we owed two hundred thousand in back taxes.

Thinking I had a good sum of money coming from what Louie and I stashed at the bank in Florida, I drove to his office. He didn't give me any money. What I got was an itemized bill listing the time he spent representing me, and every possible office expense, from copy paper to paper clips. That's when he told me that my share of the Florida money all went to satisfy his bill. There was nothing left.

Considering all the money Louie had been paid and what he took from me, I wasn't very happy, but I could not dispute the bill. I had little choice but to chalk it up as a learning experience. I hired him, so part of the blame was on me. Looking back, I probably should have hired a good business lawyer. Who knows?

That experience caused me to be much more selective when I hiring a lawyer in the future and to learn about the law myself. In the long term, that proved to be a benefit.

* * *

My probation was out of Albany, but because I lived in San Francisco, my file was transferred there to an office on Golden Gate Avenue. The probation officer (PO) laid the rules down and gave me six reporting forms. I was to submit one by mail each month and report to him personally in six months. That was a real blessing because reporting in person is such a pain in the ass.

Rosemary and I were living in Pacific Heights. I hung out a lot on Union Street in the Marina District. It had numerous cafés and restaurants, and it was always busy. I was able to make a lot of good contacts on Union Street. With my troubles in New York no longer hanging over my head and the Asian Yellow Pages showing potential, things appeared to be going pretty well.

Below the surface there were problems with Rosemary that I felt in my gut. I can't tell you all of them with certainty, but I believe there may have been some lingering animosity over the abortion I insisted she have. There was also a lot of jealousy between us, and it wasn't all about concerns over other men or women—we were jealous of each other, too. She was a very beautiful woman, and men's heads turned when she walked into a room. Back in New York, that wasn't too much of a problem because making moves on another man's woman was not allowed. Not so in California—they played by a different set of rules.

In addition, Rosemary's refusal to come to Syracuse with me for my court appearance hurt me bad, and I hadn't gotten over it. These may all have been contributing factors to our troubles; however, there was one thing that bothered me the most—I thought Rosemary was cheating on me.

One night I came across a matchbook she had left at home. It was from the restaurant where I knew she and the guy she was with in Vegas used to meet (when I first met her). He was a Vice President at Bank of America.

Two of my guys drove to the Bank of America parking garage and waited for Rosemary's friend to come to work. The brothers grabbed him, brought him to the limo, and put him into the backseat with me. Was he scared? Sure.

We had a talk. Although there was no rough stuff, the unspoken threat of it was in the air. He admitted he'd had dinner with Rosemary, but swore there was nothing more to it than that. Rosemary had initiated the meeting, saying she was concerned that she was losing me and needed someone to talk with. Neil was her friend and agreed to see her.

His explanation made sense. I believed him. Their relationship probably was just being friends. In a rather odd twist, he and I later became friends and met for drinks now and then at O'Henry's.

I decided to try harder to make the marriage work, but Rosemary wanted to have kids, and I did not. Neither of us was willing to change our position. Eventually, I told her that since we couldn't resolve our differences about having children, the only logical thing to do was to get divorced, and I wasn't very nice about it. My divorce suggestion included the provision that she not start dating until the divorce was final.

Rosemary couldn't do it, though. She started seeing a car salesman and friends told me about it. I was tight with so many people in the area that I was always being told where Rosemary and her friend went for dinner or drinks, and even what they ordered.

I decided to let her indiscretions slide. I had my own irons in the fire that needed attention.

* * *

Some of my associates and I wanted to get into the gambling business. The plan was to get a truck and put a casino in it. The operation would be completely portable, so we could switch locations frequently and keep a step ahead of the cops. I did a lot of research on how much it would cost to purchase and refurbish a rig, where there were relatively safe areas to set up, if there were cops who could be bought, and other operational matters. I talked with a lot of people.

One night I went to O'Henry's Restaurant to meet

my partners. They were very nervous. Some old, Italian wise guys in North Beach (North Beach is the Italian area of San Francisco) had put out the word that they wanted to see me right away. Their message included the name of a restaurant where they would meet me.

I went to the meeting alone. When I got to the restaurant, I was led to the kitchen, where three older Italian-looking guys were sitting at a table. I joined them.

The man who seemed to be in charge said, "We've been hearing your name quite a bit, but so far you haven't been a problem and we've left you alone. This gambling business is different, though, and it isn't in our interests to let it get started."

I knew I was in big fucking trouble.

He continued. "Who are you with that you think you can come here and do this kind of thing? We need a name. Now."

I didn't invoke Sonny Franzese's name very often, but if there was ever a time to use it, this was it. When I said his name, the effect was stunning, and reflected the high regard in which Sonny was held by mobsters all across the country. The three guys exchanged glances, and then the boss said, "If you're with Sonny, you can do what you want here."

We had dinner and I left the restaurant under my own power. I was a very happy camper.

After that meeting, I lost interest in the mobile casino idea and decided it was time for a change of scenery.

Go figure.

Los Angeles Bound

It was 1983 and I was again leading the single life. Every morning David Savin and I met at O'Henry's on Union Street. Like me, David always dressed in a suit and tie. It was actually kind of funny. Two guys dressed up every day with no place to go, but at least we looked good.

One morning, David saw an ad in the paper that the Better Business Bureau (BBB) Yellow Pages Directory was opening offices in Los Angeles and looking for managers. Figuring we had nothing to lose, we got into David's Mercedes (his pride and joy at the time) and drove to the Yellow Pages office on Howard Street. The elevator doors opened into the company's reception area, and we asked to see the company president, Don Wolf. He wasn't in, so I gave the receptionist my name, said

I'd like Mr. Wolf to contact me, and then we left. As we got to the elevator, two large men got off and passed us. It turned out one of them was Don Wolf. The receptionist gave him my message. He'd heard of me through my involvement with the Asian Yellow Pages, wanted to talk and ran for the elevator.

David and I were walking down Howard Street when we heard my name being called. We turned around and saw this three hundred and fifty-pound man running toward us. When he caught up, he identified himself as Don Wolf, and he asked us to come back to his office with him, which we did. The gist of the conversation was that Don's expansion plans called for initially opening two offices in the Los Angeles area—one on Venice Boulevard right off Interstate 10, and the other in Torrance. He needed experienced managers for those offices, and he felt David and I were well-qualified. We accepted his offer to manage the Venice Boulevard location.

We packed up and headed for L.A. in David's Mercedes. Living in hotels initially, we put our efforts into getting the office up and running, with the first imperative of putting together a sales staff.

My personal rule regarding hiring sales people is that once you take your want ad out of the paper, you are out of business. I say that because commission sales positions are high turnover. You might hire and train twenty people, and two weeks later only three or four of them are still there. So you have to constantly recruit. It's tedious, but necessary.

Los Angeles is a big, diverse territory, and we hired people of varying ethnicity to best fit specific areas. However, for some reason they all wanted to work in either Beverly Hills or the better parts of Hollywood. This created a problem that David and I had to address.

To make a point, I told David, "Tomorrow, you and I are going out in the field, and we're going to work Watts."

The color drained from his face, indicating he wasn't enthused about entering the mostly minority-populated neighborhood. His concerns didn't matter, though. We had to set an example for the sales staff.

The next morning, David and I were dressed to the nines. In addition to a suit and tie, I also had on my French cuffs and was flaunting a Rolex and a diamond pinky ring. David thought I was nuts, and he tried to talk me into taking the jewelry off. I didn't fear blacks or Hispanics, and I wasn't prejudiced.

"Don't worry about it. Everything will be okay." I said.

When we got into Watts, I saw palm trees and homes and businesses that looked well maintained. I said, "So this is Watts, huh? Hell, the east side of New York City doesn't look this good."

Our first stop was at a locksmith shop. I made that sale and then hit every business up and down the street, getting orders at almost all of them. The owners were intelligent and fantastic to deal with. It was a fun day and very profitable as well.

At the sales meeting the next morning, I showed everyone the figures David and I had generated in Watts. They were amazed and realized good commissions could be made in areas other than Beverly Hills. Problem solved.

David and I got an apartment in West Hollywood. We worked hard, but we also played hard. Every night after work we went out drinking in restaurants and clubs. I spent a lot of time with my friend Emilio. He was a real party animal and served as my bodyguard when needed.

After David and I got the BBB office up and running, we stayed for a little while, and then left to try our luck at other endeavors.

* * *

David always had a tendency to meet people in some sort of con or another. One day he introduced me to a guy who was living in the Magic Castle Hotel on Franklin Avenue, which was right next to The Magic Castle Nightclub. The guy's brother was supposedly the original Marlboro Man.

Anyway, he had this idea to take pictures of aspiring actors and tell them that for a hefty price, he'd get them the acting jobs they were looking for. He needed twenty-five thousand dollars in financing to get his scam started. He wanted David and me to put up the money. Although we didn't have the money, I thought his scheme had potential and figured I might be able to get the cash if I went to New York and pitched the plan to Sonny.

David and I flew to New York on the low-cost People Express Airline. We got there on a Friday, and I told David I was going upstate to see my children and mother, and I would be back on Sunday. I knew he had a credit card with a little room left, so I said for him to get us a nice hotel for Sunday night. In the meantime, he could stay with his old partner George Zozzaro, who was then living in New York City.

I flew into the City on Sunday night, and David told me he had reservations at a place right on Central

Park. Fantastic, right? Wrong. He had us booked into the YMCA—community bathroom and all. I got very little sleep that night, and in the morning, I called my old haunt, the Warwick. I told the manager I was in the city and need a place to stay, but I had no money. He told me to come to the hotel right away.

All the business I'd given the Warwick in the past paid off. We were comped a suite with a wine and a cheese plate thrown in. On top of that, the valets refused to take our tips. "Not from Mr. Spado," they said. This is unheard of in New York City.

I then called Sonny and asked for a meeting. He agreed to see me and David at the Trattoria Siciliana. After I made the introduction, I asked David to go to the bar and let me talk with Sonny alone. When David left, I told Sonny how much money I needed and why.

He said, "I'll give you the money, but do you think it is right to take money from these kids (wannabe actors)?"

When he asked, I realized I hadn't thought about it as right or wrong. I'd only thought of the potential profits.

"No, it probably isn't right," I admitted. "Let's forget about it."

"I think that is best. It doesn't satisfy your need for money, though, does it?"

I shrugged. "There will be other things. I'll find something."

"I'll tell you what. I'm going to give you the name of a bookmaker. Go see him and tell him I want him to loan you fifty thousand dollars. When he gives it to you, give me half and you keep the other half."

I must have looked confused, because he smiled at me and said, "When he comes to you for repayment, tell him you gave the entire fifty thousand to me. That will be the end of it."

I did as Sonny said. We got twenty-five thousand dollars each, and the bookie got screwed. There was no way he'd make a move against Sonny. He had no choice but to take the loss and keep his mouth shut.

* * *

We stayed in the City for over three weeks and made contact with several of my old pals. One of them, Eddie Gardner, came over one night. He had a line of credit at one of the Atlantic City casinos. He gave me his card and said, "If you want to go there and are able to use it, let me know, and afterward I'll report it as stolen."

It happened that David and Eddie were very similar in appearance, and David was good at duplicating signatures. We took the bus to Atlantic City and David practiced Eddie's signature all the way. We banged the card out for several thousand dollars, then took a limo back to the City. I ran up twenty-five hundred dollars in additional charges at the hotel, which I paid, and the next day, we left for California.

Poor Eddie didn't make out very well, though. The casino didn't buy his report that his card had been stolen. Their security cameras back then were primitive by today's standards, and they maintained that the guy shown in the footage was Eddie. They took the money out of his savings account and his wife went ballistic. There was nothing he could do, though, and had to eat the loss.

* * *

Not long after I got back to Los Angeles, I learned I had additional problems in San Francisco regarding Rosemary and her love life with the boy across the street from her mother's.

Go figure.

Another Divorce

After Rosemary and I split, she moved in with her mother in the Mission District. I was just back in Los Angeles from New York when I got the word that a young guy (early twenties) living across the street from her had fallen in love, and they had started an affair. I got the guy's phone number and called him. I explained that Rosemary and I were still legally married, and I didn't want her seeing anyone until after our divorce was finalized. My contacts told me that the relationship had stopped, but the guy was still in love and having a hard time letting go. I figured the best way to resolve the matter was for me to fly to San Francisco and meet with the guy.

I called him again and told him to meet me at a bar on Mission Street, and to come alone. I had a good description of him, and when I walked into the place, I spotted him at the bar. I also noticed some guys at the tables, and my instincts told me they were with him. I ordered a drink and told the bartender to give the lover boy one, and his friends too. The expression on the kid's face was one of surprise. He had to be wondering how I knew the other guys were his buddies. He probably found it a bit scary, which was fine with me.

I told him again that I didn't want my wife involved with another man until after we were divorced. If he wanted a long-term relationship with Rosemary—or perhaps even marriage—he was going to have to be patient. I left right afterward, figuring I'd made my point.

It turned out that his feelings for Rosemary were stronger than his fear of me, because he went to North Beach to try to find someone to kill me for ten thousand dollars. His mistake was that he approached the same guys I'd met with regarding my mobile casino idea. They turned him down and explained I couldn't be touched without getting proper permission first, and that would never happen.

One Saturday I got a call from him. He was crying like a baby and told me he had a gun and was going to kill himself.

I said, "You really have a gun with bullets in it?"

"Yes."

"Okay, I'll help you through this. Listen close and do what I say. First, though, I need to know if you're right-handed or left-handed."

"Huh?"

"Which had do you use, right or left?"

"Right. Why?"

"I want to take the gun in your right hand, put the barrel against your right temple, and then pull the trigger. You won't feel a thing and your troubles will be over."

That may sound cruel, but I didn't think for a minute he'd actually do it. In fact, I doubt he even had a gun. He hung up and I never heard from or about him again. I hope he's doing well and found a woman his own age.

* * *

Rosemary got the divorce papers on a Friday, and I flew up to San Francisco. We met in a huge booth with a privacy curtain at Harry's Bar. We ate, signed the divorce papers, and made love right there in the booth. I flew back to Los Angeles that night.

Rosemary and I remained friends for a long time after the divorce. She loved Las Vegas and in those days, I was in Sin City almost every weekend. I had a deal at the Maxim Hotel & Casino on Flamingo, and she and one of her girlfriends often met me there. I'd get them a comped room and Rosemary and I would always find time to make love—it was what we did best.

Years later she called me and said she'd met a guy very much like me. He was from Brooklyn and always dressed in a tie, French cuffs and a scarf, just like I did. He wanted to take her to Spain. She'd also run into a guy named Jose, whom she went to school with. He was going to law school and was interested in dating her. She wasn't sure what to do.

I said, "Forget about the guy who reminds you of me. You'll never get what you're looking for with him—

the house with the white picket fence and kids playing in the yard."

She ended up marrying Jose. They bought a house and had a baby girl. With Jose's approval, I was allowed to call their home every so often to keep in touch. One day when I called, Jose answered. He was very abrupt and put Rosemary on the phone.

"Is Jose pissed off about something?" I asked.

"Yes. We got into an argument over something he did, and I said you would have handled the situation differently."

"No wonder he's upset. He's your husband and you shouldn't have said that your ex would have done a better job than him. I'd be pissed off, too, if my wife said that to me. I think it might be better if I don't call again, but if you ever need me, all you have to do is call. If you have any trouble reaching me directly, you can always contact me through my daughter."

We never spoke again after that. I wish her well and hope she and her family are happy.

* * *

After my trip to San Francisco I returned to L.A., where I was still unsettled and living from place-to-place as my finances dictated. Emilio had a home in Pasadena with a spare bedroom and bath upstairs. He and his wife, Yolanda, invited me to stay there, and they treated me great.

Emilio told me he was driving for a guy who was originally from Rochester, New York. His name was Peter Azer, and Emilio thought I should meet him. That Friday, Emilio drove me to Peter's house, but he had company and was short on time because he was flying to Las Vegas later that evening. He asked me if I could come back Monday, and then he said, "How are you fixed for cash?"

The question took me by surprise. Embarrassed, I said, "I'm upside down at the moment."

He took out his wallet, removed five hundred dollars and handed it to me. "Is that enough for the weekend?"

I couldn't believe it. I've known the guy for maybe ten minutes, and he gives me five large with no question asked!

I went back to Peter's home on Monday. He had me wait in the parlor while he was in the next room talking to some guys. I heard him giving them instructions, telling one to take a check to a certain check-cashing place, and the others to take cash or checks to various banks.

After the guys left, Peter joined me in the parlor.

"Did you hear us talking?" he asked, nodding toward the adjoining room.

"Yes. You're kiting checks (a form of check fraud), aren't you?"

He smiled. "Emilio said you were sharp. That's exactly what I'm doing."

Peter and I became instant friends. He told me he'd been kiting checks since the age of thirteen and had become a master at it. For cover, he told people he was in the seafood business. That consisted of a freezer outside in the back of the house where he kept shrimp, which he gave to bankers. He also had an office not far from his home.

I said, "Why not actually get into the seafood business? Somebody's got to supply all these restaurants. Why not you?"

Peter thought for a few moments, then said, "You're the sales expert. How would I go about it?"

I'd learned from my days at the Ori Agency, women could be a valuable asset when dealing with clients. I routinely provided women to the car dealers I worked with.

I said, "You're right, I have sales experience. If you let me handle it for you, I'll assemble a small sales force featuring good-looking women. If you agree, I can guarantee you I'll be able to lock in some of the best restaurants in the area."

"Go for it," Peter said.

I decided that David would be my only male salesperson. The others would be women. They wouldn't be hookers, but they would be attractive because restaurant owners love beautiful women. And around Hollywood, there was no shortage of good-looking women. I hired Robin, who was an aspiring actress, and another knockout named Elaine, who I ended up having an affair with. They gave me an edge on the competition. In addition, I offered the lowest shrimp prices around.

Those girls and David sold the hell out of the fish, and we ended up with the best places in town as customers, restaurants such as Spago's, L'Ermitage and Le Dome. They all paid on delivery as agreed except one, Nicky Blair's on Sunset. Nicky was a friend of mine, and his place was always jammed. It was a great place to pick up women, and I often hung out there myself. As nice as his restaurant was, Nicky was slow when it came to paying his bills, at least to us. He always had an excuse.

California | Another Divorce

Eventually his tab got to over five grand, and I knew it was time for a talk. So on a Friday I went to the restaurant and asked to see Nicky. He was upstairs in his office, and I walked in and gave him the bill. I said, "You need to settle this. Now."

He paid on the spot. After I got the money, I told him we wouldn't be delivering anymore, and he needed to find a new supplier. We stayed friends, and when Nicky had a problem at the place that he opened in Las Vegas, he called me to take care of it for him, which I did. I never went on the hook with him again, though.

* * *

Peter was generous with me, and for the first time in a while, I was in pretty good shape financially. I got a big apartment on Beverly Glenn, and David took the spare bedroom. David and I have remained close friends, but I need to say this—the thing that sticks most in my mind about him is the way he could cry the blues when he was broke—he is the best at it. I'm sure he'll chuckle when he reads this.

David now lives in Orange County and is married to a woman who keeps him on the straight and narrow. He visits me at least once a month.

* * *

While I was in the fish business with Peter, a guy from Canada reached out to me on a deal regarding purchasing some of the government's gold reserves, which he said were up for sale. He said if I could arrange for him and his partner in San Diego to meet with the president of Indonesia, they'd deposit fifty million dollars in a bank account for me.

Through the fish business, I became connected with a former CIA agent named Benny Persitz—I called him Benno.

He ran a similar operation in Seattle. He had gone with Nixon and Kissinger when they went to China to open trade in 1972. He knew a lot of people, especially in that part of the world. I called him and told him what was going on.

We checked and found out that Indonesia was in fact planning to sell off some of its gold and use the money to purchase oil well drilling equipment from Texas.

Benno said, "Ori, get fifteen thousand dollars from those guys. Tell them you and I will fly to Indonesia and meet with President Suharto. We'll have dinner at the palace with him and his wife. That's how close I am with them."

I told the Canadian to bring his partner so we could talk in person. When we met, I asked for the money. *They didn't have it!*

I said, "You're talking about depositing fifty million in an account, and you can't come up with fifteen thousand?"

"No, we can't."

"I'll tell you what, then. Give me the names of the buyers you're working with, and Benno and I will go to Indonesia and make the deal for them. If we do, *I'll* put fifty million in an account for you."

They wouldn't give me the names.

When I told Benno, he said, "If we can find a buyer, we'll do the deal ourselves. Do you know anybody with the kind of money it will take, and is willing to spend it?"

There were only a handful of people in the whole world who could come up with that kind of money. I remembered a former associate of mine with connections to the Vatican. I called and asked him to see if the Vatican had any interest. He called me back in a few days and said the Vatican would buy as much gold as the Indonesians were selling. Benno and I would have to set it up and arrange for delivering the gold to the Vatican.

Benno planned the delivery. He said we'd take it by ship to a free zone in London, and from there to the Vatican. Due to piracy on the ocean, we'd have to hire fifty mercenaries from Thailand—who he said were the best—to provide security. We'd do a test run first, minus the gold and mercenaries, to make sure his plan would work. I said to go for it, and he started making the arrangements.

At this point, the only people who knew the details of Benno's delivery plan were him and me. So I was totally surprised when on a Sunday afternoon, my ex-wife Rosemary called in a panic.

She said, "You're going to get on a ship, and everybody is going to die. Don't go!"

How in the hell did she know I was going on a ship?

Rosemary's next-door neighbor was a radio show host named Lark Williams. She had a friend who was a psychic named Jackie visiting her. When Rosemary stopped in, she was wearing the ring I'd bought her. The psychic read me from that ring like she knew me, and then mentioned the boat trip that would end in tragedy.

Rosemary gave me Jackie's phone number, and I called her that night and she read me over the phone.

Her accuracy stunned me, and the thing about the boat trip unnerved me. I was having second thoughts about setting foot on a ship.

The next day, I found a psychic in Beverly Hills and got a reading, primarily to see if he'd confirm what Jackie told me. His reading was almost the same as hers except for the ship. But he told me something about as scary. Somebody was going to die in the Caddy Eldorado I was driving.

I called a friend who loaned money to people who weren't able to get traditional loans to finance their cars. If the customer turned out to be a deadbeat, he'd repo their car. I told him I had to get rid of the Eldorado and asked if he had something to swap. He said the only thing he had for me was a Subaru. I wasn't excited about it, but not wanting to take a chance, I told him I'd take it.

The following Sunday he sold my Eldorado to two guys who happened to be drug dealers. That same night they were shot and killed while sitting in that car.

After that, I was quickly becoming a believer. I read everything I could get my hands on about psychics, beginning with Shirley MacLaine's books.

In spite of my reservations, I still planned to do the gold thing with Benno. Fate intervened—Benno suffered a heart attack and died while making love to a young lady on the floor in his office.

Without him and his connections the deal fell apart.

Go figure.

Writing (Checks)
for Profit

I loved California, especially the Bay Area and Los Angeles. They were two entirely different places, but each had qualities that I appreciated. Los Angeles was my favorite, though. It was clean, and the palm trees made it the very image that I'd always had of where I wanted to be.

Once I got established in L.A., I always lived in nice areas, beginning in Westwood on the Wilshire Corridor, which was loaded with high-rise condos and apartment buildings. The rents were high, but the accommodations were worth it. The apartments I took always had two bedrooms and two baths.

I will never forget the time Peter asked if I would do him a favor. He said there was a girl in town from Canada, and she needed a place to sleep for a couple of nights. Since I had a spare bedroom, could she stay at my place? I said that would be okay.

She came and slept at my place, and that's all there was to it. I don't remember her name, only that she drove an old green Mercedes and was clean and cordial.

Many years later, before he passed away, Peter was living in Georgia. He called me one day and asked if I remembered the girl. I said I did, but couldn't recall her name.

Peter said, "She was Celine Dion."

I hesitated a few seconds as what he said sank in. Then I said, *the* Celine Dion? You gotta be kidding"

"Not at all," Peter laughed. "She was just starting out, then. Look at her now."

I have no reason to doubt what Peter told me, but I guess I'll never know for sure. If it really was her, I'm happy I was able to help.

* * *

Jimmy Caci and I became close friends. Originally from Buffalo, he moved to L.A. and became a street boss for the Los Angeles Mob. He had the upstate New York accent, and people always said we looked enough alike to be brothers.

Like Sonny, Jimmy was a serious man and, in my opinion, was the only wise guy in Los Angeles who had balls. He was well-respected. His brother Charlie was a member of his crew and also sang professionally under the name of Bobby Milano. Charlie was married to Keely Smith and was a friend of Frank Sinatra.

Jimmy owned a house in Palm Springs and frequently

drove to L.A. to see me during the week. He always had some kind of business deal in the works that he'd tell me about, and I was able to convert his business deals into money.

Jimmy was also in love with the horses. He was actually addicted to them, in my opinion, and was one of the best handicappers I ever met. Unfortunately, he didn't always trust his own predictions and often changed his mind on the way to the betting window. When he did, his first pick almost always won.

Jimmy wasn't very good at handling his money, either. Whether he made money at the track or through one of his other deals, he was usually broke by the next day.

Between Sonny in New York and Jimmy in L.A., I was solidly connected on both coasts.

Jimmy and Sonny were both good men in my book. I'd known Sonny longer, but he was in prison so much that our communication was often limited to monitored phone calls or letters. Sonny also had a lot of baggage because of his immediate family, namely his wife Tina and son Johnny. Tina was always putting me in the middle of situations while Sonny was locked up. Numerous times Tina would call me with Sonny in prison on the other end of the line. This was mainly to bail Johnny out of jail, or some other jam he had got himself into.

Johnny was a constant headache. He didn't really want anything to do with *the life* his father had chosen. However, sometimes he tried to get into *the life* a little, and he wasn't very good at it. He should have just walked away from it as a man, and not worn a wire on his father, me and others.

Jimmy, on the other hand, did not carry that kind of

baggage. We spent a lot of time together and grew very close. We made money and watched each other's back.

When Jimmy told people I was with him on the West Coast, it tended to piss Sonny off. Sometimes he reminded me that I was a New York guy, and I was with him everywhere. He said the Los Angeles guys weren't even recognized by the New York families. Truthfully, though, my only interest was making money. I didn't give a damn about the egos involved, and I would never allow anyone to "claim" me, as they say in *the life*.

* * *

Jimmy introduced me to a guy named Vern Stevens, who later became a police informant. Vern and I teamed up for a scam he was running. He ordered all kinds of merchandise on credit and had it delivered to warehouses he owned. He never paid the bill, and we sold the stuff at flea markets or similar venues. Not a bad gig.

Another thing I got into and was very good at was cashing bad checks. I was so smooth I could almost write a check on a napkin and get it cashed. I cultivated a bartender in a joint in Beverly Hills right next to a bank. The bartender knew the bank manager, and we formed a partnership. I'd bring the checks to the bartender, and he'd take them to the bank manager and get them cashed. He and the manager split fifty percent of the take, and I got the other half. It was a good source of income for me.

One time when Sonny was in prison, his son Johnny was living in an apartment in Brentwood that Michael had arranged for him. Johnny observed what I was doing, and he decided to try it himself. He stole a bunch of checks from other apartments in his building and brought them to me to get cashed. I wasn't able to use most of them for one reason or other, but there was one for five thousand dollars made payable to Bally's Casino in Las Vegas. I looked in the phone book and found a guy named Bally. I told Johnny to insert the guy's first name on the check in front of Bally's. He did and it looked really good. I told Johnny to wait for me while I went to see my bartender friend and get the check cashed. I got the money, came back, and gave Johnny his end. He disappeared for a few days on a drug binge and came back broke.

* * *

In the early '90s—I believe it was 1991 or '92—Vern came to me with some very large checks—a hundred grand and more—from his contacts in Nigeria. The scam was an early form of identity theft, which the Nigerians are the best at. They obtained personal information about homeowners and used it to apply for second mortgages, or straight loans with the property as collateral. The loan checks were then sent to Vern to be laundered.

Those kinds of checks are tough to get cashed, and my friendly bank manager didn't want any part of them. So I went to a Greek guy I knew who was a gambler and had bank accounts. He took one of the checks to his bank and deposited it, but they put a thirty-day hold on the release of the funds. That wasn't really a problem because on paper there appeared to be sufficient equity in the deal, and the check cleared. After running the first check through, I got more checks from Vern and had the Greek deposit them. They all cleared before the homeowners found out what happened. Our end was right around a hundred and fifty thousand.

In addition to checks, I was good with credit cards too, especially American Express. I once had five AMEX cards in my wallet at the same time. They were issued in variations of my name with different Social Security numbers.

I remember going to a men's store to buy some clothes. At checkout I gave the clerk one of my cards to swipe. When he asked for my SSN, I couldn't remember which card I'd used and gave him a number that didn't match. That killed the purchase, and I left the store in a hurry. Lesson learned.

* * *

After pulling off the Nigerian check scam, Jimmy said he was planning a trip back east in December and asked me to go with him. He said we'd be driving, and it would be a combination of business and pleasure. The itinerary included Phoenix, Fort Lauderdale, New York City, Buffalo and Chicago. I'd be able to stop in Rome to see my kids and mother too. I told him I'd go.

We left on December 14 and spent the first night in Phoenix, where Jimmy had a friend who owned a restaurant. We left early the next morning. When we got into Texas, I was tired and asked Jimmy to stop for the night. He said he was going to keep on going. I thought he was kidding, but he was serious. Jimmy loved to be behind the wheel and could drive like nobody else I've ever met. People in Palm Springs joked that if Jimmy asked you to go for a ride, you shouldn't because you might end up in Buffalo.

We got to Fort Lauderdale at around 11:00 p.m. on December 17 and checked into the motel. I had a toothache that was killing me, but there wasn't much I could do about it at that time of night. Jimmy came to my room to wish me a happy birthday, and then took me out for a drink. That temporarily eased the pain.

Jimmy came to the rescue again the next day when he used a friend of his to get me an emergency appointment with a dentist. Jimmy sat in the room while the dentist worked on me and gave the dentist his opinion on exactly what I needed to have done. I thought it was funny, but the dentist wasn't amused.

With my tooth fixed, Jimmy introduced me to more of his friends and took care of his business. Then we headed to New York City.

Jimmy was not an extravagant person and did not like big hotels, but I convinced him we should stay at the Warwick. Jimmy made some calls and several of his friends came over. They were guys I'd heard about but never met before. In the afternoon we went to Rao's Restaurant in Harlem and met with some more guys. I always made it a point not to remember the names of people I met through Sonny or Jimmy. That way, if I was ever questioned if I knew someone, I could honestly say I didn't.

That evening we had dinner at a restaurant owned by Jimmy's friend, Joe Dente. Joe lived in L.A. but was in New York at the time. There were seventeen of us, including Joe, at a huge table. The food was fantastic!

Joe told Jimmy the dinners were on him. Jimmy is a hardhead, though, and as we were getting ready to leave, he grabbed the waiter and asked for the bill. The waiter said it was already taken care of, but Jimmy insisted. Joe was offended and I was pissed, because Jimmy and I had to split a bill that was over two thousand dollars.

The next day, December 23, we drove to Rome. Before leaving California, I mailed a package to myself at my daughter's address. It contained ninety thousand dollars in cash, which was my end of the Nigerian check scam.

The arrangement between Jimmy and I was that we split our scores evenly. Jimmy had hooked me up with Vern and was entitled to his cut. I gave him forty-five thousand. Then, as I always did, I gave money to my children and mother. Jimmy headed on to Buffalo, and I spent that night and Christmas Eve with my family. The next night I took the train to Buffalo to meet him.

Jimmy picked me up at the train station and took me to the Charter House Hotel, where we knew the owner, and Jimmy got my room comped. The next morning, Jimmy called and asked me to take a cab to an address downtown. I suspected the worst when the taxi pulled up in front of an off-track betting parlor, and Jimmy was pacing back and forth in front of it.

I got out and said to him, "Please don't tell me you blew the forty-five grand."

"It's gone," he admitted.

In two days he lost it all. That was Jimmy, though.

We spent a couple of days in Buffalo, where it seemed just about everyone was Jimmy's cousin. He also had a daughter living there. She was a beautiful girl, but she had MS. She loved lobster, and every time Jimmy visited he got lobster for her. I'll never forget Jimmy picking her up, putting her in the kitchen chair, and feeding her by hand. She loved it. It was a side of Jimmy not many people saw, but I did, and he is one of the best friends I ever had.

After Buffalo we went to Chicago and took care of some business. It was so damn cold that I didn't believe it was unfit for humans. Jimmy wanted me to go back to Buffalo with him for New Year's Eve. I had to turn him down because I really couldn't take the cold and snow. I told Jimmy to take me to the airport so I could get back to Los Angeles, and I'd see him there. Grudgingly, he agreed.

I found out later that the FBI knew every place Jimmy and I were at and who we met with from the time we left California. Other than Jimmy and me, only one other person knew that information. I'm not going to give his name, but he was a guy Jimmy was doing a favor for, and Jimmy called him regularly. This guy had to be the FBI's source—there are no other options.

I'm sure the feds thought one of the reasons for our trip was that I'd become a *made* man, and Jimmy was taking me on an introductory tour to meet some of the major players. I can understand why they'd have come to that conclusion, but it wasn't true. Perception is not always reality.

* * *

Also in the 90s, I was introduced to a guy in the music business named Danny Sims. He was a producer, publisher and promoter. Danny had recently returned from Africa, where he'd moved when a number of radio people were being indicted for payola in Los Angeles.

Danny was from Hattiesburg, Mississippi—a handsome guy and very intelligent. He was respected in the music business as the discoverer of the famous Jamaican singer, song writer and musician, Bob Marley. He was married to model Beverly Johnson. Danny and I had several mutual acquaintances, including Sonny.

Danny had spent time in London, and when he was there, he was connected with underworld figure Joey Pyle. When he was in Los Angeles, he was connected with me. Danny never paid me any money directly, but I always made money around him.

I never truly appreciated how big Danny was in the music business until one night he called and asked me to go to a club where Polygram Records was located. When we arrived, the Polygram executives had just finished a meeting and were coming down the stairs. Danny and I were standing at the bottom.

As each of the bigshots passed us, they stopped and paid homage to Danny as though he were a King. I was in awe. Danny graciously accepted their accolades and then introduced me as his "partner." That gave me automatic stature, but I wondered why he was going with the partner thing.

Danny decided to move to London again. After he set up shop there, he called me often. Many times he put me on the phone with Joey Pyle and his son Joey Jr. I loved their accents and really liked talking with them.

* * *

Around that same time, Sonny contacted me. He wanted to meet Richie Marone, a U.S. Marshal I knew who was being transferred from Los Angeles to their office in Brooklyn.

I hooked them up when Richie got to New York. You'd have thought Richie had met God. He started hanging around Sonny morning, noon and night. He seemed to feel glorified that he was keeping company with such a powerful mobster.

When I was in New York I met with Sonny. I said, "You can't have this guy (Richie) with you all the time. It doesn't look right. I told Richie that, too."

"Buddy, it looks good for me to be spending time with a U.S. Marshal. And he can be valuable for us."

I don't know who Sonny thought it looked good to, but apparently the Marshal Service wasn't impressed. About the same day Sonny got arrested for one of his parole violations, Richie got fired. Here was a young guy whose career was destroyed because he thought it was cool hanging-out with Sonny.

On top of that, Sonny had asked Richie to co-sign on a car loan for a friend of his. He did. The guy got a nice BMW but never made a payment. Richie's credit went down the toilet along with his job. The last I heard, he was working at a telemarketing room in Florida.

Go figure.

Kiting

I still went back to San Francisco every so often and would usually meet Rosemary for lunch or dinner. She was working for a lawyer in the First Interstate Bank building. On one of those occasions we got together for lunch in the restaurant on the building's first floor. As we were eating, one of Rosemary's girlfriends stopped by our table. She worked in the new account section of the bank.

After the girls left to go back to work, I came up with an idea. I went to the bank and asked to see the girl I'd just met. I told her I wanted to open an account, but that I'd left my ID at home. Rosemary had introduced me to her as Ori, but didn't give my last name. So I proceed to open an account under the name of "Ori Pado." When I got back to Los Angeles, I used the new account to help

Peter Azer with his check kiting operation.

Check kiting is a form of fraud that, back then, used the time it took banks to clear checks to pull off the scam. It worked this way. The kiter wrote a check from an account with insufficient funds at one bank and deposited it into an account in another bank. Before that check cleared, he deposited another rubber check from the second bank into the first account to cover the first check. The process was repeated over and over so that it always appeared the checks were covered, but there was actually no money in either of the accounts. It was called playing the float, and for the kiter it amounted to an interest-free loan.

I used a fairly small check at first. I think it was for about five thousand. Peter's operation was so big—he had several guys working for him, all opening accounts and giving him checks, and he had so many accounts it was impossible to keep track of how much he was floating. In addition, we had people with real accounts and money give us checks that we used for a few days, and then we paid them hefty sums for the use of their checks.

Friday was our best day, and we would end up at a bank on Vermont and Wilshire, where Peter was friends with the operations manager. When the bank closed down, our bogus account showed as being even. What a relief that was. Peter was so excited he had the guy give me a cashier's check for twenty-five grand (I don't remember how we did it, but we covered that check) and we all went to Vegas. He was truly a fun guy with a personality that made everybody love him, and he always had a lot going on.

One time I went to Peter's house, and when I pulled

up, a guy jumped out of his car and asked, "Are you Peter Azer?"

Figuring he was a process server, I said, "Yes, I am."

He handed me Peter's summons. I went into the house and we looked the paper over. Peter was being sued for several million dollars by one of the banks he was using for his check kiting. Because I received the papers and not Peter, the service was no good, and there was nothing to worry about, right? Wrong.

In addition to the civil suit, the bank had initiated a federal investigation of Peter, and the FBI was on the case. That didn't stop Peter.

We had a great girl working with us at a bank on Ocean Boulevard in West Los Angeles. Peter was in the need of ninety-five thousand dollars, so I gave him a check for that amount from my San Francisco account, knowing he'd cover it out of the float before it bounced. Then Peter gave me another large check from someone else and told me to get a cashier's check from the bank on Ocean. When I got to the bank, I found out the girl had been transferred to their branch in Panorama City.

I drove to her new location, and when I walked into the bank, something didn't feel right. I looked around at the supposed bank officers siting at their desks, and my instincts told me they were FBI agents. I approached our inside girl anyway, gave her the check, and she issued me the cashier's check. I left the bank without incident. Maybe I'd been wrong about the FBI being there. I wanted to get the cashier's check deposited as soon as possible, though, just in case.

There was a First Interstate Bank branch across the street, so I went in to make the deposit. My hunch had been right. The feds had already stopped payment and the check bounced like a basketball.

We knew the kite was over. The only question was what would happen next.

* * *

Peter was eventually indicted and ended up getting five years. He was sent to the federal prison in Lompoc, California, and later to a facility in Denver. Before he went away, I told him that if he had any problems inside, he could use Sonny's and my name, but only when absolutely necessary.

Peter didn't follow my instructions, though. He started bragging that he was connected to Sonny and me and throwing our names around. I heard about it and it pissed me off. Word got to Peter that I wasn't happy. He must have been embarrassed about what he did, because he never even called me when he got out of prison.

In the meantime, Peter's wife, Marie, got involved working for a female doctor with offices in Beverly Hills. When Peter was released, he started working for the doctor, too. In fact, they developed more than a business relationship. He had an affair with her and left his wife, something I never thought he'd do. I cannot tell you how bad I felt for Marie. She was like a saint. She kept the family together while he was in prison and deserved better.

One day I was in a Rite Aid drug store in Beverly Hills and saw my friend Emilio in one of the aisles. At the same, time I noticed a familiar figure duck down another aisle—it was Peter. Emilio told me he was working for Peter and Peter was afraid to face me. I told him to tell Peter not to worry and to come over and talk. We chatted cordially for a minute or so and then went our separate ways.

* * *

In the late 1980s, using money raised by a dentist I knew, I started a business called American Check Guarantee, with an office on Wilshire Boulevard in Beverly Hills. We guaranteed checks for businesses and paid them on bad checks after they bounced the first time. However, most checks cleared the second time, and that became my cash flow. As usual, I hired and fired lots of sales people, but those I kept did quite well financially.

The business grew, and I had seventeen people working for me. It was also time to get computerized. I bought the computers and hired a programmer. One day he didn't show up for work, and we couldn't access the computers because he had the codes. It turned out he was trying to shake me down for more money.

I had two of my guys go to his house. When they walked right into his home, he got so scared he almost pissed his pants. He hung on his chair and wouldn't let go. They actually picked him up and brought him to my office still sitting in his chair. He unlocked the computers and then I fired him.

That didn't end my problems, though. My dentist friend screwed me up by putting some of the investor money into other businesses. That prevented me from buying the additional equipment and software I needed to get my accounts organized and running properly.

To top it off, my former computer programmer filed papers with the Labor Board alleging he was suffering health problems due to work-related stress caused by me. On the day of the hearing, I arrived a little early and brought a friend with me. The programmer was in the waiting room. I walked over to him and said I wanted him to meet my friend. Then I walked outside and left them alone.

A few minutes later the programmer left after withdrawing his complaint. My friend had convinced him he'd made a mistake.

Because I wasn't able to get the financing I needed, I decided to see if I could find someone sharp enough with figures to operate the business manually. David Savin told me he'd met a young guy named Scott Flansburg, who was from Herkimer, New York. Scott was down on his luck, had lost all his belongings, and he couldn't pay his bill at the place he was living. That aside, David said the kid could add, subtract and multiply quickly and accurately. I said to bring him over to my office. I gave him a stack of checks about eight inches high, which he added to the penny in a matter of seconds. I knew he was the guy I needed.

I hired him and arranged for him to move into an apartment with a friend of mine who needed a roommate. I also found him a car to drive. Things went well for about three weeks, and then he stopped coming to work. His roommate said Scott had left and taken all the clothes, including his.

A couple of weeks later I got a strange call from an out- of-state banker asking me questions about my company. He explained that Scott had applied for a loan and said he was the owner of my business. I straightened the banker out, but had to give Scott credit for having a lot of balls.

The next time I heard from Scott he was in jail in West Palm Beach, Florida, over an unpaid hotel bill. He wanted me to bail him out. I sent a friend from Boca Raton to West Palm to post the bail. Scott got out and vanished again. He later turned up in Arizona teaching kids at a school.

In 2001, TV personality Regis Philbin dubbed Scott "The Human Calculator." He holds the Guinness World Record for adding the same number to itself more times in fifteen seconds than a person can do using a calculator.

My business didn't do as well. I ended up moving it from the office to my apartment, but I couldn't bring it back and had to close it down.

It was now 1991, and I was on a downer again financially. I was off probation and decided it was time for another change of scenery.

Go figure.

PHOTOS

All documents and pictures in this book can also be viewed
at *www.theaccidentalgangster.com*

Orlando "Ori" Spado

Ori as a young boy in Rome, New York.

Ori in the Army, 1963.

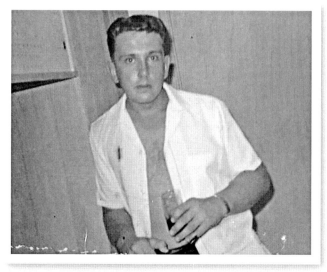

Ori visits home while on leave, 1964.

Ori and his father at Ori's first wedding.

Frank Costello (Ori called him uncle Frank);
they met at the Waldorf hotel in New York with Frank Russo.

Dino De Laurentiis – famed independent producer.

Frank Russo, the friend who introduced Ori to all the bosses.

Sonny Franzese, Ori's friend of over 40 years and
the underboss of the Columbo crime family.

Town and Country Motel, New Orleans,
where Ori met with Carlo Marcello.

Russell Bufalino, the crime boss Ori had lunch with
at the DeMarco's Restaurant in New York with Frank Russo.

Attorney Frank Russo with Producer Dino De Laurentiis.

Ori, 1978.

Ori's friends, Ralph Serpe (film producer) and Frank Russo.

Ori's friends, Jimmy Caci (underboss of Los Angeles) and Joe Todaro
(crime boss of Buffalo)—taken when Jimmy and Ori went back east
and Ori went on record with the tapes he had done on the FBI.

John Daly, famed film producer, director, Oscar winner,
and Ori's dear friend.

Ori's son, Anthony, film producer John Daly,
Ori's best mate in London, Joey Pyle, and Ori.

Jerry Zimmerman, Ori's dearest friend:
"I miss him, and we certainly made a lot of money together."

Hank Bennett, Ori Spado, Johnny Masiello, Jimmy Caci,
and Mario Cudemo.

Ori's son, Anthony, with Joe Pyle.

Ori's best mate in London, Joe Pyle, with Ori.

Ori and his three greatest loves, his children—
Ori, Gina, and Anthony.

Ori with his son, Anthony, at Anthony's 40th birthday:
"A moment that I will always cherish."

Gina and Ori.

Ori and his son, Orlando.

Ori's dear friend, screenwriter and author Nick Pileggi,
with Ori at Ago's Restaurant in Los Angeles.

Ori and his pal, Charles Torrent, who traveled the world
with him and kept him safe.

Bobby Derien and Ori at The Montage.

Author and investigative reporter, John Connolly.

Jack Gilardi , Ori Spado, Thorsten Kay,
and Pooch Hall (in the background).

Ori and Thorsten Kaye.

Ori, Giulini, and Anthony Spado.

Wyclef Jean and Danny Sims at the opening
of the Bob Marley exhibit on the Queen Mary.

Ori's first ride without cuffs or shackles after being discharged from Lompoc. His son, Anthony, and Chris Muto picked him up.

Ori Spado

Gotta Do
What I Gotta Do

In 1991, I moved back to Florida for two good reasons. Things were not going well for me in Los Angeles, and my sons were living there with their mother. I felt a little guilty about not spending much time with them, and I thought it would be a good chance to make up for it. I got a place in West Palm Beach to be near them, and Orlando Junior decided to move in with me.

I loved having my son living with me, but I remember one thing that used to drive me a little crazy. He was in high school at the time, and this girl was always calling him. They'd be on the phone most of the night. I asked him who she was, and he said she dated a friend of his and just wanted to talk. That girl, Christa, is now my daughter-in-law, and they have three wonderful children, Gianna, Antonia and Orlando Giovanni.

Anyway, I needed to earn. So one of the first things I did was contact my friend Don Ritz at his restaurant on Singer Island. He loaned me seven thousand dollars and, more importantly, told me that an old acquaintance of ours from Utica was in Florida and looking for a partner. His name was Ralph "Ralphie" Centinela.

In the old days Ralphie was one of the best armored truck robbers around. He got busted and served time in Attica (New York) prison during the riots there in 1971. In Florida he was still stealing, but his target was jewelry, not armored trucks. Don contacted him and arranged for us to meet.

Ralphie explained that he was doing some robberies and burglaries, and some other things, with inside help. What that meant—and what most people don't realize—is that not all robberies are planned by the thieves. Many are setup by the business owners themselves.

Here is how it worked. When a jewelry store or pawn shop was having financial issues, one way to relieve the pressure was to have a robbery and collect the insurance money. Ralphie had a tipster—another guy formerly from Utica named Tony—who was in the jewelry business. When he heard of an owner looking for an insurance job, he'd tell Ralphie. After Ralphie and the store owner reached an agreement, the owner gave him the code to the alarm system.

Prior to the theft, the owner removed the cash and any high-value pieces of jewelry that they wanted to keep from the store. They left pieces they knew could be fenced for a hundred and fifty thousand or so. That was his pay. The owner made out by keeping some of his inventory and collecting an inflated insurance claim. It was a win-win for everybody but the insurance company.

I liked the operation and told Ralphie I wanted to work with him. He took me on, and we started on a nearly year- long crime spree.

* * *

We did several jobs that stick in my mind. One was at a jewelry store in a shopping mall. The store opened at ten o'clock, and Ralphie and I got there at nine-thirty. The owner was there and let us in. To make it look good, we tied him up and put him on the floor in a small storage closet.

We had just started emptying out the display case when a UPS guy came to the door. We let him in, tied him up, and put him in the closet with the owner. The interruption cost us valuable time. We needed to hurry in order to be out of there before customers started showing up. It wasn't to be, though, because a couple of minutes later FedEx was at the door. That guy was the third one to go into the closet, which was so small he had to go on top of the others. By then it was ten o'clock and a customer came. We now had the closet stacked four-high. We finished loading all the merchandise and cleared out before anyone else came in.

Afterward, Tony the tipster and I rented a car and drove to New York where we sold the stuff in the jewelry district. He negotiated a price while I stood there. If I agreed, I'd nod my head. If not, he'd negotiate some more, or we'd go on to another buyer. When everything was sold, Tony (or any other tipster) got ten percent, and Ralphie and I split the rest.

* * *

One day while Ralphie was having coffee at a donut joint on Okeechobee Road, a guy I will call "Tim" approached him. Ralphie knew who Tim was and that I detested him for trying to cause me problems in the past. Besides that, Tim was someone you could not stand being next to for very long because he had terrible body odor.

Tim told Ralphie he had a friend who worked at a bank that handled money for a major drug dealer from Wellington (Florida), who also ran a legit real estate business. His friend told him there was a major deal in the works involving two million dollars in cash. Ralphie came to me, and we talked it over. We weren't sure how far Tim could be trusted, but if his story was true, we had to try to get the money. We put a plan together to make our move when the drug plane landed at the small airstrip on the dealer's property.

However, as the time for the alleged deal got closer, Tim came up with a different story. He said that the DEA had got wind of the deal, found out the location of the house where the money was stashed, and taken over control of the home next door. We couldn't be sure Tim's information was true, though, and there was too much money at stake to just fold our plan.

On the evening the drug plane was to come into Wellington, Ralphie, Tim and I were on the other side of the dealer's airstrip where we had a good view of everything. For transportation we had my car with switched plates and Tim's van. Ralphie and I knew we might end up in a shootout, and we made a pact that if that happened, we'd go down fighting. When we shook hands on it, Tim just about shit his pants, but knowing we were prepared to die on that airstrip, he realized we were serious guys.

The plane with the drugs appeared, but right behind it we saw the fucking DEA plane with no lights on, so it could not be seen by the drug plane.

Ralphie and I made a quick decision—the only choice we had was to alert the drug plane. I had Tim drive me around to the home of the dealer and flash his lights all the way around the private airport. The plane turned around and headed out over the Atlantic.

Tim pulled up in front of the house, and I went to the door. When I spoke with the dealer, I said, "You don't know who I am, but I just saved you a lot of money. I'll see you at your real estate office tomorrow."

In my mind, I'd just lost two million dollars and he'd saved two million, so I figured I was entitled to something. But when I met with the guy the next day, he was sharp. He denied everything and I came away with nothing.

* * *

On another occasion, Ralphie told me that we had to meet with an old friend of his in Miami at four in the morning. I thought that was a crazy time for a meeting, but I trusted Ralph, and he said that was how it had to be.

The guy we met was named Joe, and his brother was a skipper (capo) with the Bonano family in New York. He said he had a source who told him about a Miami nightclub where seventy to a hundred thousand dollars was left in the safe every night. He wanted us to help him steal it.

Ralphie told me Joe was excellent at getting through doors and a master safecracker. With Joe's expertise, it sounded like an easy score, so we agreed to do the job.

Ralphie and I drove to Miami every night and met Joe across the street from the club. Then the three of us staked it out. We noticed that about one o'clock each morning, a guy would leave the club carrying a briefcase, get into a Jaguar, and drive away.

I told Joe, "There goes the large (the money) sure as hell."

"No. My guy guaranteed me the money stays in the safe," he said.

After a few nights we had the club's schedule down and knew when the last employees left. It was time to go in.

Joe proved to be as good as Ralphie said at getting doors open. The club was in an old movie theater with staircases off each side of what was once the lobby. We went to the second floor where the office was. We looked the safe over and Joe said he had to go out and get his tools. I let him out the fire door on the side of the building where his car was parked. He opened the trunk, then closed it and got in the car and drove off. I wondered what the fuck he was doing—leaving us?

He came back about a half hour later. He said he had to go to a grocery store to get boxes to put his tools in. We got the boxes upstairs, and he went to work. All of the sudden, I heard a lot of loud bangs. He wasn't cracking the safe; he was peeling it (removing the outer skin)—not exactly what I expected from a "master safecracker."

As Joe worked on the safe, the time flew by, and it was starting to get daylight. Around dawn, the lady in charge of the cleaning crew let herself in. I brought her upstairs but didn't have anything to tie her up with. Ralphie cut the telephone cords and I used them.

Ralphie had a good way of putting people at ease, even in the middle of a robbery. He spoke to the woman and let her know she wouldn't be hurt. She seemed to relax and didn't give us any trouble.

By the time Joe got the safe open, the rest of the cleaning crew was waiting outside the door, not knowing their boss was being held prisoner upstairs. We grabbed the cash and got the hell out of there using the side door.

We went to Joe's house to count the money. Our "guaranteed" seventy to one hundred-thousand-dollar score turned out to be a measly three thousand, all in one-dollar bills.

We each took our thousand dollars. Then Joe said, "What about my tipster? We've got to take care of him."

Ralphie pulled out his gun, removed a bullet and handed it to Joe. "Here," he said. "Give this to your tipster for giving us bum information."

* * *

Orlando Junior was turning sixteen, and I wanted to get him a car. I promised I'd get him one and found a good first car for him. He wasn't really excited about that Subaru but bought it anyway for nine hundred dollars. When the guy delivered the car, I gave the money from the nightclub job to Ori and told him to pay the man. I went into my bedroom while the guy made out a bill of sale and counted the money. I could hear him count the bills out loud—nine hundred times. My son Ori was embarrassed, and he did not even like the car.

* * *

Later on, Joe brought us another tip. This one was for   a jewelry store on Las Olas Boulevard in Fort Lauderdale. According to Joe, there would be around two hundred thousand dollars in the safe.

Ralphie and I drove to Fort Lauderdale to check the store out. Las Olas Boulevard reminded me of Rodeo Drive in Beverly Hills—strictly upper class. We parked our van near the store and watched. We already knew from Joe that the jewelry store owner was a very attractive woman, and that there was one employee. Also, she operated by appointment only, so there was no random walk-in traffic. After some of our past experiences, that was a plus.

After a while, I noticed a guy on the corner opposite the store scoping it out. I looked up on the roof, and there was another guy.

I said, "Ralphie, who are all these other guys watching the store? Maybe the cops got wind of this deal."

It turned out they weren't cops. They were thieves we knew from Miami. Apparently, we weren't the only people Joe had put out the job to. We decided to leave, but agreed we'd come back the next day and be the first robbers in the door.

We were back in Fort Lauderdale early the following morning and saw the owner and her employee enter the store. We waited and watched, ready to move as soon as the right opportunity presented itself.

After a couple of hours, the employee left the store. We knew no customers were inside and the owner was alone. It was time.

I was always the front man on jobs like this, nicely

dressed and respectable looking. I went to the door and pushed the buzzer. Through the intercom I told her I'd been by the store the previous day but didn't have time to stop in. I said I'd come back because there was a piece of jewelry I really wanted to look at. Although I didn't have an appointment, she let me in. As soon as I got inside, I pulled my thirty-eight revolver and Ralphie was right behind me.

He shut the door and took the owner to a back room where the safe was. While he worked his magic on her and put her at ease, I started cleaning out the display cases. I thought the stuff was crap, but the big score was supposed to be in the safe. She opened it for us. *Nothing!*

Once again, Joe had provided us with wrong information, and we were fucking pissed.

The robbery was reported on the TV news that night. There was the owner, describing the robbery between sobs. She estimated her loss at a half million dollars. It was a good score for her.

Ralphie and me were fortunate to get twenty grand for what we took. We, along with the insurance company, took a beating on that one.

There was one good thing, though. When they flashed a picture of the suspect on the screen, it was a Cuban guy that looked so much like me we could have been twins. Apparently, he was out there robbing, as well. It seemed like almost every time there was a jewelry store robbery the Cuban got credit for it, whether he did it or I did.

* * *

We got a tip that a pawn shop on Okeechobee Boulevard in West Palm Beach was full of cash and jewelry. It was a free-standing small building located between two automobile dealerships. The tipster said there would be a minimum of a half million dollars. We got inside with no problem. Then we ran into trouble.

The store had an Israeli safe. In those days they were the toughest safes to get in, and there was no way we would ever be able to peel it. In order to get it open, it would have to be removed and taken somewhere it could be worked on—something we didn't have the ability to do. We left the pawn shop without taking anything.

A couple of weeks later, on Thanksgiving, I was reading the Palm Beach newspaper and saw that pawn shop had been hit. It was incredible. The thieves went in through the roof. Using a truck with a crane, they lifted the safe out of the building and drove away.

Ralphie and I attributed the job to a crew consisting of a father and his sons out of Rhode Island. They were probably the best in the country, and always worked alone. Whoever it was, they earned my respect for being able to pull off that score.

* * *

I had a friend who came to me with a paint can full of cocaine paste. He wanted to know if I could do anything with it. I told him I didn't know anything about cocaine paste, but I'd hang on to it and check around. I put the can in my freezer.

The next time I spoke with Joe, I asked if he knew anybody who could do something with the cocaine paste to make it profitable. He said he could cook it up and convert it to powder for sale on the street. We met, and I gave him the can of paste to work on.

After a while he called and said he had something to show me. We got together in the parking lot of a motel off the Florida turnpike. He opened his trunk, and it was filled with wrapped packages of cocaine he'd converted from the paste.

He said he had a buyer for it, and I told him to go ahead and sell it. We'd split the profits and take care of my friend who gave it to me.

I kept in touch with my psychic friend, Jackie, in Las Vegas. We talked on the phone shortly after my meeting with Joe. She told me not to trust him; he was either setting me up or would sell me out.

Sure enough, a couple of days later I got a call from him. He said he'd been driving around in some development when the cops got him and found the cocaine in his trunk. There was going to be trouble.

I called Jackie again and told her about it.

She said, "Don't trust him. Get out of there right away." I'd done a lot of good scores in Florida in a short time. I agreed with Jackie, though. With the Cuban guy that I looked so much like robbing stores almost every day, and now the problem with Joe, it was time to leave.

The following day, I packed my clothes and told my son that I was going back to California. He could sell anything we'd bought for the apartment and move back with his mother.

That next morning, I was gone—back to Los Angeles.

Go figure.

22

The Gangster Squad Makes Its Appearance

While I was running American Check Guarantee Company, Peter asked me to hire a girl named Deborah. She came from a wealthy Palm Desert family, was recently divorced and had a son. What I did not know when I hired her was that she had drug and alcohol issues. Only after we began having an affair and she moved in with me did I learn about her problems.

As I learned more about Deborah, I thought I was going to be the hero who saved her from her demons. I put her into multiple rehabs, but none of them worked. Eventually, I concluded that when dealing with people in her situation, the person you are trying to help has to want to get better. If they're not committed to getting cured, all the rehabs in the world won't help.

I'll never forget the day she was drunk and fell while

we were at the swimming pool where we lived. I took her to the emergency room, and while we were sitting there, an LAPD detective from the Gangster Squad came over (I don't recall his name). He showed me his badge and asked me to go outside with him.

He said, "Mr. Spado, I'm with the Organized Crime Intelligence Division, and I'm delivering a friendly message. I'm here to tell you we know a lot about you. We know you're connected to Sonny Franzese. I'm here to tell you we do not like people like you in our town. If you try to practice your trade here, we'll get you. Now you know."

Practice my trade? What the hell was he talking about?

I was more annoyed than concerned about the cop's message. I didn't think too much about it until I was approached again. It was quite a while after the ER encounter, when I was having dinner at Monty's Steakhouse with Jimmy Caci. Two guys stopped by our table to introduce themselves and make their presence known. They were detectives Steven Sewell and his partner, a guy named Banister, from the Organized Crime Intelligence Division. Apparently the first detective hadn't been bluffing.

I did some checking on the Organized Crime Intelligence Division (OCID), and the more I found out, the more seriously I took their involvement. The OCID is the elite unit put together by Chief Parker years ago to go after Italian criminals. They were good at what they did—very good. There have been movies based on the OCID, one of which was *Mulholland Drive*, with Nick Nolte. More recently, Sean Penn played Mickey Cohen in *The Gangster Squad*.

I wasn't simply on their radar. They were actively watching me, as I would soon find out.

My credit wasn't the best and I needed a car. I asked Mel Russo (Frank Russo, Senior's nephew), who was in Los Angeles and staying with his cousin Frank Russo, Junior, to put a car in his name for me. I got Mel's credit pre-approved by phone, and we drove to a dealership in Claremont to pick out a car. I settled on another Caddy and walked around in the showroom while Mel signed the papers. After getting the keys to the Caddy, I told Mel to drive it over to my place. I'd meet him there and take him out to lunch.

As I started to back out of my parking space, a car pulled behind me and blocked me in. I got out of the car and guess who is standing there? Detective Steven Sewell, that's who.

He said, "Mr. Spado, how are you? Do you remember me from Monty's?"

I just stared at him and didn't reply.

Sewell continued, "We haven't bothered you because you were always a loner. But now you're hanging out with a lot of people who are known to us, and you're becoming well known. That's troubling to us. We also know you got this car with fake financials and ID."

Then another car pulled up with more detectives. They had Mel with them. He was handcuffed and obviously scared. I felt sorry for him because he'd done nothing wrong. They brought us to the local police station—which only had about three cells, a conference room and some candy machines— and put us in separate cells.

They took Mel to the conference room for questioning. He stopped in front of my cell as he passed. I told him,

"Tell them the truth. You did nothing wrong."

He did as I told him. They checked him out, realized who he was, and that he was clean. The car deal was legitimate and wasn't part of a scam. They had no choice but to let him have the Caddy, and they drove him back to the dealership.

Then they brought me into the conference room and began asking questions, which I answered. They had nothing on me and let me go. When they dropped me off, Sewell said, "We'll be watching you."

Watch me they did. In addition, the FBI was keeping an eye on me, too. I could go out on my patio, look down at the street, and see the detectives and agents parked there waiting for me to make a move.

Although it was an uncomfortable way to live, I must say this. I learned from Sonny how to interact with law enforcement. He said, "They have a job to do. Therefore, they should be respected, and in turn they will respect us."

That's exactly what I and most of the wise guys I knew did. Cops and agents are people, too. They wake up and leave their families and loved ones every day to protect us, not knowing if they will go home at the end of their shift. They deserve our respect for doing what they do. Yes, there are some bad ones, but they are few. Every profession has some bad apples that can and should be weeded out, and law enforcement is no exception. There are procedures in place to do just that.

Yet today, it seems to be open season on cops—all cops. They are being murdered and attacked relentlessly. It's crazy and it is not right. There is no respect anymore. Respect used to be passed down from the parents to their children, but somewhere it has gone wrong.

Economic conditions are horrible, and the middles class is dwindling quickly. I am not an economics major, but I recall the words of my friend Tommy DeMare, Senior, from many years ago. He told me our country was set up for only low income and high income—we were not to have a middle class.

Homeless numbers rise daily, and it is scary. In Beverly Hills there are homeless people all over, and it's like that across the country. It's just not right. Here in Los Angeles, people complain about the homeless, but when the city wants to build places for them to live and get them back into society, those same complainers sue the city and say that the housing shouldn't be too close to the park, school, or wherever. Some of them definitely have mental issues and should be in a hospital, but who closed all the mental hospitals? It was President Reagan. However, most are just hard-working people who could not pay the exorbitant rent here in Los Angeles and got evicted. The citizens and everyone in government think it's a big deal that on Thanksgiving and Christmas they feed them a decent meal, but for the rest of the year they are forgotten.

* * *

When Deborah got on a real bad drug or booze binge, I would have to throw her out of my apartment, but I could never just put her on the street, though, so I would put her in a hotel.

One time when I had her in the Beverly Terrace Hotel, I got a call from the manager telling me that two guys were in her room. I drove over and found Deborah passed out on the bed. On the table were papers with phone numbers for Detective Sewell, one for his office and the other for his cell. It turned out Deborah had called the OCID and offered to serve as a paid informant, providing them with information about me. She did this to get money for her drug habit, and they gave it to her.

I took the notes, packed up Deborah's things, and moved her to another hotel. After I got her settled in, I left and called Sewell.

I said, "Let's get something straight. You're the good guy, and I'm the bad guy. Why don't we play this the right way? If you catch me doing something illegal, arrest me. But if you think you're going to use what a drunk and a junkie says against me, one who has a longer rap sheet than me, I'll spin you around in a courtroom."

Sewell agreed, and I think we developed a mutual respect that day.

I tried my best, but the revolving door of rehab and treatment centers continued with Deborah, and we finally split. Her mother then went through the same thing with her again. She died of an overdose in July of 2007. I was told that when they found her body. it was surrounded by empty Vodka and pill bottles.

* * *

I first heard of Jerry Zimmerman shortly after I moved to Los Angeles. Sonny was in prison for violating his parole, and his wife Tina called me one night for a favor. She said this Jerry guy owed some money for something to do with her son Michael. She wanted me to go see him, and she gave me an address. I sensed this was something I did not want to get involved with, but I did take a drive to the address she provided. It turned to be a warehouse, and a couple of guys were moving things inside that appeared to be artwork. I suspected it wasn't really valuable. The guys told me Jerry wasn't around. I went home, called Tina, and told her what I'd found. I had no intention of getting involved unless Sonny asked me, then it would be a different story.

Sonny did want me to meet Jerry, though—not about Michael, but as a business contact. Sonny and I spoke by phone several times a month, and more than once he mentioned connecting with Jerry. He called Jerry and gave him my phone number.

Jerry reached out and asked me to meet him at Jerry's Deli on Ventura Boulevard. He was a very impressive guy, standing six feet, five inches tall with a head of silver hair like you've never seen before. In addition, he was a great talker. Those attributes made him very good at what he did. He was the best con man I ever met, and I met a lot of them.

* * *

As Jerry and I got to know each other I learned he was from the streets of Brooklyn. As a young man, he was a stand-up comic in the hotels in the Catskills. Like many other great comedians, he was also a manic depressant. He was amazingly smart—another guy who I believe could have been successful at anything he set his mind to. However, he loved what he did.

He had a warehouse where he stored merchandise

until he auctioned it off. He made some money at it, but in reality, it was just a front.

Jerry's main income was from a scam that worked like this. He ran ads in some of the smaller newspapers around the country that read, "Money to Loan." The targets of his ads were other scammers—"mooches" as we called them— people who were fraudulently taking money from their victims for phony projects.

Let's say a couple of guys wanted to look for suckers to invest in developing oil wells where there was no oil. In order to get the plan up and running, they'd need money to form a company and open an office to make everything look legitimate. This could take a big financial investment, and they'd need a start-up loan.

When these guys contacted Jerry, he gave them the impression that he had organized crime connections and could help them get mob financing—for a price. The "clients" had to come up with his fee for making the arrangements. The big thing was to get the borrower to write the first check. It might be only five hundred dollars, but Jerry (and later me) would go back for more, citing additional expenses, and most of the time we would get it.

For one such meeting, I drove to Jerry's office. The lights were off except for a lamp on his desk. The two victims were sitting in front of his desk, and Jerry had a chair for me set up next to him. I sat down, and Jerry told these guys that I would be getting them their loan money. They were to show their respect by coming before me, getting on their knees, and kissing my ring. They did it. It was all I could do to keep from laughing.

The beauty of the con was that when the loan didn't

materialize, the victims weren't able to complain to the authorities. After all, they'd been trying to get money for their own illegal purposes.

* * *

Here are a couple more of Jerry's capers.

It was a Friday and I decided to take a ride out to see Jerry Zimmerman at his warehouse. It was a warm summer day, and by the time I got to Jerry's, it had already been an unusually quiet week for us. We hadn't made a dime. We decided to take a ride around the San Fernando Valley.

Jerry and I were driving on Van Nuys Boulevard, and Jerry was watching all the civilians (in *the life* we call normal people with jobs getting weekly paychecks *civilians*) going into different banks to cash or deposit their paychecks. Suddenly, he said, "You know, it's not fair that all these people get a paycheck on Fridays and we don't." Then he asked me, "Do you have your check book with you?"

"Yeah, why?"

"Write me a check for a thousand dollars."

I had maybe a hundred bucks in my account, but I wrote him a check. I drove Jerry over to Laurel Canyon Boulevard where his brother did his banking. He went inside, cashed the check, and came back out and gave me $500. That seemed to change our luck. Money started coming in, and I was able to cover the check by Monday.

Jerry could find things for us to do like no other person. He was funny, but he was able to do things nobody else could get away with. He just had that kind of personality.

* * *

One time when I went to see Jerry at his warehouse, there was an Asian guy in his early to mid-twenties sitting in the waiting room. Sometimes when you look at someone for the first time, your gut sends you a warning. That's the way it was when I saw this guy.

Jerry showed up almost immediately, grabbed me and took me to the back of the building. He told me the kid in the waiting room was Kenny Kaneko. Kenny was involved in the porn business, and sometimes he brought in films for Jerry to sell and Jerry could always pick up a few extra bucks. He added that Kenny had been a low-level drug dealer since the age of fifteen when he sold drugs in school. He told me that Kenny had been an informant since he was 15 years old, and advised me not to trust him or do anything illegal with him. I didn't, but Jerry made money from Kenny and acted like he was his friend.

Jerry turned out to be right about Kenny. Using the name of Kenny "Kenji" Gallo, he went on to become an FBI informant and wore a wire against Teddy Persico and others, back in New York.

Later, he started saying things about me in his online blog—that I was an informant or a rat. It wasn't true, but if anyone had believed him, it could have gotten me killed. However, what he and others did not know is that I was already on record for being taped by the FBI with Joe Todaro and Jimmy Caci. Kenny's charges were serious enough that Sonny called me back to New York to ask me about these allegations. I told Sonny what I did and to check with Joe, which he did. He also wrote a book that contained a lot of untruths about me and others.

After Sonny went back to prison yet again for another parole violation, Kenny wrote him a letter saying he could get him out of jail. When he got the letter, Sonny had someone call me wanting to know who Kenny was. I sent word back reminding him that Kenny was the rat who had written the bullshit blog posts. Sonny didn't respond to him. When I got arrested and taken back to Brooklyn, I was approached by some guys who Kenny had written that I was associated with. It was the first time we'd ever laid eyes on each other.

"So, you're Ori Spado? It's nice to actually meet you." We all had a good laugh.

Another lie Kenny told was that he was in Jerry Zimmerman's office and answered the phone when Sonny called for Jerry to contact me. *Bullshit!* Not in a million years would Sonny call Jerry and leave a message with someone he didn't know. If Jerry or Jerry's daughter didn't answer the call, Sonny would have hung up and tried again later.

Kenny couldn't get to Sonny without my help, though, and he had a tremendous amount of jealousy and animosity toward me. He once told someone he was going to kill me, but I knew he didn't have the balls.

Jerry and I became very close friends and remained so until he passed away in 2000.

Before his death I visited him in the hospital nearly every night. Jerry was not a person to take his medicine, and he had kidney problems and was on dialysis. Then he quit that on his own. He ended up in the hospital, I recall during one visit his wife Eileen was a nervous wreck. I saw that Jerry's arms and legs were strapped to the bed. Eileen explained that he was agitated and because of his size, the hospital staff were afraid of him and applied the restraints. She asked me to talk to him and calm him down.

I told her to go get a cup of coffee. When she left the room, Jerry looked at me and asked me to cut the straps. "I'd do it for you," he said.

I didn't cut the straps, but before I left, I did loosen them so he could slide his arms and legs out. I knew it was wrong, yet I just couldn't walk out and leave him like that.

Something told me this would be the last time we'd speak, and it was. He died shortly afterward.

* * *

Not long after I met Jerry, my old friend Peter Azer called and said he needed to see me right away. He and his doctor girlfriend had a place on Elm Drive in Beverly Hills. When I got to their place, I was shocked by how far Peter had fallen. They were both heavy into drugs, and she was having some kind of problem with the law.

Peter said he needed to get to a drugstore in Century City and wanted me to drive him. I don't know for sure what drug he picked up, but it might have been morphine. With his girlfriend being a doctor, she could order anything they wanted.

After we pulled away from the drugstore, Peter took the drugs out of the bag, filled a syringe, and injected himself in the thigh right through his jeans.

Peter was my friend, and I tried helping him and his girlfriend. I got Peter into a rehab in the Marina, and her into the Betty Ford Center. She had a lot of legal problems and Peter asked me to get a lawyer for her. I got my lawyer at the time, Kevin McDermott, to represent her; however, after she was in Betty Ford, she hooked up with another guy and started saying that I was a gangster and got her a mob lawyer, Kevin was doing a good job for her, but that ended quickly. She had a son who was a good kid that she basically abandoned, and as she had some money in the bank that her son was to take. I had him buy a ticket to fly back to Australia and live with his grandparents.

Go figure.

23

──◦◦◦──

The Queen Mary & Titanic—One

I n early 1993, Jerry Zimmerman called and asked me to go with him to meet Joe Prevratil, Chief Executive Officer of the RMS Titanic Foundation, Inc., and the new leaseholder of the Queen Mary. The famed ocean liner had been docked in Long Beach since 1967, and most recently had been serving as a floating hotel and tourist attraction. Jerry said Mr. Prevail needed a loan of three million dollars to make necessary renovations to the ship. Jerry hoped I'd be able to get the money through my contacts in New York.

Jerry and I drove to Long Beach and met with Joe and his Chief Financial Officer, Howard Bell, aboard the ship. The first thing Joe did after the introductions was hand me an envelope with a thousand dollars to cover my time and consulting. Then he told me the story of the Queen Mary since it had been in Long Beach. It turned out Joe had been involved at the very beginning.

He explained the ship was first leased by a wealthy family from Beverly Hills, and they hired him to manage it for them. Then the Walt Disney Company took over for a short period of time, until they discovered the property wasn't large enough for their purposes and closed it down.

While the Queen Mary sat idle, Joe was in charge of the Port of Long Beach. The city offered him an opportunity to lease the ship, and he accepted on behalf of the RMS Foundation. However, the lease was for only five years, making it difficult to borrow money. That was why they needed me.

Joe then gave us a tour of the ship, and his knowledge was impressive. As we made the rounds, Joe told us that although the Queen Mary was one of the largest tourist attractions in Southern California, it was also known as a "one stop" destination. That meant once you took the tour, there was really no reason to go back, and the tourist numbers were dwindling. He wanted to reverse that trend and give people a reason to revisit the ship, and that took money. After the tour, I told Joe I needed to make some calls and I'd get back to him.

A couple of days later, I went back to Long Beach alone to discuss my ideas with Joe. I told him the short-term lease was a big drawback to getting a loan, but in spite of that, my New York connections might be willing to take a chance. This was a ticklish deal that I needed to handle in person and not by phone. That meant going to the City at least once, and probably several times. I said my fee would be twenty-five thousand dollars, plus expenses. Joe agreed and gave me the money.

Sonny was in prison and couldn't help me, but I knew several other people in positions to make things happen. I began making numerous trips to New York to meet with them and pitch the deal. After each trip I told Joe I was making progress but needed more money. Eventually, Joe's payments to me totaled a hundred fifty thousand, which I split with Jerry Zimmerman.

I was finally able to get a coalition of three people who would loan Joe the three million. They were all in the garbage business, but I didn't give Joe their names. I went back to New York yet again to arrange for a wire transfer for the money. I was at the Warwick waiting to close the deal, but no one was returning my calls.

I found out why the next morning as I walked past a newsstand on Sixth Avenue. I saw the headline on one of the papers—everyone in the trash business had been arrested. The loan was dead. I flew back to California to tell Joe and Howard what had happened.

It was a day I'll never forget. I was exhausted from all my coast-to-coast trips and knowing the law was constantly behind me. When I got to the pier I sat in my car for a few minutes, looking at that massive, beautiful piece of steel. Suddenly a thought came to me. The Queen Mary could still be a gold mine for me—my way to earn a steady, decent living. With an idea in my head, I boarded the ship.

When I broke the news, Joe and Howard weren't surprised. They'd already read about the mass arrests and figured their benefactors were probably among them.

Next, I pitched them my new idea. What if I could bring the ship to life by providing live entertainment and giving visitors a reason to come back? They liked the idea and said they'd be willing to compensate me if I came up with a workable plan. I left that meeting exhilarated and ready to try my hand in the world of entertainment, this time to attract tourists.

Joe never asked for any of the hundred and fifty thousand dollars back. However, I later paid him seventy-five thousand—my half—by having him withhold ten percent of my earnings until it was all paid. Jerry had already spent his share and didn't make any reimbursement.

In addition to the money Jerry made on the deal, he was impressed with how I handled it and started using me more and more in his scams.

* * *

While I had been working on Joe's loan, Jerry had been contacted by some guys from Minnesota who were looking for *big* money—something like twenty-two million. He asked me to see what I could do to bilk them out of some money. I recruited my old Polyglycoat partner, Walter Fiveson, to help me. I'd kept in touch with him, and when the Minnesota thing came up, he was publishing a magazine advertising strip joints and other adult entertainment. He welcomed the chance to come onboard.

I told one of the guys from Minnesota to come to New York and bring me fifty thousand dollars, and then I'd start working on his loan. He came to my suite at the Warwick with a bag of cash. Walter was there with me, but I introduced him as "Sal."

The guy offered the bag to me and I told him it wasn't mine, to give it to Sal.

After he handed the money over, he said, "I'm pretty short of cash. Can you loan me five hundred?"

Here is a guy who just gave up fifty grand and doesn't have anything for himself. *Unbelievable.* I wondered who had given him the fifty thousand. I told Sal to give him the five hundred and said I'd be in touch.

After the guy left, I stuck my hand into the money bag. Normally the money would be in bundles of five thousand dollars each, so I grabbed a bundle and gave it to Walter. He thanked me profusely.

Only after Walter left did I realize the money was in bundles of ten thousand dollars, which meant I'd paid him double what I had intended. There was no way I'd ever ask him for half the money back. I called Jerry and told him about my mistake. He laughed it off and I sent him his half of the score. The loan, of course, never came off.

Walter was associated with a guy from Scarsdale named Greg DePalma. Greg once owned the Westchester Premiere Theatre in Tarrytown, New York, and was friends with many celebrities, including Frank Sinatra. He was also a *made* man in the Gambino family. Walter kicked up a thousand dollars of his end of the Minnesota scam to Greg. This connection came in handy later on.

* * *

I believe it was in early 1997 that Jerry contacted me with another deal. He wanted to introduce me to a guy named John Joslyn, a producer of several TV documentaries, including *Roughcuts* (1984), *Al Capone: Chicago's Scarface* (1986), and *Live from Transylvania* (1989). Later, he produced *Titanic: Secrets Revealed* (1998). He was also one of the original partners in RMS *Titanic*, Incorporated. It's my understanding that the company was founded in 1987. Other partners included George Tulloch, who lived in Connecticut, and one of the French Piaget family that produced luxury watches. When Mr. Piaget died, George Tulloch reportedly flew to France and purchased his rights relating to the Titanic from his widow. The story goes that he did this without informing John Joslyn.

Tulloch also brought in an investor from Greenwich, Connecticut, named Bill Gasperini, who owned Post Road Iron Works. He put up two million dollars. John was living and working in Los Angeles and wanted to sell his third of RMS for a million dollars. He wanted me to help him with the sale. I did some research and concluded that the logical buyer would be Bill Gasperini. He was already invested in the business and had the money to buy John out.

I made an appointment to meet Bill on a Monday morning at his office in Greenwich. I took the early train out of the City, looking very business-like in a coat and tie, and carrying a briefcase.

Bill ushered me into his office, and almost as soon as we sat down, he said, "I know who you are."

He then mentioned several Italian names and asked if I knew them.

"I may have seen them in the papers. I'm not sure. My business here, though, is to offer you a chance to purchase Mr. Joslyn's RMS stock."

"How about Anthony Megale, do you know him? He's a friend of mine."

I was getting uneasy and ran my hand under the table checking for a microphone as I said, "Sorry, I don't. Again, I'm here regarding Mr. Joslyn's stock."

Finally, we got down to business and I made my pitch about John's stock. Bill said he'd have to think it over and would get back to me with an offer on Friday. Afterward he gave me a tour of his operation and then took me to lunch.

I waited in my room at the Warwick all day Friday, but Bill didn't call. At about quarter to five, I called his office and was told he had left to spend the weekend at his home in Mexico. I was pissed that he stood me up. I was able to get his phone number in Mexico and called. I don't remember exactly what I said, but some of it may not have been very nice. I closed by telling him I had to go back to California for a few days, and I'd be back the following week.

When I returned and went to check in at the Warwick, the desk clerk said I was already booked into a two-bedroom suite, and that it was charged to my American Express card. I was totally confused because I knew I hadn't checked in, and I didn't have an American Express card.

I went to the suite and the mystery was solved. There in the second bedroom was Walter Fiveson, with all his personal possessions. He explained that he'd had a fight with his girlfriend and moved out. Knowing I was coming to the Warwick, he put the two-bedroom in my name and put it on his credit card. He told me he was going to drive to Los Angeles after I finished my business in New York and move in with me. This wasn't exactly what I had in mind, but I couldn't say no.

After I recovered from Walter's announcement, I asked him if he'd take me to meet Greg DePalma. We drove to Greg's construction company in Scarsdale, and Walter introduced me. Greg and I hit it off right from the start.

After some initial small talk, I said, "Do you know a guy named Anthony Megale?

"Yeah, I know him well. He runs things in Connecticut for the (Gambino) family."

"I'd like to meet him."

Greg arranged a luncheon at a restaurant (Italian of course) on the border of New York and Connecticut. A private table was set up for us in the kitchen, and Anthony Megale and a couple of his friends were waiting for us.

After lunch I asked Anthony, "Do you know Bill Gasperini from Greenwich?"

"I don't know him, but I've heard of him."

"I met with him a couple of weeks ago and he dropped your name. He said you're friends."

Anthony got visibly angry. "That's not true! You can do whatever you need to do with this guy. I don't know him, and I won't bother you. You've got free rein in Connecticut."

When we left the restaurant, I had Walter drive me to Bill's office. When we got in to see him, I said, "Remember all those names you mentioned the last time I was here? Well, I happen to know them all, and I just met with Anthony Megale. He said he doesn't know you, and you don't have permission to use his name."

The color drained from Bill's face. No doubt he was scared.

Having Bill's attention, I asked what he'd decided about purchasing John's stock. He did make me an offer, but it was a very low figure and we couldn't reach an agreement.

* * *

Although I couldn't get John's stock deal done, there was something else he asked me to help him with. He wanted to get the rights to film the Titanic salvage for a TV documentary. This required getting George Tulloch to sign off. George's office was in the City, and since I was there, I figured I might as well stop in and see him. I called John to give him an update and tell him I was going to talk to George. He said that wouldn't be necessary. Now I was confused again. John was paying me good money, and he doesn't want me to try to get him the film rights?

As I thought things over, I started putting two and two together. How did Bill Gasperini know who the hell I was? Maybe he found out from John. I suspected that after John hired me, he started tossing my name around to scare people. That was not the right thing to do, and the more I thought about it the madder I got.

I decided I was going to find out what was going on, and George was the closest to me. I got hold of Walter and had him drive me to George's office.

I told the receptionist I wanted to see George and gave her my name. When I did, the door behind her closed and I heard the sound of a lock.

"Mr. Tulloch isn't here," she said.

I walked past the receptionist and busted through the door. George and a guy who turned out to be his lawyer were cowering in a corner of the room. I said something to them, and the next thing I knew, Walter was pulling on my arm.

"Come on, we've gotta get out of here," he said.

We left and that was the end of my dealings with John and his associates. John ended up shooting the Titanic documentary, and today he runs the world's largest Titanic exhibit in Branson, Missouri. God bless him.

The Titanic and Queen Mary came back into my life a little later, though, and this time the outcome was much better.

* * *

In spite of the setbacks on John's stuff, I made money on the deal and developed a good contact in Greg DePalma.

Before I went back to California, we had a private talk in his office. He said, "I like you. I want to be involved with you and you with me. I'm going to meet with John Gotti, Junior, and I'll get you on the book with them (the Gambinos)."

We talked about my connections with Sonny and Jimmy Caci. I said I appreciated his offer but preferred to be a loner. He accepted that and we became friends until his death in 2009. He always seemed to know when I was in the City and we'd get together. In later years he'd sometimes ask me to go to the nursing home with him to visit his son, who was in a years-long coma. I always came up with an excuse not to go, and I thank God for that.

Greg turned his son's room into a meeting place and the FBI had it bugged. On top of that, Greg had been taken in by an FBI undercover agent named Jack Garcia. He introduced him into his crew, and even proposed him to be *made* into the Gambino family. Garcia ended up sending Greg and thirty-one of his associates—including Anthony Megale—to prison.

Go figure.

24

Cable TV Boxes—
Frustrating & Costly

In 1994, Jerry had these guys from Florida in the cable box business who were in the market for a certain type of cable TV box. Neither of us knew anything about cable boxes, but we did some research and thought maybe we could have the boxes made. We called Kevin McCarthy, who was in the movie business, and asked if he could make the boxes we needed, but he couldn't. That seemed to be the end of it.

Then one Sunday I got a call from Kevin's wife. She said, "Kevin's doing a movie at the old Los Angeles City Jail. He said to tell you there are cable boxes stored in all the empty cells."

"Tell him to bring a few home with him tonight, and I'll stop by with Jerry and look at them."

I went to Kevin's that evening. There were various

types of boxes that I thought might be of use to the Florida guys. I had Kevin take the boxes to the warehouse and invited them to come to town and look. They showed up, selected what they could use, and gave us fifteen thousand dollars for them. It was not only a nice payday, but now we knew exactly what they wanted and the serial numbers to look for. If we could loot the jail, we'd make a score that could reach a million dollars or more.

Kevin took Jerry and me to the jail and, just as he'd said, it was loaded with boxes the cops had found or confiscated. I told Kevin to change the locks on all the cells so we could secure the boxes until we figured out a way to get them all out.

I devised a plan in which we'd rent the facility under the pretext that we were going to shoot a film there. Coming up with a few real actors and some rented equipment was no problem. A friend who was in the porn business could be used as the director, and Jerry said he could arrange for a pal of his to play producer. We'd have a crew ready to move the boxes while the filming was in progress.

I had someone rent the place and invited the customers from Florida to come back out. I put them up in one hotel, I stayed in another, and Jerry in yet another. As I recall, we all used beepers in those days in case we needed to reach each other.

On the day we planned to remove the boxes I had four trucks with crews positioned down the road from the jail. I even had a catering wagon on site to feed the actors and make it look realistic to anyone watching. Inside the building we had guys positioning the boxes to load onto the trucks, and my special effects guy used smoke screens, so the actors did not know what was going on behind the scenes.

The Police Academy was located across the Los Angeles River from the jail. I posted a guy on a motorcycle there to act as a lookout. I told Jerry's producer guy to shut the set down at midnight. Unfortunately, he liked to drink and was drinking that day. He thought he was really filming a movie, and wouldn't close down so the trucks could pull up. I cursed and yelled at Jerry to straighten his guy out. Midnight quickly became two in the morning, and three of my four trucks had disappeared. It was turning into a nightmare.

At four o'clock, the set was finally shut down. The remaining truck pulled up, and there was a scramble to get it loaded with as much as possible and be out of there when our rental expired at six. In the rush, a lot of boxes we didn't need got loaded while the ones we could have sold didn't. A little before six, the truck pulled out and went to a pre-arranged location where the guys from Florida picked out what they wanted. After all that, they only paid us forty thousand.

Let me remind you I was on the hook for paying the actors, the moving crew, and the facility and equipment rental. After all the expenses were paid, Jerry got nothing, and I broke even.

There were still a lot of sellable boxes in that building, though, and I wasn't ready to give up on getting my hands on them. I vowed there would be another day with a different outcome.

* * *

When a friend of mine named Clarence was released from prison, we hooked up and I gave him a few bucks to help out until he got back on his feet. I did this for a lot of guys, as well as putting money in their commissary while they were locked up.

Clarence told me he had a friend (I'll call him Roy) who was a vice president of Comcast and wanted to introduce me to him. We met at a restaurant in Burbank. During our conversation the subject of cable TV boxes and their value came up. We decided to meet again and talk some more. However, unbeknown to me, Roy was having legal problems—he was under investigation for being a pedophile. After the meeting, he called the cops and asked if they had any interest in me. They did. From then on, when I met with Roy, he was wearing a wire.

During subsequent meetings with Roy at the same restaurant, we talked about how I could get the cable boxes from Comcast. He would give me phony papers on Comcast letterhead authorizing removal of the boxes. I'd drive a truck to the storage yard, show the papers to the guard, load the boxes and drive away.

I told him it was a good plan, and we had to get it done soon because I'd heard that a rogue police detective— whom I identified by name—had some guys stealing boxes for him and was selling them on the streets. I also told him about the cable boxes at the old Los Angeles jail and how I planned to get them out of there. My idea was to get a phony court order transferring the boxes from Los Angeles to another closed jail in San Pedro. Of course, they would never get there. He had all this stuff on the wire.

While Roy and I were having these meetings to

finalize our plans, I met with Jerry. He didn't want to get involved in the Comcast deal and tried to talk me out of it.

I told him, "If you're that suspicious, when I meet Roy to pick up the transfer papers, I'll go into the restaurant first. Then you come in, take a seat at the bar and observe. If you see or sense something that doesn't seem right, leave and beep me. I'll bail out."

Jerry agreed.

Roy called me on a Thursday and said he had the paperwork ready. We agreed to meet at the restaurant that afternoon. I had a date with a gorgeous chick after I finished my business with Roy and was really looking forward to it.

I went to the restaurant and sat at the bar. As planned, Jerry came in a few minutes later and took a seat across from me. Then Roy showed up, we went to a table where he handed me an envelope with the papers. I looked them over and everything looked good except the date Roy had dated them for Friday. I told him I'd heard that the guy in charge at the storage yard was on vacation and would not be back until Monday, so I wouldn't be able to pick up the boxes until then. He wasn't happy about it, but changed the papers to Monday's date.

While Roy and I were talking, Jerry left. I didn't get a beep, so I felt all was okay. A few minutes later, Roy left, and I wasn't far behind him.

I walked to my car, and as I bent forward to unlock the door, I heard the sound of racing engines followed by screeching tires all around me. I threw the counterfeit papers under the car.

The vehicles surrounding me were operated by officers of the detective squad. One cop cuffed me and put me into his car. He said to the others, "You know what to do." Then he pulled away.

I knew enough not to say anything, and we rode in silence. I wasn't familiar with the area we were driving through, I and didn't know where he was taking me. Then he pulled into a place called Griffith Park (a huge municipal park covering 4,310 acres, located in the Los Feliz neighborhood of Los Angeles).

My first thought was that maybe it was a shortcut of some kind. It wasn't. When he pulled onto a dirt road I said, "I don't know of any police station here."

He pulled over and stopped the car. Then he looked at me and said, "You know who I am you Guinea bastard! You've been blabbing my name on a wire."

Then he told me his name.

Oh shit! This was the rogue cop who was stealing and selling cable boxes.

I was pretty sure I wouldn't make it out of Griffith Park alive. As I was contemplating my fate, his cell phone rang. He talked a few seconds, disconnected and threw the phone on the floor.

He said angrily, "This is the luckiest day of your life. They want to talk to you at Parker Center (LAPD headquarters). Maybe there will be another time."

He was right—it could very well have been my last day. I found out later that I was saved by a fluke. One of the cops who was at the restaurant had made the mistake of announcing over the police radio that I was in custody. Detectives Sewell and Bannister of the OCID heard the transmission and ordered that I be brought in.

When I got to Parker Center, I was cuffed to a file cabinet while they tried to figure out what to charge me with. The cuffs were tight, and they wouldn't loosen them. Although it was uncomfortable, I was sure it was mild compared to what would have happened to me in Griffith Park.

I dozed off and was awakened when Roy was brought in and put in a chair next to me. That confirmed it. Jerry had been right, I'd been set up. I kicked Roy's chair and said, "Get this fucking rat away from me!"

They removed him, and a few minutes later Sewell and Bannister came in.

Sewell said, "Mr. Spado, I told you we were watching you. I said that if you so much as spit on a sidewalk in some hick town in Missouri, we'd know about it."

I looked up at him and said, "Thank you."

He and Bannister exchanged puzzled glances.

I didn't say anything more—nothing about the rogue cop or the visit to Griffith Park. They probably wouldn't have believed me even if I had.

A little while later I was formally charged with conspiracy to commit the theft of the cable boxes. I asked how much my bail would be and they said fifteen thousand. I was then taken to booking and afterward allowed to make my phone call.

I called Jerry and told him to get hold of Rocco, my bondsman, to get me out.

"How much is your bail?"

"Fifteen thousand."

"Don't embarrass me," he said, and hung up.

That was Jerry. He could make a joke out of almost anything.

I called him back a few minutes later and he said Rocco was on his way. After posting my bond Rocco drove me to my car. I got home around eleven-thirty, just wanting to take a shower and go to bed.

After showering I decided to call Clarence and tell him he introduced me to a rat. As I was standing nude in my living room talking to Clarence, somebody started pounding on my door. I hung up the phone.

"Who is it?" I hollered.

"Detective Sewell, OCID. We're here to execute a search warrant. Open up!"

"Okay. I have to get a robe on and then I'll let you in."

"Open the door now or we'll break it in. You can worry about a robe later."

I opened the door and stood there, naked, as Sewell and the rest of the search team entered, including two very attractive female officers.

Sewell brought me my robe. "Okay, Spado, you know the Procedure. Sit down and relax until we're finished."

He escorted me to my recliner, handed me my cigarettes, and left a cop to keep an eye on me while he joined the search. They had obtained the search warrant while I was still at Parker Center being charged and processed. They were looking for stolen cable boxes and anything else they could use against me. As usual, they found nothing. They would always ask me where my gun was, and I always answered that it was in the same place as usual. When they left, they would put it back where I kept it. I did not have a license for it, and they knew it, but they always just put it back.

I hired a lawyer, and we went to court for the arraignment. The DA was late, so when my name was called, my lawyer requested a future date and the judge granted it. We were starting to leave the courtroom when the DA walked in. My lawyer grabbed my arm.

"Let's get out of here fast," he said. "He (the DA) will want to raise your bail to at least seventy-five grand." And sure as hell that's what he tried to do, but my lawyer took me down the stairs and out of the courthouse, otherwise I would have been locked up waiting for bail again.

It was early 1995, and the OJ Simpson criminal trial was just underway. The courthouse was mobbed with news crews from all around the world, so rather than wait for an elevator we ran down the stairs and got out to the street.

In the end, I took a plea deal with a sentence of three years of probation. One of the main reasons the DA was willing to settle was that he didn't want to go to trial with a pedophile as his chief witness.

Go figure.

25

Turning Up The Heat

Although I'd gotten off with only probation for the cable box deal, 1995 saw a marked increase in the attention I was getting from the feds, and they were watching me more consistently.

When I returned to my apartment one Friday morning from a collection I had to make on Westwood Blvd., Swall Drive had a lot of cars parked on it because of the temple on the corner. As I was pulling into my parking garage, I noticed a car with two guys. I had no idea who they were, so I backed out and pulled up so close on their driver side that the driver wouldn't be able to open his door. When the driver rolled down his window, the passenger hollered my name, then opened his door and got out.

I thought—who in the hell are these guys? Are they the law? Or are they here to whack me?

I drove away fast not knowing if they were law or two guys trying to whack me. As I did, I noticed my apartment manager walking her dog. I drove to a coffee shop and called her. She said that after I left, two other cars pulled up, each with two men in it. The six men talked for a few seconds, and then they all took off.

I called my probation officer and asked if he was looking for me. He wasn't.

I waited a couple hours and then went home. I got my suitcase and headed for Palm Springs. I came back late on Monday and didn't spot anybody who was out of place.

Early Tuesday morning I got up and left for a restaurant in Beverly Hills where I frequently had breakfast on Canyon Drive. I turned out of my garage, and I saw a car parked at the side of my building with one guy in it, reading a newspaper. I decided to stop and confront him.

I rolled my window down and just stared at him, when he noticed, he held up his badge. "FBI, I just want to talk to you."

"What do you want?"

"The two guys in your driveway on Friday were agents from New Jersey. Your friends in Florida are informing on you, and we have the tape they are giving us with information on you. You should listen to it.

"Tell them to come to my apartment this afternoon around two o'clock and let me hear it."

"We will be there."

The lead agent was named Michael Wachs—an exceptionally sharp individual. His partner played a tape that was a conversation that Frank, the cable box guy, had with an undercover agent.

When I heard it, I laughed "Frank wasn't intentionally informing on me. He thought he was talking to a customer. Your agent sucked him in, that's all. If you think I'm going to roll on him or anybody else, you're wasting your time. By the way, you've got your other guy sitting out there in a car. Why don't you have him come in?"

Wachs and his partner appeared surprised that I'd noticed the second car. Spotting tails had become second nature to me, though.

The third agent came in. He was young and very aggressive. He wanted me to be an informant and wasn't happy with my answer.

"I'll get you for transporting stolen cable boxes across state lines," he said. "I'll see you arrested, chained, shackled, and put on Con-air and flown to Brooklyn."

I wasn't worried about that threat because I'd never transported any stolen boxes across state lines. I laughed, but I shouldn't have. It took twelve more years, but that agent Scott Gariola kept his word. He happens to be the same agent that got Whitey Bulger.

* * *

The following Thursday, Michael Wachs came to the Four Seasons where I was having coffee. He sat down and handed me an envelope.

He said, "I know you go to Palm Springs quite often. Here's a little extra spending money for you. No strings attached."

You've heard that if something seems too good to be true, it probably is? This was, but like an idiot I took it, thinking I was smarter than the FBI. I wasn't.

When I returned from Palm Springs on Monday, Wachs called and said he wanted to talk to me at the Hilton in Beverly Hills. I met with him and he made a pitch for me to become a paid informant. I could make big money, he said.

Wachs was a seasoned agent and had infiltrated Carlo Marcello's organization in New Orleans. As I said, he was very sharp and convincing. He also had an envelope with him with five thousand dollars in it.

What if I take their money but don't do anything in return? Taking from the FBI, how cool is that? No way can I refuse.

I took it.

Wachs gave me a recorder to tape my phone calls and said I'd be working with the younger agent who had threatened me previously.

I never taped anyone, but one day when I was a little short on money, I taped the Oprah Winfrey show. I called the agent and told him I had something for him, and I wanted five-grand for it. It was on a Friday afternoon after five. He was pissed off but told me to meet him in an hour. He gave me a thick envelope with the money, and I gave him the Oprah tape.

When I got back to my apartment, the phone was ringing. It was him and he was in rage, yelling: "What the hell is this tape? It sounds like a TV show."

I said, "As I told you, I'm not experienced using recorders and must have recorded a TV show instead of the phone." In the meantime I was taping him.

I played the recordings of my taped calls with the FBI agents to my lawyer, and then to Jimmy Caci. They both got a big kick out of it. Jimmy was going on a trip to Buffalo, so I gave him a copy of it to play for the guys back there. I knew I needed to go on record back east with what I was doing. Jimmy met with the boss, Joe Todaro (Senior), at Joe's pizza restaurant. They called me, and Joe laughed and suggested I keep recording the FBI so we would know what and who they wanted. However, when Jimmy returned to L.A., he said I should stop taping because I'd probably get into a lot of trouble. He was right.

The agents weren't the least bit amused. They said they were thinking about wiring my house to avoid mistakes in the future. Then they called me to a meeting at a Denny's restaurant in Santa Monica. I told Jimmy about it.

He said, "You're playing with fire. You'd better take a lawyer with you."

I agreed with Jimmy and we contacted a young lawyer named Mark Mazie. Mark was basically an entertainment lawyer, but he served the purpose. Mark and I met with the agents and Mark did all the talking. He told them that I would not be an informant, and if they had anything on me, let him know and he would arrange for a time and location for me to self-surrender. They were really pissed and walked away.

However, no sooner did I got home then Mark called me and said he got a call from one of the agents stating that I had one more chance to play ball with them, "or else." I wasn't sure what that meant, but as I sat and thought about it, I figured they'd put the word out on the street that I was an informant. I told Mark to tell them that I said to go fuck themselves. And he did exactly that.

In case I was right, and they were going to try to

hang the "rat" label on me, I figured I'd better get my story out there first. I went to Frankie's restaurant on a Tuesday evening, knowing there would be some guys there I needed to talk with. I got two of them in private and explained what was going to happen. I told them I was on record back east and said, "If someone tells you I'm working with the feds, that person is the real rat. Get back to me with whoever it is."

I didn't really care about the California guys, but I wanted to make damn sure the word got back east so I'd be covered. With Sonny again in prison and unavailable, I knew I was on record with Joe, so I was covered.

I started getting feedback that the feds were doing what I suspected they'd do. They stopped a friend of mine on the streets in Las Vegas and told him to work for them like I was doing.

He spit at them and said, "Spado is no rat!"

I got a call from the guys I met with at Frankie's restaurant, and they told me that Kenny Gallo was telling everyone I was working with the Feds. My thoughts were accurate, and we also found out who was working with the Feds, Kenny Gallo.

Kenny Gallo was on their side, and he started writing bad stuff about me in his blog.

I wasn't happy about all the bullshit going on, but I still had to go on and bring in money. With the law always nearby it became more difficult to earn, but dealing with being under constant surveillance eventually became a normal part of my life.

Go figure.

Collections

I found that helping people collect money that was owed to them a lucrative business. I'd done a lot of it when I ran American Check Guarantee, so I had the experience. If I did my homework, recovery jobs didn't require a lot of time. I never used a gun or any other weapon. Instead, I used my head—reason, logic and more logic. And my voice and looks helped for sure. I didn't use a gang of guys, either. I worked alone and didn't do or say anything to the debtor that could get me into trouble with the law. My clients included doctors, actors and bookies.

There were a few basic rules I followed when deciding whether to get involved in a debt collection. The debt had to be legitimate; the money owed had to be enough to make my effort worthwhile; and the person owing the money had to have the ability to pay.

After I had collected the money, I always shook the person's hand and told them to call me if they ever had a problem of any kind, as I could help them. Sometimes they would call me when they were having trouble recouping their money, providing me with additional opportunities to earn.

Most of my collection jobs were what you might call routine. There were some that stick in my mind, though, because of the people or circumstances involved. In addition, I would get 50% of the money, and for larger sums, I required a retainer. I have a rule. There are three sides to every story, and I have had an occasion where the individual asking me to collect was not actually owed the money. There were times when I had to hire a private investigator to get me more information, or when I had to have people sit and learn the habits of the individual that owed the money.

There was a famous movie actor—I'll call him Sam—who was trying to get two million dollars released from one of the largest agencies in Beverly Hills. The money was owed to him for a movie deal, but the agency refused to release it to Sam or his lawyers until a dispute with one of the producers of the film was resolved. I met with Sam at his home, and after getting all the details, I said I would handle it for him. Although my fee was not discussed at that time, I assumed he would do the right thing.

My next step was to call the producer and ask him to meet me at the Four Seasons Hotel in Beverly Hills. In the '90s and early 2000s, I used the Four Seasons as one of my main places to meet with people to discuss potential business deals and hang out. The valets and other staff knew me, and I actually had my own table on the patio lounge. You could find me there almost every afternoon at five o'clock.

I had to meet with this producer and his partner a few times before I convinced them that what they were doing was wrong. In the end, though, he agreed to call the agency holding the money and tell them it was okay to release it. Good job and big bucks in my pocket, right? Wrong. I didn't get a dime.

Here's why. Johnny Franzese and I were out in my car, and although I never told Johnny much about my business because of his drug issues, he had met Sam through his father, and Sam was very fearful of Sonny. Johnny said he wanted to talk with Sam about something and asked if I had his phone number. When Johnny got Sam on the phone, he mentioned he was with me and that I was a close friend of Sonny's. Following that call, Sam started avoiding me.

Then I found out Sam was involved with some people in New York whom I knew, and he was testifying against them. I smelled trouble and decided it would be best to keep my distance from him. I made no further attempts to contact him.

It turned out to be a good move. Sam had once been a major action star and had got there with the help of certain people of influence. After he made it big, he forgot about what they had done for him and went against them. He started screwing the wife of a big-name guy in the music business, which was way out of bounds. He even went so far as to testify against his benefactors in court.

I wasted a little time on the deal, and I got nothing in return.

* * *

I had a great relationship with a bookie named Herb. One time, Herb had this guy who tried to double-bet with him using another name. Herb knew it was the same guy, and he owed Herb fifteen thousand dollars. Herb and I went to this guy's office and he promised to pay the money a few days later.

On the due date, Herb was with me in my car when the guy called Herb's cell phone and asked for a postponement. I told Herb to keep him on the line while I drove to his office. I went into the building, took the elevator up and walked in on him. There he was, sitting behind his desk talking with Herb.

I said, "Hang up the phone, we need to talk."

After he disconnected, I continued, "Before we get down to business, is that a real watch you're wearing?"

"Yes, it is. Why?"

"I'd like to take a look at it."

He took the watch off and handed it to me.

I looked at it and then stuck it in my pocket. This was one way I used to intimidate people I was collecting from to make them realize this was for real. I didn't mention the watch again, and neither did he. Message delivered.

Next I said, "I have good news and I bad news for you. The good news is you no longer owe Herb the money. The bad news is that now you owe it to me."

The color drained from his face. He didn't say anything. He just stared at me.

"Apparently you can't come up with the full amount at one time, so here's how you're going to pay me back. Every Monday you'll pay me three percent of what you owe. That comes to four hundred and fifty dollars. That will be easier for you, won't it?"

"Yes," he said weakly, "that will be easier."

"Okay, I'm glad we have an agreement. Don't forget, four fifty next Monday and *every* Monday after that. And that's just the juice payment—none of it goes on the principal. If you want to pay down the loan, you've got to pay more. Understand?"

"Yes, I understand."

"Good. Have a nice weekend."

That conversation took place on a Friday. The following Monday, Herb called me. He said the guy had found the fifteen grand and we should come to his office and pick it up. I got a third of the money—five thousand—for my help. I had different terms with different people, but with Herb that was our standard deal.

* * *

The only time I came close to a problem was when a friend of mine from New York wanted me to go with him to see the owner of an auto repair shop in Westwood (California) who owed him some money.

He said, "I'll show you how we do it in New York. When we get to his apartment, let me do the talking. Okay?"

"Sure. It's your show."

I drove him to the guy's apartment building. The repair shop owner answered the door and my friend stood there talking with him instead of walking inside.

I stood there looking past the guy to see what I might be able to take to intimidate him and get his attention. It didn't get that far, though. He told my friend to come to his shop the next morning and he'd pay him off.

As we left my friend said, "See how easy that was?"

I laughed. "That guy bullshitted you. You're not going to get the money tomorrow, and he'll probably have the law there waiting for you."

The next morning, I rented a car and we went to the shop earlier than scheduled. I drove around the building and sure enough, the cops were there, waiting. I'm sure they were counting on arresting us on extortion charges. I beat it out of the area and my friend had to write it off as a loss.

* * *

One day I got a call from a friend in Florida. He told me about a doctor in Las Vegas who also dabbled in the gold mining business. He supposedly got some of his colleagues to invest fifty thousand dollars with a guarantee they'd get their investment back if things didn't pan out. However, when the investors demanded their money back, he refused to pay.

My two sons had just arrived to spend the summer with me. I was broke and on top of that, coming down with the flu. I wasn't in a good mood.

When I called the doctor in Vegas, I wasn't very nice. I told him he needed to do the right thing and return the money, as promised. I must have been convincing, because almost immediately he agreed to pay. He said he'd have a cashier's check ready at two that afternoon.

I caught a flight to Vegas and then took a cab to the doctor's office on Flamingo Road. I walked in and the receptionist had an envelope ready for me with the cashier's check in it. I asked to see the doctor, thanked him, and gave him my usual spiel about calling me if he ever needed my help.

I made it back to Los Angeles in time to get to my bank. I cashed the check from the doctor, taking twenty-five thousand in cash for myself, and getting a cashier's check for the other half to send to my guy in Florida. That followed my rule of always getting my end right off the top.

* * *

In June 1994, I had just moved to a place on Palm Drive in Beverly Hills. My son, Orlando Junior, was getting married, and I planned to go to Florida the next day for the wedding. While I was still unpacking from the move, I got a call from a friend in Buffalo who knew my plans. He said a friend of his had been ripped off for thirty-five thousand dollars by a telemarketing room out of Fort Lauderdale. As long as I was going to be in Florida, would I try to get his friend's money back?

I took the victim's contact information and gave him a call. We reached an agreement that I'd try to get the money back and, if successful, I'd get half. I wrote all the information the guy gave me on a piece of paper, put it on my desk, and returned to unpacking the boxes that were all over the place.

Suddenly, there was a loud knock on my door. I answered it and found detectives from the OCID were there serving another fucking search warrant. I found out later that other detectives had hit Jimmy Caci's house in Palm Springs at the same time.

It was the same routine. A Beverly Hills cop kept an eye on me as I sat in my recliner and smoked while the detectives went about their business. They found nothing of evidentiary value regarding anything Jimmy and I were involved in, but they did see my notes about the collection job in Florida and wrote everything down. I didn't think it was a big deal.

Shortly after the cops left, I got a phone call from Christa, my future daughter-in-law. She said there were guys in a parked car watching their place in Florida. I wasn't sure what was going on, but figured it was an FBI operation. I told her to call the local cops and make a suspicious vehicle complaint.

My son Ori came up with a better idea, though. He ordered pizza and brought it to their car. He told them he figured they were probably tired and hungry and could use the snack. He also told them I wouldn't be there until the next day. They left.

When I got to Florida several family members from Rome and Syracuse were already there, including my daughter and her husband Larry. He's a prison guard in upstate New York, solidly built and very strong. I asked him to take a ride with me.

We drove to Fort Lauderdale and went to the telemarketing room. The owner wasn't in, but the manager got him on the phone. When I talked with the owner, I made sure to speak loud enough for the manager and sales crew to hear what was being said. The owner promised to make things right.

Since I was in Fort Lauderdale, after we left the

telemarketing room, I stopped to see Frank, the guy I had gotten the cable TV boxes for. From there, I met another old friend at a Denny's restaurant.

At each stop I was pretty sure I was being watched. I couldn't spot the tail, but I knew it was there. I later started getting calls from everyone I met with that the FBI had stopped at their homes and offices asking questions about me. It wasn't until much later I found out that Frank had been unknowingly doing business with an undercover FBI agent who was posing as a buyer of cable boxes. Frank's phones were tapped, and the FBI knew of me and my attempts to get the cable boxes from the old Los Angeles City Jail.

The next day was the wedding. It was a great day, and I was very proud. The reception was held at a country club in West Palm Beach. Christa's father, who was a photographer, took a lot of pictures. He wasn't the only one using a camera that day, though. The FBI was taking lots of photos, too. I'd sure like to see those photos and add them to the wedding album.

* * *

When I got back to Los Angeles, I got a call from my friend in Buffalo that his buddy got a check from the telemarketing room in Fort Lauderdale for all his money. That meant I had seventeen thousand five hundred dollars coming. I never got it, though.

The OCID called the Buffalo police and had them intimidate my friend. They told him not to pay me and scared him enough that he didn't, but he did call and tell me.

How in the fuck did OCID know about the money?

On a hunch I called the phone company and said I was having a problem with my phone. They sent a repair guy. He found nothing wrong on my end, so he went to the box on the corner, and I went with him. There it was—an *illegal* tap on my phone. I gave him a hundred dollars to disconnect it. This was a practice the Gangster Squad used more often than you might think. When the cops didn't have enough probable cause to get a court order for the tap, they tapped the phone anyway. Because it was an illegal tap, they couldn't use the information they obtained directly, but they got a lot of useful intelligence.

I wasn't happy, but at least I knew how the cops found out about the payment I had coming for the Florida job.

Go figure.

A Bad Collection

Jerry Zimmerman was always on the lookout for new opportunities to turn a profit. He saw potential in the auction business and formed a relationship with an auctioneer named Steven Brown. Some other guys and I served as buyers during the auctions, sitting in the audience and bidding on items we knew were of the most value—a rather common practice.

Another of the auctioneers was Berry Sweet. In my opinion, Steve was a much better auctioneer, but Berry was the money guy. He had a home in Santa Barbara where he still lives, yet he always cried the blues about money like there was no tomorrow.

One day when Jimmy Caci and I were visiting Jerry, Berry was also there. He said a guy who ran a small computer repair business owed him twenty-five grand

and wasn't making any effort to pay it off. Berry wanted to know if Jimmy and I could help him collect.

Even though I preferred to work alone, it sounded like an easy earn that Jimmy and I could split. The trouble was that I was coming down with some bug and just wanted to get back home and in bed, so, I wouldn't be able to do my usual research until I felt better.

After we left Jerry's, Jimmy said, "Since we're near the deadbeat's office, why don't we pay him a visit right now?"

"Let's wait until next week. That will give me time to check everything out."

"This is a piece of cake deal—you don't need to do any checking. Let's just go and get the money."

Against my better judgment, I gave in and drove to the guy's office, which was in a small strip mall, and parked my car facing his window. We went inside. The owner was alone in the shop area, and we started talking to him about his debt. While we were talking, the guy said something I didn't like, I picked up a plug adapter and put the prawns between my fingers and got up and hit him. When I did, the heel of my shoe got stuck in the carpet. I lost my balance and we both went down on the floor, with me on top. He got up, ran into his office and picked up the phone.

Jimmy said, "Go talk to him."

"Bullshit! He's calling the cops. We've got to get the hell out of here."

We beat it, but the guy was able to get my plate number through his office window before I pulled away. When the cops got there, they ran my plate and found the car was registered to me. Then they called the OCID. Detectives came, showed the guy my picture, and he

ID's me as the guy who hit him. They also showed him a photo of Jimmy, who was out on bail on a previous arrest regarding a telephone operation in Palm Springs. But the victim did not identify Jimmy.

When a victim identifies a suspect from a picture, he is required to sign that photo. The guy signed my picture but not Jimmy's. My lawyer found out later that the cops signed Jimmy's picture themselves so they could lock him up and his bail would be revoked.

They took Jimmy in right away for violating the provisions of his bail. They weren't in that big a hurry to grab me, though, which I didn't understand. I was still on probation for the cable box thing, and they could have taken me in, too. They decided to play a couple of head games with Jimmy before they arrested me, but he'd been locked up too many times for those kinds of tricks to work.

First, Jimmy called me from jail and told me two new guys were placed in his housing unit and came to him saying that I hadn't been arrested yet because I was informing on him. He said one of them looked familiar, but he couldn't remember from where. Sensing they were plants, he punched one of the guys out—he didn't take crap or lies from anybody. The guards removed both of the new arrivals from the unit.

Later, we found out that the one Jimmy hit was an FBI agent. The other guy was a restaurant owner from Westwood who'd done checks with us previously, and that's why he looked familiar to Jimmy. He got caught up in a drug sting in Florida, flipped, and was working for the feds. That goes to prove what most good criminal defense lawyers tell their clients who are going to jail for the first time: don't ever discuss your crimes with anyone. You never know if the person you're talking to is an agent, cop or a jailhouse snitch.

Jimmy told me they tried one more time. When he was being taken to a court appearance, FBI agents told him they heard I was giving information to the cops, and he should start cooperating with them. He said he told them, "You can go fuck yourselves. Ori is not talking."

Then he added, "Ori has been recording you guys and has seven tapes."

Remember, at this point the only people who knew I taped the FBI were Jimmy, Joe in Buffalo, and my lawyer. When Jimmy broke the news to the FBI, they got pissed off because they knew my tapes could cause them problems.

Anyway, the cops were finally getting around to me. Jimmy heard about it in the slammer and called me.

"They're coming for you. Get yourself a lawyer," he said.

I got out of my place and in a few minutes my beeper went off. I called the number, and it was the Forest Lawn Mortuary. I hung up and the beeper went off again, showing a different number. I called and it was the FBI office.

I said, "Go fuck yourself," and hung up.

I drove around for a few hours. When I was sure no one was following me, I checked into a hotel. The next morning, I went back home.

Jimmy was right. A slew of cops showed up and took me in on the computer guy's complaint. The worst thing was that the guy didn't really owe Berry a nickel—it was not a legitimate debt. Berry had already sued the guy and lost in court. He didn't bother to tell us that, of course. Still, if I'd had the time to do my usual research, I'd have found that out, and all these headaches for Jimmy and me could have been avoided.

Anyway, I got myself a sharp lawyer, and we prepared for my case to go to trial. Three times the complainant failed to show up in court. If he missed one more date, the case would be dropped automatically. He appeared the next time.

As we were sitting around waiting for a room to become available for jury selection, the DA approached my lawyer. He said the computer guy only wanted to be compensated for his injuries. For three thousand dollars the case could be resolved. I agreed.

We went in front of the judge and presented the settlement.

She said, "Mr. Spado, do you have the money with you?"

"I don't, Your Honor."

"In the past people have left us checks that bounced, and then they've been nowhere to be found. So I'm going to be very careful here."

"Do you accept cash?"

"Certainly," she smiled.

"I have the money in my apartment. If it's okay, I can have my lawyer deliver it to you this afternoon."

"That is acceptable, Mr. Spado."

As we left the courtroom, the computer guy stopped me and said, "I didn't want to go through with this, but the FBI came to my house and told me I'd better be in court today."

"I understand. You did what you had to do, no problem."

At this point, I would like to say to everyone, don't ever think you're smarter than the FBI. If you do, you'll end up in even worse trouble. These guys are smart, and they have more money and time than you do. Even though this was a local charge, they wanted to see me behind bars and stuck their noses into it. I came out on top that time, but the feds have long memories.

As for Berry, although his lies created that whole mess, he never came up with a penny to help with the legal expenses. Berry was all about Berry. Everybody else could go fuck themselves. When I was released years later, I was flat broke. I reached out to Berry for a loan—a measly five grand. He whined about how tough things were and said he didn't have the money, yet he was always out of town on cruises or vacations. Yeah, to Berry loyalty is a one-way street.

On a positive note, although Berry Sweet was a bust, Jerry did introduce me to some very good people. One of them was an old friend of his named Bob Barich. Bob was a very intelligent and quiet guy. He is a syndicated writer for over two hundred fifty newspapers, was a writer for the *Hill Street Blues* TV series, and was also one of the writers for the 1983 horror movie *Mausoleum*, which Michael Franzese and Jerry were involved in.

I heard that there were a lot of financial problems during the filming, but Michael convinced some of his New York friends to invest, and Jerry and Bob secured the additional money needed to complete the project. I think it grossed somewhere around twenty million. However, when you did business with Michael, neither the investors nor anyone else ever got their money back— Michael kept it all.

Bob and I became and remain close friends. I am currently involved with him on a screenplay that is near completion.

Of all the contacts I made through Jerry, Bob is one of the best.

Go figure.

28

The Queen Mary & Titanic—Two

I t was now 1997. Walter Fiveson was living in Beverly Hills, publishing a magazine about local strip joints. I hadn't given up on my idea of doing something with the Queen Mary that would make some good money for Joe Prevratil and me. I discussed the situation with Walter, the marketing genius. We came up with a workable plan that would increase Joe's business, and I scheduled a meeting with Joe and Howard Bell aboard the ship.

I opened the meeting. "Walter and I have developed some ideas we think will make the Queen Mary a place that visitors will come back to time after time. What you need is to provide a variety of entertainment options so that virtually any audience will find something that will appeal to them. The ship is so big and has so many venues to put on shows, singers and bands that the potential is almost endless.

"By adding entertainment to the museum and restaurants you already have, you'll have one of the biggest draws in Southern California. If you agree, Walter and I will start lining up the talent for your approval. All we'll need is a fifteen-thousand-dollar retainer to get started."

Joe said, "Ori, I like your proposal, but I can't pay you fifteen thousand. However, if you can arrange with George Tulloch for us to get artifacts from the Titanic, I'm sure we can all make a lot of money."

I was speechless. I'd busted through the door of George Tulloch's RMS Titanic office in New York a few months earlier and gone on a rant. I didn't know if Joe knew about it, but I suspected he did. Now he was suggesting I contact George to work out a deal for some of their artifacts. I didn't think that was very likely to happen.

I said, "Joe, you and George are pretty much equals. I think it would be better if you called him."

"I don't think so, Ori. Negotiating this kind of a deal is something you're better at than I am."

"Okay, I'll contact George and get back to you."

As Walter and I were leaving the ship, he said, "Kid, how in the hell are you going to pull this off?"

"I have no idea, but I'll figure something out—I've got to."

* * *

Joe and Howard had told me that not many artifacts from the Titanic had been recovered yet, and some that were being stored in Virginia. Other than that, I knew very little about what might be available, much less how to go about getting any of it.

I decided I needed to learn more about George Tulloch, try to get inside his head, and figure out how to approach him. I got lucky when I stopped at a store for cigarettes and found George staring at me from the cover of a magazine. He was in the crow's nest of a ship that was doing salvage work on the Titanic. I bought the magazine, read that article about him, and found several more. When I was finished with all my reading, I knew for sure that he loved the Titanic. In fact, he was consumed by it. Confident that I understood George's mindset, I came up with an idea I didn't think he'd be able to refuse.

I didn't want George to know I was involved in the deal, at least not to begin with. I had Walter call him, and while they were on the phone, I whispered in Walter's ear what I wanted him to say. It was all stuff that glorified the Titanic and would play to George's love of it. I was surprised at how quickly George agreed that he and his lawyer would come to Long Beach to meet with Joe and Howard.

We arranged their flight and transportation from the airport to the Queen Mary, where their suites were waiting. Walter then called and told them to meet him at the Promenade Café at eight-thirty the next morning, and the breakfast meeting would start at nine.

When Walter and I got to the restaurant, George and his lawyer were waiting at a table with big smiles on their faces. I was behind Walter, and they did not see me at first. The way their smiles disappeared when I stepped into view was almost comical. I walked over to their table and sat down.

"Gentlemen," I said, "There is nothing to be afraid of or nervous about. I was retained to do a job. When I'm paid to do something, I get it done. That's why we're here today. So, let's be friends and cut a good business deal. And if you ever have a problem in the future that I can help you with, all you'll have to do is call."

They relaxed and we shook hands all around.

Next I said, "Here's how it will work. RMS Titanic will supply the artifacts you have on hand in Virginia—I believe there are about thirty-five of them—to the Queen Mary. They will assure the artifacts are properly maintained and kept in a climate-controlled environment. All proceeds resulting from the sale of admission tickets to the exhibit, minus the initial cost of transporting the artifacts and necessary modifications to the Queen Mary, will be split equally between RMS Titanic and the Queen Mary. My fee will be ten percent, which will come off the top."

George and his lawyer agreed. Joe and Howard then joined us, and the deal was made.

I was pleased, but didn't see this as the big money-maker Joe did. I was still looking at setting up the entertainment on the Queen Mary as my best shot at making some decent money. Boy was I wrong.

While we were preparing the exhibit to open on the Queen Mary, James Cameron was filming *Titanic*. When it was released later in the year, it became a smash at the box office, and that success carried over to the exhibit. Every day we had long lines of people waiting to get inside. Howard told me they made a profit of a million and a half dollars that year. And that was the only year it did make a profit to this date. I was very happy, as I was getting checks every month for between $15,000 to $20,000 a month.

* * *

Joe Prevratil invited me to dinner at Sir Winston's, the premier restaurant on the Queen Mary. He told me that the Long Beach Chief of Police contacted him. He told Joe everything about me and advised Joe to be careful.

I was always straight with Joe, though. Even before the cop warned him about me, I'd made a deal with him to withhold ten percent of my fee from the exhibit to repay the money I owed him from the failed attempt to get him a loan.

My arrangement with Joe and the Queen Mary was probably the best gig I ever had. I made good money— fifteen thousand a month or better—and it was all legitimate.

* * *

A lot of other things happened for me in the '90s, and many of them involved Jerry Zimmerman. How he was always able to come up with money-making opportunities was beyond belief.

You were never broke when Jerry was around, but sometimes his deals turned out not to be profitable, like the time Jerry met a guy fresh out of prison that had a lot of baseball memorabilia in storage in Newark, New Jersey. Jerry got me an airline ticket using his brother's frequent flyer miles and I flew to Newark. I spent a whole day filling a tractor-trailer with the merchandise and shipping it to Jerry's warehouse. It filled the place from floor to ceiling.

The plan was to get the stuff insured and then have a fire. It had the potential to be a good score, but somehow the law found out about the plan. Jerry got a visit from the fire department, and they told him, "We understand there is going to be a fire here." That was a warning, and we knew it. We had no choice but to sell the stuff at a flea market for three grand. It wasn't worth our time or effort.

These kinds of things were infrequent, and overall, being around Jerry was kind of like having your own ATM machine.

Go figure.

1999

In 1999, my son Anthony grew tired of Florida and decided to move to Los Angeles. That decision turned out to be great for me because I've learned a lot from him, and having him near has helped keep me young. If I sound proud, it's because I am. My children are the best and greatest thing in my entire life.

John Franzese was also living in Los Angeles and was temporarily sober and off drugs. Johnny was adept in the music business, and he and Anthony opened a business called J&A Entertainment. This lasted only a short time, though, before Johnny started doing drugs again.

I can't tell how many rehab homes he was in, how many times I bailed him out of jail, or how many times I had to go look for him on the streets. Tina, his mother, would hook me up on a three-way call with her and

Sonny (she moved back to New York and he was in prison) and ask me to help find Johnny when he went missing.

I knew one place not to look: at his stepbrother Michael's. Although Michael was also living in Los Angeles, Johnny never went to him when he was high. Maybe it was because Michael had already had his fill of Johnny and all his baggage.

When Johnny was into drugs, he was a real piece of work. He would go to everyone I'd introduced him to and ask to borrow money—not a lot, just forty dollars, the amount he needed to score his drugs.

He worked a scam on cab drivers, too. He'd call a cab from his apartment which Michael got for him in Brentwood, and have the driver take him to McArthur Park (notorious for gang activity, murders and drug dealing). He'd claim he'd left his wallet at home, and ask the cabbie for forty dollars. When the driver took him back home, he promised to pay it back plus a healthy tip. A lot of the cabbies went for it. Johnny would score his drugs, and when the cabbie took him back to his apartment complex, he'd go inside and disappear. The cabbie would be out his forty dollars and the round-trip fare.

Another source of drug money for him was hookers. He'd borrow the forty bucks from them and say that "Uncle Ori" would pay it back. When they showed up at my place, I'd chase them away. His debts weren't my responsibility.

Tina called me one night in a panic. It seemed the cab drivers Johnny had ripped off had compared notes. They decided that the next time one of them spotted Johnny, they'd converge on him and get their money back. That night, six or seven of them had him trapped at a market at the telephone booths, not far from my apartment. Tina pleaded with me to go there and pay Johnny's debts, promising she'd reimburse me.

I went to the market and had the cabbies come to my place, where I paid them off. I didn't think for a minute Tina would pay me back and she didn't. I did it because I didn't want to see Johnny get his ass kicked by a bunch of angry cab drivers.

Another time I was having lunch with some friends in a restaurant on Camden Drive in Beverly Hills. Johnny stopped in, and I introduced him to my friends and the bartender. When I got home, my phone was ringing. Johnny had got the numbers from my friends, and then he went to their offices and borrowed forty bucks from them, as well as the bartender. I paid them all back. At first, I couldn't figure why he always borrowed forty, but eventually I realized that was the price of a bag of crack at the time.

* * *

With Johnny, it never stopped. He got arrested again and Tina got me on another three-way call with Sonny asking me to bail Johnny out. I did, and this time Michael pitched in by finding Johnny a free rehab in Lancaster. Once again, it didn't last long.

Anthony was promoting a party at a local night club when Johnny showed up at my door stoned out of his mind.

He said, "I'm going over to that club where Anthony is. I have to meet someone there."

A drug dealer?

"No, you're not!" I said. "I don't want you near my

son ever again. This is his livelihood, and you're not going to fuck it up."

Then I took him to Cedars Sinai and checked him in for evaluation. Next, I went to the club where Anthony was doing the promotion. I waited around until I spotted a guy I'd seen Johnny with previously, a guy I figured for a dealer.

"Are you looking for Johnny?"

"Yes, I am."

I grabbed his arm. "Come with me."

When we were in private, I had a talk with him. He had literally pissed his pants. I was pretty sure he wouldn't sell Johnny any more drugs. But he was only one dealer and there were a lot more of them out there.

The hospital released Johnny around four the next morning, and he ended up back at my door. I didn't want to see him on the street, but I wouldn't let him inside either. I got dressed and drove him to Santa Monica with the intent of checking him into a motel, but I couldn't find one with a vacancy. We went to the Coffee Bean on Wilshire Boulevard where I had a long talk with Johnny.

I told him, "I don't want you around me or Anthony again until you're straightened out and sober."

After a few cups of coffee, I felt he was okay to turn loose. I knew Michael lived not too far away, so I dropped Johnny off a few blocks from Michael's home because Michael told him that he did not want anyone to know where he lived.

I learned later that as he was walking down the street, he heard voices coming from one of the houses. He investigated and found himself in a substance abuse center. He hit it off with the group and ended up staying with them.

Was finding that group divine intervention or simply coincidence? Whatever it was, it turned Johnny's life around, or so I thought?

* * *

I didn't hear from Johnny again for a year, then he called and told me about the rehab program, and that it had been successful. He had been off drugs for a year. He invited Anthony and me to attend a meeting with him at the center to mark his one-year anniversary.

At that meeting, Johnny gave a spectacular speech. He said, "My Uncle Ori and cousin Anthony are here. I hope that now I'll be allowed back in his home."

He was.

There was more positive news. While in the program, Johnny met a girl named Deborah and married her. It was a small wedding at the home of one of his rehab program mentors. I gave them a five-hundred-dollar wedding gift. When Michael and his wife came, we exchanged a brief greeting, and then Anthony and I left.

Johnny then took Deborah back to New York to meet Sonny and Tina.

I believe it was after he straightened out that Johnny became an informant for the Los Angeles County Sheriff's Department, and he also worked with the FBI. He started traveling back and forth between New York and California and wore a wire in both locations.

After I was indicted and had access to evidence during the discovery process, I heard the recordings he made of several people, including me and his own mother and father.

He didn't get much of value on me because I didn't trust him, and almost anything I told him was bullshit— like one time when I met him at a diner, and he was wearing a wire. I made up a story about a truck coming in from Mexico filled with weed, and that I planned to rob it. It sounded interesting to the law, but there was no truck and no robbery. There was nothing they could use.

The feds did try to use something Johnny told the L. A. Sheriff's Department, though. Supposedly I'd given him a gun one time that he put to his friend's head. He also claimed that on another occasion I sold him a gun.

At no time was I ever in the gun business, and I never gave a gun to anyone. Even though the sheriff's department couldn't produce one of the alleged guns or a tape to support Johnny's stories, they showed up as uncharged crimes on my pre-sentence investigation report.

I can't help but wonder if Johnny became an informant as a result of the rehab program. Did the counseling he received make him feel he was better than his father and the rest of us?

Go figure.

30

⚜

My London Connection

The early 2000s were busy times for me. In spite of being under continuous scrutiny by the law, I was doing pretty well financially. That was due in large part to my ability to multi- task—doing several things simultaneously and knowing at all times what's happening with each and every one of them. The expanding use of cell phones also made conducting business much easier and faster.

Joey Pyle and I talked almost every day by phone. He introduced me to other Londoners such as gangster Dave Courtney and convicted robber and killer Freddie "Brown Bread Fred" Foreman, among others.

One day Joey, his son and Danny Sims got me on the line to announce they were representing singer Mark Morrison, best known for his hit song *Return of the Mack.* They had made a deal with Warner Brothers, and they asked me if I'd watch over Mark while he was in Los Angeles and make sure he got to the recording studio as scheduled.

Joey explained that Mark liked to fight and had been banned from most of the hot spots in London. Joey had been able to make arrangements for the ban on Mark to be lifted. In addition to getting into fights, Mark had numerous other run-ins with the law. In spite of that, Joey insisted Mark was really a great kid.

My son Anthony was roughly Mark's age and very adept in the music business. I figured it would be a good match and said I'd be glad to help out.

Mark flew in and took a room at the Mondrian on Sunset Boulevard. Anthony and I met with him there. He and Anthony warmed up to each other right from the start. Anthony took him around to the clubs in Los Angeles, and there were never any problems. Mark didn't miss any recording sessions, and everybody was happy.

Joey and I were developing a close bond, even though we'd never met in person. It was kind of a mutual trust thing. I knew he'd look out for me, my family or friends if the chance arose, and he knew he could count on me to do the same. It was an unspoken promise that existed between us until Joey died, and continues with Joey Junior.

* * *

Danny moved back to Los Angeles again and stayed with me for a while. On his way, he stopped in New York and met Haitian singer and producer Wyclef Jean of the Fugees. He also met Jacques "Haitian Jack" Agnant.

Jack was pretty connected to the hip-hop world going back to Tupac Shakur and beyond.

Anyway, Danny brought Haitian Jack back to Los Angeles with him. He was a good-looking guy and a smooth talker—or maybe I should say a bullshitter—and he wanted to be a gangster in the worst way. When Wyclef came to L.A., Jack introduced me to him. I thought Wyclef was a class act, but Jack seemed to have some kind of hold on him that I could never figure out.

I have a rule when it comes to guys hanging around me and trying to impress me as being tough, as Jack did. When someone tells me how many guys they have killed, I know immediately they never killed anyone. Jack was just a petty thief who took credit for the work other guys did. He ended up living with me for a year, sleeping on my couch, making money by stealing from people in the music business, and robbing drug dealers.

* * *

In 2001, I had an option on 250,000 music CDs which were overstocked at Universal Studios. Joey Pyle put me in touch with a guy in London named Ron Winter, who was the distributor for Death Row Records in England. Ron said he wanted to buy the CDs, and on several occasions, he promised to wire the money to my bank account. I kept checking my account, but the money didn't show up. I came to the conclusion Ron was a hustler who thought he was a little sharper than anybody else. I wanted to talk with him in person, but whenever he came to L.A., he didn't let anyone know where he was staying.

And then a friend of mine in the movie business told me

he had a meeting scheduled with Suge Knight—founder and CEO of Death Row Records—at the Beverly Wilshire. Prior to seeing him, Suge would be meeting with none other than Ron Winter. He said Suge and Ron were getting together because Ron was always behind in his payments to Suge. I told my friend I wanted to go to the Beverly Wilshire with him and give Ron Winter a real surprise.

When we got to the hotel, my friend went up to the room to tell Suge I wanted to see him about Ron. Suge came downstairs to meet me. We had a drink at the bar, and I told him about my issues with Ron. He asked me to let it drop and he'd include me in something else where I could make more money.

It turned out that Ron owed Suge millions of dollars, and he wanted Joey and me to help him collect it. We agreed.

By the time Joey got the first million from Ron, Suge was in prison for a probation violation. He wired the money to Death Row Records, and the very next day Suge had a hundred grand sent to me as our collection fee. I immediately sent Joey and Joey Jr. their share.

Later, we wanted to discuss the handling of future payments with Suge. Joey Jr. flew over from London, and he and my son Anthony drove to the jail to visit him. They weren't on his visitor list, though, and weren't allowed to see him.

I know Suge has had his share of legal problems. However, in my dealings with him, he always kept his word. While I was in prison, whenever he saw Anthony he'd say, "Make sure you say hello to your Pops for me."

* * *

Shortly after the terrorist attacks on September 11, 2001, Wyclef went to Oakland to produce for Carlos Santana. Wyclef's birthday was October 10 (the same as my daughter's), so I decided to take a drive up and help him celebrate. I booked a room at the Fairmont Hotel in San Francisco.

Before I left L.A., I got a phone call from my friend Danny Florio. Danny was originally from Florida, but I didn't meet him until after he'd moved to Las Vegas. He was in the music publishing business, and although he wasn't a gangster, he did know Sonny and that I was connected to him. Several months earlier, Danny asked me to do him a favor that could have gotten me whacked.

When Danny relocated to Vegas, he assembled a group of girls who sang country music. He was promoting them, but was having trouble with a connected guy named Johnny who wanted the action for himself. Danny was afraid of the guy, and asked if I'd go on record as their manager and take him off the hook. I agreed.

Not long after that this John guy called me from Vegas, yelling and screaming. He ended with, "I'm going to call the Gambinos and have them send some people to Los Angeles to see you."

That pissed me off. Nobody is going to threaten me. I don't care who they are or who they know.

I said, "Do yourself a favor. Buy your boys one-way tickets because they won't be coming back to New York."

It happened that Jimmy Caci was in Vegas at the time and was friends with John, who was part-owner of a big Italian deli. He stopped in the deli the next day, and while they were talking, John mentioned that he was having a couple of guys out of New York go to L.A.

on a hit. Jimmy asked who the target was.

John said. "Some wiseass named Ori."

Jimmy said, "Hold up! Ori's my friend. Ain't anybody going to whack him."

He told John to call New York and put a stop to things. He did.

Shortly after that, Jimmy and I were in Vegas to meet with some people about the garbage business. Jimmy took me to John's deli and introduced us. John and I quickly became friends and spoke on the phone almost every day. From that first meeting on, no trip to Vegas was complete without a visit to his deli.

As so often happened in my life, my enemy had become my friend.

Anyway, Danny said he'd like to meet Wyclef, so I had him fly in and meet me at the Fairmont. We went to the recording studio where I introduced him to Wyclef and Carlos. We had a great time, and Danny was impressed at the amount of respect those guys had for me.

He told me he'd like to put on a concert in Las Vegas if it could be put together at the right price. Would I set it up for him?

I said it wouldn't be a problem. I was sure I'd be able to get Wyclef Jean at the "family rate" (about half of his regular hundred and fifty-thousand-dollar payment). My fee would be twenty-five thousand.

Danny said to go for it. He reached out to the Aladdin Hotel & Casino. They agreed to all the terms, or so I thought, and a concert date of March 16, 2002, was set. The problem was that Danny had failed to tell them about my twenty- five thousand. So I had already booked Wyclef, R&B singer Jimmy Cozier, R&B and hip-hop trio City High, and the English electronic dance group, The Prodigy—only to find out there was no mechanism for me to get paid.

I flew to Vegas and met with the Aladdin executives. They refused to add my fee to what had already been agreed upon, so I ended up agreeing to what is called a "two wall," where the Aladdin fronted the money, and I became a partner. They gave me seventy-five grand as half down for Wyclef and the other entertainers. I took my ten percent booking fee off the top. The concert was on.

Joey Pyle decided to attend. He had tried to enter the U.S. via Los Angeles previously, but had been denied entrance and sent back to London. This time, he tried a different entry point and was allowed in. He brought his fiancée, Julie, Joey Jr., and around thirty of his associates with him. Because I was now one of the promoters of the event, I was able to get comped rooms for Joey and his entire party.

In addition to attending the concert, Joey had a job he wanted me to do. Someone in Seattle was causing problems for one of his London mates, and the guy asked me to have someone talk to that individual and straighten things out. He'd given Joey the money to cover my fee.

Rather than carry all the money himself, Joey had split the money among his entourage. When everyone was settled in their rooms, Joey collected the money and gave it to me. The only trouble was it was all in British Pounds. Anthony and I split it and went from casino cage to casino cage, exchanging unobtrusive amounts at each one.

When Joey got back to London his friend changed his mind and canceled the job. Of course, Joey and I did the right thing and kept the money.

It was a fun trip for Joey and his people. As icing on the cake, Joey and Julie got married at Treasure Island in a ceremony arranged for them by a friend of mine.

* * *

I ran into problems with the concert itself. For one thing it was college spring break weekend—a very busy time in almost all tourist destinations. I learned later that when the hotel rooms in Vegas are sold out, they don't advertise their acts in other cities. That lack of promotion is what I ran into. For a major hip-hop concert with big name performers, we sold only 850 tickets to a 7,500-seat venue. We gave 1,500 tickets away at nearby Nellis Air Force Base just to get enough people in to make it look good.

The opening act was Jimmy Cozier. I was in his dressing room with him when a hotel executive called and said we were running late—it was time for Jimmy to get on stage.

I said, "The performers haven't been paid the balance of their money yet. Where is it?"

They rushed to cut me a check. Then I demanded they cash it for me, which they did. I took my ten percent and then paid everyone what they had coming. Finally, the concert went on, and all the acts did a hell of a job.

The concert lost something like $175,000. However, for reasons unknown to me, the Aladdin did not ask me to participate in the loss.

Go figure.

31

Joey Pyle,
My Best Mate

Joey Pyle was a man among men. He was the crime boss of London for over four decades. When author Kate Kray interviewed Joey in July 2000, she asked what kind of weaponry he used.

He replied, "My brain is my biggest weapon."

He was right. You can get more from someone by using your brain than you will with threats of violence or a gun.

Respect, trust and honesty were the basis for our relationship. If I needed help with something in Europe, Joey took care of it for me. When he needed assistance with something in the States, I was there for him—no questions asked.

As Joey and I bonded I began going to London frequently to visit him. London is a fantastic city, and

Joey took good care me whenever I was there. He always had some of his people around me in the event there was a problem. I got to meet many of the guys I'd previously spoken with on the phone. We partied a lot and, believe me, they could drink.

In those days English gangsters were like celebrities, and it wasn't uncommon for citizens to ask them for their autograph. One Sunday we had brunch at a restaurant and pub down the street from where Joey lived. After eating, Joey and I were standing at the bar when this young kid came over from a table with a paper and pen. He stood there looking at me.

I said to Joey, "What's this kid want?"

He laughed, "Your autograph."

I signed the piece of paper and the kid walked away happy. That never would have happened in America. In London, though, Joey, and his associates and friends were legends.

* * *

In 2005, *Joey Pyle: Notorious – the Changing Face of Organised Crime* was published in England. A financier from Beverly Hills named Michael Mendelson heard about the book and went to London to see Joey and try to get the film rights. When they talked, Joey told him to go back to Beverly Hills and deal with me.

Joey told me Michael asked him, "Who is Ori Spado?"

He answered, "You know who I am here in London?"

"Yes."

"That's who Ori is in Hollywood."

When Michael and I met, he said I needed to get a

script written. I contacted several writers and ended up hiring the sister of a friend of mine from Florida. What a fiasco that turned out to be.

She had to go to London to meet Joey but was afraid to fly alone. I had to have one of my guys go to Florida and then fly to London with her. Joey and I paid for the trip.

After she met Joey, things got complicated because she fell for him, but he wasn't interested in anything but business. On top of that, she wrote a two hundred fifty-page script. For those of you who don't know, the average script is between ninety and a hundred twenty pages. Nobody in Hollywood will read a script that long. It was a total waste of time and money.

I next got an Englishman to write the script, but Joey developed ALS (Lou Gehrig's disease) and passed away in 2007. Before he died, I promised him I would get the movie made and I'm determined to do so. Joey Jr. and I are partners on the project and are getting close to finishing it as I write this.

* * *

One of the many people Joey introduced me to was actress and singer Terri Vasiliou. Her daughter (now known professionally as Laura V) had one hell of a voice, and I firmly believed she had superstar potential. However, at the time Joey introduced us she was too young, and I wasn't able to help advance her career.

Several years later my friend Rusty Lawrence came to see me after a trip to Chicago. He said he'd met some people there who were managing a hot young singer from London. They told him they were trying to promote her and wanted my help. Their client was Laura V. Her mother also reached out and asked me to assist Laura with getting her career up and running in the States.

Joey had since passed away, but Joey Jr., my son Anthony and I decided we would give it a try.

Terri brought Laura to Los Angeles. I arranged for a girl who had formerly managed Madonna to meet with us to discuss a management contract. However, when we all got together, something in my gut said that she wasn't the right one and we didn't go any further with her.

Next I called Benny Glickman, who is a music manager. He loved Laura and we formed a partnership to manage her. Laura had to relocate to L.A., which meant getting everything set up for her. If you've never managed a performer, let me tell you it requires a lot of work and expense to get started. Benny and I got her an apartment and stocked it with food. We also had to rent a studio for her. Laura had a skin condition that required treatment, so I arranged for her to become a patient of world famous dermatologist Dr. Harold Lancer.

Laura was in L.A. for six months and then had to return to England. Shortly after she left, I got arrested on federal charges and wasn't able to work with her further.

I really feel that if I hadn't gone to jail Laura would be a superstar today. I guess that's something I'll never know for sure, though.

Go figure.

Ghosts & Informants

I had a lot going on with the Queen Mary. I brought in a young, sharp kid to open a club on the ship and bring in quality entertainment. I also wanted to put on shows in the Queen Mary Dome (the same dome that at one time housed Howard Hughes' airplane Spruce Goose). The dome had 75,000 square feet of space, 130-foot tall ceilings, and a capacity of up to 2,160 people. It was an incredible venue. However, I found out that Long Beach had so many restrictions on the use of the facility that it was almost impossible to bring in good acts.

And then, I found the perfect entertainment solution. It would be popular, and the performers didn't have to be paid for their time or expenses. Ghosts were already there and worked for free.

I started running ghost tours and brought in the

famous psychic Peter James. I also invited ghost hunters from England, who filmed several episodes of their paranormal TV show there. They called the Queen Mary the most haunted place in the world, claiming it had over six hundred ghosts aboard.

The ghost tours proved to be highly successful and profitable. The Queen Mary continues to offer several paranormal programs to its visitors. I was actually making decent money, and this gig was all legit.

* * *

In the meantime, Haitian Jack was still sleeping on my couch. Around Christmas, Wyclef called and asked if I would help a friend of his, Naomi Campbell, who had a problem with a stalker. The victim was and still is a very famous model. The situation was serious and had been mentioned in the local papers and TV news, as well as all the trade magazines.

I told Wyclef I'd speak to her. When I called, she said she was hosting a Christmas party, but would see me anyway. I drove to her home near the Beverly Hills Hotel. She took me into her office, and she gave me the story and information on the stalker, who lived on Long Island.

I later learned that after I left, she told her guests I was "The Godfather," and she'd just met me. I assume Wyclef told her that and she believed it. See how easily things can get out of hand?

Anyway, I made a few calls to New York and found the guy. I called a couple of my friends and asked them to go to his home and get him on the phone with me. They found the house and got in. He was scared but they got him on the phone with me. I explained to him that I was not happy with his conduct and his stalking of Naomi. He'd either have to straighten out, or the next time he saw those guys, there would be no talking and it would not be pleasant. Meeting my friends and hearing from me apparently got his attention, and he promised to back-off immediately. He was definitely scared and realized the consequences of exactly what he was dealing with.

Jack was there on the couch and overheard the call. He later called Naomi and told her he'd resolved the problem for her. That's the kind of guy Jack is, taking credit for the work of others.

* * *

Another time Jack asked me to introduce him to some people in the music business. I thought it was a chance for all of us to make a few bucks, so I arranged a meeting at the Four Seasons. One of the guys I'd never met before rolled up in a wheelchair. The first thing he wanted to know was why was I there (I was the only white guy at the table).

My acquaintances explained who I was, and then he launched into a tirade about a guy he knew being shot in a bar in New York. He said the bar was owned by "people like you" and they did nothing about it.

I had no idea what he was talking about, but it was obvious he had an attitude toward me. I excused myself and moved to another table. After I left, the other guys told him about a Jamaican kid I knew and did a big favor for.

The kid had been in downtown L.A. to rob some drug dealers in a high rise. He thought there were only two of them, but there were several more. When he realized what he'd walked into, he jumped out a window, breaking his leg when he hit the ground. He crawled under a parked car and spent the night there hiding from the drug dealers.

During the night he used his cell phone to call people to help him. No one would come, not even his wife. Around daybreak he called me. I drove to his location and got him into my car. Then I dropped him off at the emergency room at Midway Hospital. When he returned home, he called and thanked me.

After the guy in the wheelchair heard the story, he came over to my table, hugged me and apologized. His name is Michael Concepcion, an original founder of The Crips. He is a great guy, and we are still friends. He is totally legitimate and one hell of a businessman. The only thing he didn't understand from that first meeting was why I would get involved with Haitian Jack.

Michael wasn't the only one to question my relationship with Jack, though. Others in the music and fight business in L. A. called and asked why I was hanging around with a rat. I was damn glad when he got his own apartment and moved out of mine. The only trouble was that his new place was in my building, so I wasn't truly rid of him.

* * *

With Wyclef's help, Jimmy Cozier signed with record producer Clive Davis. And then, in my opinion, he made a big mistake by taking Haitian Jack on as his manager. Jimmy is a great singer and the girls love him. He should have been a superstar, but I think Jack brought him down and Davis eventually dropped him.

Jack robbed a big load of weed from some Mexicans and took it out of state to Ohio for someone else to sell for him. When Jack got back to L.A., he was flush with cash. I was on my patio when I overheard Jack outside talking to Ricky Lee, a Jamaican who lived in our building.

Ricky asked Jack, "You're gonna take care of the Old Man (meaning me), aren't you?"

"Fuck the Old Man," Jack said.

I called Jack. "Bring my son's car keys back. Now! And I want you out of this building by tomorrow. There's only one real gangster here and it's not you."

He brought the keys back and wanted to talk with me, but I refused.

I said, "Slide the keys under the door and be on your way. Don't forget to be out of here by tomorrow night."

The next day he got a U-Haul and moved. Later, when I was in prison, my son found an article written by a former New York cop who wanted to write a book about Jack. I was mentioned in the article. It was obvious Jack was talking to the guy because there were certain things in the piece where Jack had all wrong information. I called Jack from prison and he lied and blamed Jimmy Henchman, but I knew Jack was lying. The information he told the detective was all wrong, from the hotel I was at to the area of town I was in to the people I met with. Jimmy knew where I stayed, as he came and visited me when I was in New York.

Jack was feeding information to the FBI, much of

which he made up. I guess they eventually got tired of his crap, and he was deported back to Haiti. He now lives in the Dominican Republic.

Some of Jack's friends started a blog with lies about me. I must agree with Bill O'Reilly of Fox News when it comes to Internet content. Anyone can write anything about anybody and post it online, and there isn't much that can be done about it. It just stays there.

I think it's wrong, but I can live with it. Every day when I look in the mirror, I know the guy I see never wore a wire on his friends or sold them out to get a better deal for himself. That's something that guys like Haitian Jack, Kenny Gallo, Johnny Franzese and Guy Fatato can't do.

* * *

I mentioned Ricky Lee, the Jamaican living in my building. I liked Ricky. He had a beautiful wife and I was the godfather to his daughter. I thought he was different from the other crooks I knew. I was wrong.

Ricky was good at making money illegally, but he turned out to be one of those guys who loved the flashy side of being a crook. They had to drive a Rolls Royce or a Bentley, hang with a lot of people, and spend money like it was water. They didn't keep a low profile and certainly didn't fly under the radar. I tried to help Ricky get on the right track by getting him lawyers to clean up his legal problems.

I told him, "You've got money invested in legitimate businesses. You don't need to do this other stuff anymore."

It didn't do any good, though. He couldn't resist *the life*.

It was in his system. He got jammed up with the feds in a cocaine deal out of North Carolina and was locked up in the MDC in Los Angeles, pending transfer back east. I hooked him up with a lawyer.

It was at this time that Guy Fatato (who Sonny was grooming) came out from New York and stopped to see me. I didn't know then that he was working for the feds.

Ricky's wife came by to talk with me while Guy was there. She said Ricky owed a half million dollars to the Mexicans for a separate drug deal in Brooklyn, and they wanted their money.

I knew the Mexicans she was talking about, and they knew me, so I had them over also. I also knew the guy Ricky had in charge in Brooklyn. I called him, and he said he had $100,000 of the money ready. Guy Fatato was sitting there through it all and said he could call Brooklyn and have the money picked up immediately. He also asked the Mexican for 50 kilos a month and wanted it steady—he would arrange the transportation. All the while, this conversation was being recorded.

I'd always been leery of the cocaine business and wasn't comfortable with being drawn into the situation. I knew that until the full half million was paid, there was no way I could get out of it. I told him to go ahead. That was a big fucking mistake.

When Guy got involved, he started telling the Mexicans he could move a lot of product back east. He discussed fifty kilos, but I knew that wouldn't happen until the Mexicans had been paid all the money Rick owed them.

I found out later that Guy collected the cash to pay the Mexicans, but it never got to them. I flew back to New York and called him. We met in the restaurant of the Warwick and I told him I needed the money. He denied having it. Guy said he would get the money, and unknown to me at the time, our conversation was being recorded, which later became part of my discovery. When Guy left, he immediately called his handler at the FBI, and when he told the agent that I was demanding the money, the agent told him to put his phone in the trunk of the car and call him from another phone. *Why* is the question that keeps popping up in my head. I can only speculate on the reason, but I cannot prove it.

This all became the basis of Michael Catapano and me being charged with cocaine distribution. What had transpired without my knowledge or Michael's was that when Guy Fatato went back to New York, he met with Michael and told him they were going to make a lot of money with Ori on big cocaine shipments coming from California, so Guy was getting Michael all worked up about all the money. However, I was never going to do anything because, in reality, the Mexicans were not going to be giving anyone more cocaine until they had the money Ricky owed them, which you can figure where and who kept that.

But Michael kept asking Guy about where all this money was, and then Guy made up the story that I was doing the deal and not paying anyone, and Michael got pissed and went and asked Sonny for permission to whack me. Not once did Michael ever call me to ask me about it, and Michael and I never even had a discussion about it. If he had asked me then, I'm sure everything would have turned out much differently. Michael and I got indicted for a charge that was never going to happen, all because of a story that the informant Guy Fatato and the FBI cooked up. Go figure.

* * *

Guy Fatato and Johnny Franzese weren't the only guys to sell me out to the feds. While Ricky Lee was waiting in MDC Los Angeles to be transferred, he called me several times a day, which made my antenna go up because you cannot just pick up the phone in prison and call anytime you want, but he was allowed.

The last time I ever spoke to Ricky Lee was while in transit, and they had him waiting, I think, in San Bernardino. He called and asked me to call our friend Jimmy Henchman and others for money for his wife, which would not have been a problem, but Ricky ended up telling him to give her money, or else. That statement told me exactly what he meant—that he would inform on everyone, and I replied that this was our last conversation, and I told him not to ever call me again.

Ricky Lee did talk to the FBI and the US attorney. He gave several proffers on everyone including me, where he told them that I was the Boss of Hollywood, and anytime I needed people for anything, I just had to make a call. Ricky's cooperation got him a way lighter sentence. He was the leader of the guys in North Carolina and he ratted them all out. I think they got 20 years and Ricky got close to five, and then he was deported back to Jamaica. He found his way back here, I was told, but he got caught again and deported. Where he is now, I really don't know, but my guess would be he is not in Jamaica.

Go figure.

33

More Government Money
& Dealing Weed

I got a call from Jimmy Caci's friend, Joe Dente. He said he needed to talk with me and asked me to come to his house. When I got there, he told me that he'd been at Frankie's on Melrose restaurant the previous night. A guy approached him and said his name was Tommy Piazza, and he was a wise guy from Baltimore. He had another guy with him using the last name of Marino. They said they were jewelry thieves, and they tried to give Joe Rolex watches, which he refused to accept. Joe wasn't sure Tommy and Marino were what they claimed to be, and he wanted to know if I knew them.

I told him I'd never heard of them and didn't think there was anyone left in Baltimore. I promised if I found out anything about them, I'd let him know.

The following week, Lloyd, a guy Jerry Zimmerman

had introduced me to, called and asked to borrow a few bucks. I was planning to go to Frankie's to get a takeout dinner and asked him to meet me there. We hooked up. I gave him the money, got my dinner and went home.

The following day Lloyd called. He said that after I left the restaurant, two guys, Tommy and Marino, were at the bar and struck up a conversation with him. They told him they were old friends of mine.

After a few drinks, Lloyd told them he wanted to make a porn film and was trying to raise twenty-five grand to get it started. They told him they'd loan him the money, but only if I would personally guarantee the loan. They told him to arrange a lunch meeting with me to discuss it. I told him to set it up, but not for a few days. Joe Dente had been suspicious of Tommy and Marino, and now, so was I. Still, I wanted to get a look at them and hear what they had to say. If two guys were at the bar and knew me, why would they not say hi? It's a small bar.

The following Tuesday I took a date to Frankie's for dinner. While we were eating, Lloyd came over to our table and told me Tommy and Marino had come in. They wanted to come over and say hello. Was that okay? Even though I wasn't there for a meeting, I told Lloyd to bring them over.

When they came to the table, Tommy did almost all the talking. I just looked at him and let him talk. He knew what to say and gave the impression we were old acquaintances. He dropped the names of people I knew and said he'd done time with Sonny in Leavenworth. Despite his act. I knew I'd never seen either of them before in my life. I didn't challenge Tommy, though, and agreed to meet with them again.

After we left Frankie's, I stopped at a payphone and called Sonny. He could tell you the name of every guy he'd ever been locked up with, but he didn't know Tommy.

"Be careful," he said.

When I got home, I called my contact with the U.S. Marshalls. I told him about Tommy and Marino and what was going on with them.

He asked, "Does this Tommy guy chew on a toothpick and wear penny loafers?"

"Yes."

"He's an undercover FBI agent. The other one is a flip flop (a criminal who became an informant) from New Jersey."

Knowing the game, I met with Tommy and Marino again at Frankie's. I told them I'd guarantee their loan to Lloyd under certain conditions. We would form a corporation, pay taxes, and not do any child porn, as that would be a serious crime. I said it all with a straight face.

They agreed.

Tommy acted really excited about our deal, flashing a wad of money and talking about what close friends we were. I leaned back in my chair, trying to look and act depressed.

Tommy said, "What's the matter, buddy. You should be happy."

"I know, but I've got a problem that has nothing to do with this."

"What is it?"

"Come outside with me where we can talk in private."

Out in the parking lot, I said, "I invested a lot of money in something with a friend of mine, and I'm really short on cash. Five thousand would straighten me out until this other thing starts paying off."

He acted a little nervous, but reached into his pocket and pulled out that wad of money. It happened to be five thousand.

He said, "This is all I've got right now. Take forty-five Hundred, and I'll get the rest to you on Monday."

I grabbed the money and said, "No problem. You're a good friend."

I ended up getting a total of twelve thousand from him and never got the porn film off the ground.

* * *

In the early 2000s I met a young guy from Fresno I'll call Ray. He seemed like a good kid and he started hanging with me. Ray was of Mexican descent but was born in the States. He was in the weed business and needed my connections in New York for distribution. Not my Italian connections, but people in the hip-hop community.

We put a plan together where Ray would rent a place in Arizona and arrange to get the weed. It was a low to medium grade called AZ. We could get it for around five hundred dollars a pound and, if all went well, we could sell it for nine hundred or a thousand. He knew a pilot with his own plane who would fly the weed to New York for us, and he could handle four hundred and fifty pounds per trip. When he arrived with the load, my people would pick it up and sell it.

I went to New York to oversee all the shipments. We were operating with the supplier on credit, and I wanted to get the stuff sold as soon as possible so we could settle and order more. I had a driver bring the weed from the airport into the City where I dispersed it to my dealers. I went to my hotel and waited for the money to start coming in. Then the problems started.

My people reported that the product was a lower quality than the supplier promised—we had to lower the price to move it. Although we weren't taking in as much, the pilot still had to be paid what he'd been promised. I sent money to Ray so he could take care of the supplier and order more weed at a better price. No product came. In the meantime, I was running up expenses while waiting around the City for another shipment.

Then I got word back that Ray was blowing the money I'd sent him and not taking care of business. I figured I had no choice but to do something to reimburse myself and make a few dollars. When the next load finally showed up, I didn't send any money to Ray. I paid the pilot and the dealers and kept the rest. Bart didn't come after me for the money, and I wouldn't have cared if he did.

Even though my partnership with Ray was over, I had proven that I could move a lot of weed and was contacted by others who needed a distribution network. I made some money, but all the people I had to deal with were thieves. I had to stay one step ahead of them or they'd screw me.

* * *

A guy from San Diego I'll call Stu, whom I met through a friend from Syracuse, got in touch with me. He said he had a load of weed in a warehouse in New York that he wanted me to help distribute.

The background was that the shipment originated in

Mexico, and then was trucked up from Texas. When the drivers left Texas, they somehow got the loads mixed up. The order that should have gone to New York ended up in Chicago, and Chicago's much larger but lower grade order wound up in New York.

The guy in the Bronx who received the load didn't have a market for the lower grade and wanted it all out of his warehouse as soon as possible. Stu heard about the situation and said he'd take it, but payment would be contingent on the condition of the product. The supplier agreed to the terms, and Stu rented space in a warehouse to stash it until he could set up distribution and invite me in. The Mexican delivery guys moved the product to Stu's warehouse and unloaded it, but the driver and his helper couldn't go back to Mexico without the money, so they were sleeping in their truck in New Jersey.

We flew to New York and I had a couple of my guys rent a truck to move the product. While I was waiting for them to do that, I worked on finding a location we could use as a distribution center. The wife of a big hip-hop star who lived in a gated community on Long Island said we could operate out of her garage. We got the load over there and set up shop. As usual, problems developed.

The weed was of poor quality, and on top of that, it was rotting. I called the supplier and tried to negotiate a lower price. Being greedy, he wouldn't budge and wanted five hundred dollars a pound. That put me in the position to not give them anything. Considering the poor quality of the product and the condition it was in, I sold it for three hundred and was lucky to get that.

While this was going on, the truck crew needed money to eat. I felt sorry for them and gave them a few bucks every day. They started following me around and became a nuisance.

The supplier was getting antsy, too. He called me and said his boss wanted to talk with me. He wanted me to meet with one of his men who would hook me up with the boss by phone. Figuring there could be a problem, I arranged the meeting in Proctor Park in Brooklyn, where I had several guys hidden to watch my back.

The Mexican showed up and put me on the phone with the boss. I didn't know exactly who the guy was and didn't really give a damn. I started off by giving him hell for the way he was treating his delivery guys, not sending them any money and making them live out of their truck. I also told him he wasn't being realistic by demanding five hundred a pound for the crap his people delivered. After my tirade, he said he'd send his son to meet with me.

Not trusting him, I agreed to meet his son at a place where nobody would have access to a gun but me—a Chinese restaurant at the top of a major hotel in Columbus Circle. They had all kinds of security, which would make it difficult for this guy to show up with a crew. He wouldn't know that the girl and her date at the next table were with me, and that the purse hanging off the back of her chair facing me contained a gun I could get too quickly.

The son showed up alone. After we ate, I told him my offer—I'd give him fifteen thousand dollars as full payment. If he agreed, I had the money nearby, and he'd get it that night. It wasn't anywhere close to what his father had wanted, but he accepted. When we left the restaurant, I told him to go to a corner where I had somebody deliver the money to him.

Although I can't say we became friends, he did call me

a few times to discuss other deals, but I'd had enough of the cloak and dagger stuff. I didn't do any more business with him.

* * *

Back in Beverly Hills, I was introduced to some left-over hippies who were growers and suppliers of high-end weed. Those guys sent some of their product back east, where they could charge higher prices for it. They hired guys to bring their money back to them in California and paid them twenty-five hundred dollars. The trouble was that the couriers were usually transporting between two hundred thousand and half a million in cash. That kind of money was too tempting a target, and their couriers vanished with all that money.

One of the growers came to me and asked for my help in getting the next payment for him and his partner. I told him I'd personally drive back east and go to each city where they had money due. I said I didn't know what would be involved, so I would figure out my fee when the job was complete, but it would definitely be a lot more than twenty-five hundred.

I brought one of my guys along and our first stop was Chicago. I don't know what the dealer there had heard about me, but he didn't want to meet me. Instead, he had one of his people deliver a grocery bag full of money to me in front of the hotel at four o'clock in the morning.

From there we went to New York City where we had two pickups, and then on to our last stop in Boston. We drove back to Los Angeles with a trunk full of cash.

I took care of my guy and then totaled up the money

from the trunk. It was a little under a half million. I drew up a bill itemizing the collections, my time and expenses, and my fee, which I decided would be fifty percent of the net. I set the expense money aside and then took half of the remaining money. My share totaled a little over a quarter million, out of which I paid the guy who made the introduction, and then I called my client to come and get his half.

When he arrived, I gave him the bill and his money. He took it, but was apparently a little confused, because a couple of days later his partner came to me and complained about the split.

I said, "Listen to me, you paid guys twenty-five hundred and they robbed you. You got nothing. I collected everything you had coming and brought it all back. I think the split was fair."

He left without an argument, but they never asked for my help again.

* * *

On another occasion, a friend from Syracuse who dealt weed called me. He said that his supplier, a Jewish guy I'll call Eddie, got busted and was being held in the Rikers Island jail. He was a big operator and bought weed by the truckload from the Mexicans. He'd made tons of money and had a lot more on the streets waiting to be collected. He'd never been locked up before, though, and was scared stiff—being one of the few white guys inside with all the blacks and Hispanics. Could I do anything for him?

I said I knew a damn good lawyer who might be able to help him. I'd make the referral, but first the guy would have to send me retainer money for the lawyer. Almost immediately I received fifty thousand dollars, which I gave to the attorney. He went to Rikers and met with his new client.

I next reached out to a guy I knew who had connections working in the jail. He made a few calls and arranged for Eddie to have decent living conditions and a good work assignment.

Eddie was so happy that he called me and thanked me. While we were talking, I said I'd appreciate it if he didn't use my name, so he started calling me Uncle. Then he explained exactly how he got busted.

He met a wise guy from Brooklyn and called once in a while. He didn't know it, but the wise guy was being investigated by the feds and his phone was tapped. They picked Eddie up and tried to get him to give them information on the wise guy, but he knew nothing that would be of use to them. Shortly afterward they took Eddie down.

Eddie later asked me to do some collections for him and, of course, I got a large cut.

The lawyer did a good job for Eddie. He served very little time and moved to Los Angeles after being released. We did a couple of things together and made a few bucks, and then he relocated to Florida.

I thought he was a nice guy but guess what he did for me when I got busted—absolutely nothing—not even a post card. The lawyer I got for him and others, whose pocket I put a lot of money in, never came near me while I was being held in Brooklyn.

Go figure.

34

Schemes, Double Crosses, & Another Charge

B efore Ricky Lee was arrested, he called me and said another Jamaican friend of ours named Tony had been arrested and was being sent back to MDC in Brooklyn. He needed a lawyer. Once again, I reached out to my lawyer buddy and he got his fifty-grand retainer. The lawyer did a good job, and instead of doing any time, Tony got deported.

What's important about this is that prior to his arrest, Tony sold a large amount of weed to people in Philadelphia and had a million dollars or so in a safe at his place. When he got deported, he left the safe with his wife, but she didn't have the combination. That's when things got really bizarre. I was at Ricky's one night when Tony's wife showed up with the safe. She said she couldn't open it and asked Rick to hold it for her until she could figure out what to do.

I think what happened from then is that Ricky contacted Tony in Jamaica and told him he had the safe. They decided that rather than Tony giving the combination to his wife, he would give it to Ricky, and they chopped the money. Afterward, Ricky gave the empty and locked safe back to Tony's wife. Then things got even weirder.

Tony's wife called me. Apparently, she was pissed off that Tony wasn't coming up with the combination to the safe, and she said she wanted to be robbed. The plan was that I'd arrange for a couple of guys to come out from New York to do the job. After the phony robbery she'd file a police report, saying guys posing as DEA agents had talked her into letting them inside and then robbed her. Then she'd call Tony and break the news. The pretend robbers would get half the money, and she and I would split the other half.

I reached out to my friend Chris Curanovic in New York and told him the deal. He said he'd come out with another Albanian, Besnik "Nick" Neza, and stage the robbery. Since it was going to be a big score, he'd kick some money up to Sonny out of his end.

Unbeknown to me then, but revealed during the discovery after my indictment, before coming out to Los Angeles, Chris told Guy Fatato all about the plan. Guy wanted Chris to bring the money back to New York where they would split it, cutting me and Tony's wife out of the deal. As usual, Guy recorded the conversation.

Even though I wasn't aware of Guy's scheme, I had a gut feeling and planned to take the safe to a place where I'd personally peel it, open it, and supervise the split.

When Chris and Nick arrived in L.A., we met at my place to finalize things. Nick would later swear that he saw me give Chris a real gun to bring with him. That didn't happen. When I gave the item to Chris, I took him into my bedroom and Nick wasn't with us.

After Chris and Nick left, I called Tony's wife and told her they were on their way. They'd be wearing DEA jackets and hats and look official to anyone who noticed them. She didn't bother to tell me that her niece would be there, too.

When Chris and Nick got inside, the niece was coming down the stairs and started screaming. Nick grabbed her to try to shut her up, and chaos ensued. The guys panicked and ran out without the safe.

Tony's wife called and told me what happened. I told her to call the cops anyway to get it on record that somebody had tried to do a robbery.

Chris and Nick took the next plane back to New York. I think the only people who made out were Tony and Ricky, if they had already emptied the safe as I believe, and the feds.

That's right, the feds. They had another charge against me. My days of freedom were ending.

Go figure.

35

Busted

On June 4th, 2008, I got up early as usual. By quarter after six my coffee was made, and I was watching the early morning news on TV. My dog, Maggie, was on the floor next to my chair, waiting for me to take her out for her first walk of the day.

Suddenly, I heard several car doors open and close, which is very unusual for that time of morning in my normally quiet neighborhood. A few seconds later, there was pounding on my door. Then I knew. It had to be the FBI.

A voice hollered, "Orlando Spado, this is the FBI. Open the door or we'll break it in!"

I opened the door holding a cigarette between my fingers. An agent knocked it out of my hand onto the floor, and then he put the cuffs on me.

The noise woke up my son Anthony, who was living with me. When he came out of his bedroom to see what was going on, they cuffed him, too. When I saw that I wanted to cry, because whatever they wanted me for had nothing to do with him. One of the agents explained that handcuffing Anthony was simply a safety measure, which made me feel a little better.

"Do we have permission to conduct a search of the premises?" one of the agents asked.

"Do you have a warrant?"

"No."

"Then you can't search. By the way, if I'm under arrest, what's the charge?"

"You're charged with conspiracy to distribute cocaine." I laughed. "I'll be out by dinner."

Little did I know I wouldn't breathe free air again for five years, and it would also be that long before I had my next cigarette.

To my surprise, when they took me down the elevator and out to the street, I counted a total of twenty-seven officers and agents from the FBI, LAPD, and the Beverly Hills Police Department. Can you believe it took all this law enforcement just to take a 63-year-old gangster down? All they had to do was call me and I would have turned myself in. Go figure

The lead agent took me and had me stand next to his Ford Taurus. He opened the trunk, took out the chains, and shackled me in the middle of the road at 6:00 a.m. in the morning. I looked down Swall drive, and right in the middle of the road was a white SUV. I knew exactly who it was, Special Agent Scott Gariola, the same agent that in 1997 told me he would see the day I was chained and put on Con-air to Brooklyn. Here it was, 2006, and his promise had come true. For the hell of it, I asked the lead agent where my buddy Gariola was, and the agent said he wanted to come but was busy—ha-ha. I knew it was him in the middle of the road enjoying me being chained and shackled.

When all the restraints were in place, he put me in the Taurus, and I looked up and there was my son, Anthony, on the patio holding Maggie. My heart just broke, and something told me I would not be home for dinner. Anthony later told me that when he went back inside, the news was still on the TV. He looked, and at the bottom of the screen where they have the crawler, he saw it. An organized crime bust of the Colombo Crime family was being made, and one man, Ori Spado, was arrested in Los Angeles.

After we drove away, the agent said, "You don't need these chains and shackles, and he took them off. I knew it was all to show Gariola that his promise had become reality.

With the shackles removed, they took me to downtown L.A. for booking. After taking my pictures and prints, I was taken into a small room with a table and chairs. They had me sit in a corner chair, and then several agents with note pads came in and sat down.

I looked at them and said, "I want to talk with my lawyer." When you say that, they cannot ask you any questions. I barely got the words out of my mouth when all the agents picked up their notepads and left. Talk about a room emptying out fast. A few minutes later I was transported to the MDC Los Angeles and placed in a cell below the courtroom to await arraignment.

Finally, at three that afternoon, I was taken upstairs to the courtroom. Anthony was there along with my lawyer, Danny Brookman, and my bail bondsman, Josh Herman.

Danny was as pale as a ghost. He showed me the indictment, and as I read it, I began to grasp the seriousness of the situation. It was a seventeen-count RICO indictment unsealed in federal court in Brooklyn, charging a total of twelve alleged Colombo crime family members and associates of a variety of crimes, including four murders.

My co-defendants were Sonny Franzese, Thomas Gioelli, Nicholas Bova, Chris Curanovic, Michael Catapano, Dino Calabro, Frank Campione, Joseph Competiello, Joseph Digorga, Angelo Giangrande and John Capolino. I knew Sonny very well, Chris and Michael, but I had never heard the other names before.

I was charged with the cocaine conspiracy and the fake robbery I'd set up with Chris and Nick. If convicted on all charges, the feds said I was facing a sentence of life in prison.

I was processed into the MDC Los Angeles and waived extradition to New York. On a Thursday morning, a little over a week later, I was among a group of prisoners taken by bus to an airport in Victorville for the first leg of the Con-air flights that would eventually land in New York.

When the bus stopped on the tarmac, it was surrounded by armed U.S. Marshals. After exiting the bus, we formed a line where all items, including our shoelaces and anything that could be used to harm ourselves or someone else, were removed. Then cuffs and leg shackles were put on. When I walked up the stairs into the plane, I saw a sign that read, "Fun Jet Tours." I suppose if I weren't one of the passengers, it would have been funny.

The con airplanes had been confiscated during government investigations of illegal activities and modified to transport prisoners. They didn't have doors on the bathrooms, so if you had to take a leak you did it with a marshal watching. If you had to do anything else, you were in trouble, because it was not permitted.

Our first stop was in Oklahoma, where a major prisoner processing center was located. The planes land right on the prison grounds, and you exit the plane right into the prison, where the cuffs and leg shackles are removed. After that, you're logged in and given bedding, a shirt, pants and shoes—all of which have been used hundreds of times before by other inmates—and then assigned to a specific housing unit and cell.

Later that afternoon another plane came in. One of the new arrivals told me Sonny had been on that plane but had been assigned to a different unit. That made sense because with Sonny and I being co-defendants on the same indictment, the government would want to keep us separated as much as possible. They flew Sonny out on Monday, but didn't move me until Thursday.

When I arrived at Brooklyn MDC, I was processed in and then assigned to spend a couple of days in the medical unit, where new prisoners are examined and tested for any communicable diseases, especially TB. While there, inmates are locked in their cells except to take their meals.

I'll never forget the first night when we were let out to eat. I looked up at the TV and there was Nicholas cage in the movie *Con Air*. I looked up and just laughed.

That same night I heard a big commotion. Several guards rushed into one of the cells and removed the two inmates. We found out the next day that a young guy had been raped by his older cellmate. I never saw either of them again.

After clearing the medical unit, I was assigned to a regular housing dorm of a hundred and twenty guys. In a dorm, everything you need, or use is contained in an area no larger than a high school gym. There are bunks, tables to eat, write or play cards at, six toilets and a few showers. So you do everything, including eat and go to the bathroom, in this one open space. The lights are on twenty-four hours a day, and it's always either too hot or too cold, and the food is horrible.

If you like your privacy and take it for granted, take a few seconds and think about living in a prison dorm. It will probably make you really appreciate what you have.

When I entered the dorm, I was approached by Anthony and Mickey, two brothers from Staten Island. They'd heard of me and asked if I'd like to sit with them at their table. As I looked at the table they pointed to, there were guys there that I felt did not belong, so I said I would think about and get back to them.

You need to understand that in prison, who you share a table with can be a matter of prestige. It can prove who you know and how you're connected. In addition, the population is heavily black and Hispanic, and you learn very quickly that it's best to stay with your own kind.

As I was setting up my locker, a guy came up behind me and said my phone number and name. I was shocked and turned around and asked him how he knew.

He shook my hand, introduced himself as Joey C, and said I was welcomed to sit at his table. I accepted, as I liked him immediately, and I asked him how he knew my phone number.

"When Sonny was in here (Sonny was ninety at the time) I used to help him out a little bit," Joe said. "One of the things I did for him was dial his phone calls. He called you a lot and told me about you. You're welcome to sit at my table."

I said, "Thanks, I will."

In addition to Joe, I soon made more new friends and reconnected with a few old acquaintances, most of whom gave me advice and assistance on how to survive in the joint and handle legal issues. Tommy, Dino, Billy, Angelo, Tommy Dono, Michael Uvino and Charles Carneglia come to mind. Thanks to them, there were actually some pleasant times. I often think of our talks, making burnt toast and playing cards. I became very close to Charles. When he was being shipped-out to serve a life sentence, they let me out of my unit to say goodbye to him. It was very emotional for both of us.

Anyway, once I was settled in, I was able to turn my attention to how I could defend myself against the charges I was facing.

Go figure.

PART

THREE

Facing Justice

The Dance Begins

In prison, you learn the rules quickly and adapt because you have no real choice, unless you become a rat, a snitch, or just a weak bastard who would sell your soul to get an edge for yourself. Doing that runs against my grain, and I can't comprehend why such weak wannabe gangsters turn into informants so fast.

I had a little advantage over most new inmates because of what I'd learned from Sonny and Jimmy Caci, who both had a lot of experience spending time in prison. I had talked with each of them about it many times over the years. Jimmy always said it was best not to talk with anyone on the inside until you knew who and what they were. He was right.

So when I got to Brooklyn MDC, I knew to keep my mouth shut until I found out who was real and who was not. For example, the kid Mickey and his brother Anthony, the ones who had invited me to share their table—Mickey became an informant in an effort to get their charges reduced. When my request for bail was denied at a hearing, the FBI said they had an informant who would testify that I would flee the country if given bail. It was a lie Mickey made up. I never made any such statement and wouldn't run and hide from anybody—not even the government.

In the justice system, the truth doesn't necessarily matter, though. Informants like Mickey make proffers to the FBI and U.S. Attorneys, who gobble it up and rehearse the informants until they can recite the lies in their sleep. In return, they get a break in their charges or sentencing. Some go into the federal Witness Protection Program and receive protection and a new identity.

According to the statistics I read in a *New York Times* article, the United States has less than five percent of the world's population, but almost a quarter of its prisoners. I think five of the major reasons for this are informants, conspiracy statutes, RICO, minimum mandatory sentencing and ridiculous drug laws.

I imagine informants exist everywhere, but most other countries do not have similar justice systems. For example, grand juries are primarily used in the United States. The saying that a grand jury can indict a ham sandwich is true. The feds, with the help of their informants, use it very effectively. They present their "evidence" unchallenged, and if the indictment they get is sealed, the target doesn't even know about it.

After you're indicted, if you aren't granted bail, you are forced to pursue your defense from behind bars. This puts you at a distinct disadvantage due to the limitations on phone calls and visits. In other words, you're basically guilty until you can prove yourself innocent, which rarely happens in federal courts.

Anyway, about a week after arriving in Brooklyn, I was chained, cuffed, put on a prison bus and transported to the federal courthouse for arraignment. After the restraints were removed, I was placed in the bullpen with my co- defendants. For the first time since my arrest, we were able to communicate in person.

When it was time, we were chained to each other, taken to the courtroom and seated in the empty jury box. I didn't have a lawyer, so I was assigned one—Donna Newman. Afterward, I retained my own lawyer, Seth Ginsberg, to represent me.

Thinking I had a good chance of having bail set, I told him to schedule a bail hearing. That's when I heard of something called the Federal Bail Reform Act. In it, the judge is allowed to reject setting bail if the defendant is a substantial flight risk or presents a danger to others.

I had a total of four bail hearings and was denied every time. The FBI attended each one, and the U.S. Attorney presented evidence that prevented the judge from granting bail. The first time I was refused bail was in Los Angeles, where they said I had outstanding arrest warrants. Danny Brookman, my lawyer, was astonished because I didn't have any warrants. The next hearing was in Brooklyn, and the U.S. Attorney began by apologizing to the court and saying the bench warrants referred to in L.A. weren't mine—it was all a mistake. *Really?*

It didn't matter anyway, because the government

had another excuse. They told the judge that because I was close to Sonny Franzese and Michael Catapano, I was a very dangerous and violent person. My record didn't back that up, but it worked for them.

Yet, in the following weeks Sonny and Michael both got released on bail.

* * *

The good thing about being in Brooklyn MDC was that there were a lot of Italians there on RICO charges, and several of them had been through the system before. They helped us new guys by sharing their experiences and knowledge. And we all helped each other with preparing motions— motions that my attorneys would not submit for me, such as for prosecutorial misconduct. With guidance from Danny Brookman, my lawyer in California, I filed one against the U.S. Attorney, and one against the FBI and their informant Kenny Gallo, which showed that Gallo posted lies about me on the Internet and that the government promoted those lies, endangering my life. I also filed a severance motion and another for a change of venue, all of which resulted in me becoming known as "the renegade client."

When represented by an attorney, motions are rejected when submitted directly by the defendant. Even so, at least Judge Cogan read them, which I firmly believe helped me throughout the proceedings, including at my sentencing, I wanted to learn all I could about the law—especially RICO—and never missed my weekly opportunity to go to the law library. When permitted, I spent time with my co-defendants reviewing discovery content, which was enormous. In addition to a mountain of documents, there were over five hundred CDs (seven hours each) containing conversations recorded by the informants. My voice was on only eleven of them, but even one is one too many.

I was surprised to find out that the recordings weren't made by taping a wire to the informant's chest like you see on TV. Instead, they had the technology to produce a mic so small it fit inside the informant's watch.

On one tape a capo (captain), Michael Catapano, is talking to the informant, who in this case was Guy Fatato. Guy adds fuel to the fire by saying, "You should see how Ori lives out in California. He's got a big apartment in Beverly Hills, drives a new Lexus, and every place he goes, everyone knows him."

Believe me, it was tough listening to this and other recordings that were made by guys who were supposedly my friends. I think it showed their greed, jealousy and lack of character. They were intentionally creating problems for me to benefit themselves. The government loves it, though, and coaches the informants on what to say and how to say it.

As the tape continued, Catapano said he'd received permission from Sonny to kill me if I didn't kick up some money from a big cocaine deal that I was not really working on. It was all made up by the informant, Fatato.

When the FBI is aware that your life is in danger, they are supposed to tell you. They never said a word to me about it. Yet, when Sonny said on tape that he gave his approval to kill John Gotti Junior, they ran and told Junior and his lawyer.

Anyway, this alleged drug deal was the one Guy

inserted himself into when he was in California and overheard me talking with Ricky Lee's wife. Ricky was my friend, and I was trying to collect the half million dollars he owed to the Mexicans for a load of cocaine. I was trying to get Ricky off the hook, not deal the drugs. The truth is I never dealt cocaine and never would, but this is where the conspiracy statutes come in.

A conspiracy is a plan or action between two or more people that is illegal, or involves a legal act committed in an illegal way. According to the feds, when Guy said he'd get the balance of the money together and pay the Mexicans off when he got back to Brooklyn—providing they gave "us" product—that made me a co-conspirator in the drug deal.

Guy didn't stop there, though. He went back to New York and talked with Michael Catapano about the cocaine. Michael never did a thing with the drugs either, and him and I never spoke about them. But thanks to Guy's recordings, Michael and I ended up as co-defendants in a cocaine conspiracy that never took place. Michael ended up taking a plea and got seventy-eight months. As far as I know, he doesn't even know what cocaine looks like. There is a saying that on a RICO indictment, someone will end up wearing one of the charges. I think that's true.

During one phone call with my son Anthony, he told me he'd read articles in various newspapers about what they called "a major bust of the Colombo crime family." The reports said that several of the defendants were facing life sentences, including me. That motivated me to spend even more time reading law books and going over the discovery.

* * *

The government offers most defendants plea bargains—that's normally what they do—however, not on our case, not for a long time. Then, finally, they offered me 97-110 months, Michael Catapano 78 months, and Chris Curanovic 84 months. It was contingent on all three of us accepting. At the time, Michael had gotten out on bail, and Chris was assigned to the Special Housing Unit (SHU) because there had supposedly been a telephone threat on his life. We thought that was probably bullshit, to make Chris become an informant, or at least look like one.

On the day we were scheduled for court, I was brought downstairs to change clothes, get shackled, cuffed and wait to be put on the bus. I didn't see Chris, but I knew his name was on the list, so I asked not to get on the bus until Chris was brought down. He finally showed up wearing his orange SHU jumpsuit. He was put into the cage in the rear of the bus, and I took a seat next to the cage so we could talk.

Chris had no idea we were going to a plea offer. In reality, he was going to what is called a "reverse proffer," where the government tells you what their evidence is against you. Their goal is to convince you to cooperate against your co-defendants in return for a lighter sentence. I told him I was rejecting my offer, which I knew was going to be something like 97 to 144 months. I also said I wasn't happy with my lawyer and was going to get rid of him, too.

We arrived at the courthouse and were separated while waiting to be called to the courtroom. When my turn came, I was brought upstairs, and my cuffs were removed. Seth Ginsberg and I stood before Judge Cogan, with the U.S. Attorney and two marshals next to us.

The judge said, "Good morning, Mr. Spado. Are you aware of the government's offer?"

"Yes, Your Honor."

"Are you prepared to accept it?"

"There is no way I'll accept this ridiculous offer. Further, I'm firing my lawyer as of now."

I stuck my hands out toward the marshals. "Put the cuffs on and get me out of here."

The U.S. Attorney said to Seth, "Talk to him. Try to convince him."

I interrupted, "No way."

The marshals led me out of the courtroom. When we got on the elevator one of them said, "Spado, you've got big balls and I think you were right."

The next day the story of my court appearance made the New York papers.

Seth was replaced by Kelly Sharkey, a court-appointed lawyer. In spite of me firing him, we remain close friends.

Go figure.

The Plea

I firmly believe that if Sonny had accepted a plea offer, the rest of us may have received better deals. I think, though, he didn't believe in his heart that his son Johnny would ever testify against him. He should have known better.

One morning I was brought to the courthouse for a hearing on various pre-trial motions the defendants had filed. When Sonny (who was out on bail) came in he sat across from me. He said, "Hey, Buddy, we've been friends for almost forty years, and now I hear you're upset with me."

"I'm not upset with you. I don't know why you would think that," I said, and then continued, "I'm a man and I understand you gave Michael permission to whack me for a non-existent drug deal, and that bothers me.

You always called me in for other things, but not for this—to ask me what was really happening because you trusted Fatato, even after you were warned about him. No, Sonny, I am not upset at all. As you see, I'm sitting here with the rest of the guys because you thought your son Johnny would never come to testify, so we all got bad plea offers. No, I don't give up friendships that easily."

Those were the last words Sonny and I ever had.

The proceedings began, and Sonny's lawyer put in a motion to sever his case from the rest of us and to preclude me from using certain discovery, including the recording in which Michael Catapano said Sonny had given him permission to whack me. This was addressed first.

Judge Cogan looked at Sonny and his lawyer and said, "There is no way I would ever sever Mr. Franzese from this trial. But I did read something in Mr. Spado's motions that perhaps indicate he should be severed."

He then said to the government attorney, "You have until noon tomorrow to explain why I should not sever Mr. Spado."

By late the next morning the government had responded, and we were all back in the courtroom.

Judge Cogan said, "Mr. Spado, I am denying your motion for severance and the discovery issues that have been raised. Before I make my decision, I want you to explain to me your understanding of the discovery matter. If you can explain it to my satisfaction, I will give you the choice whether to be severed or not."

I stood up and said, "The discovery is and can be used as exculpatory or inculpatory, meaning for me or against me."

Cogan nodded. "I'm satisfied that you understand the issue. Do you still want the severance?"

"I do, Your Honor."

"Your motion for severance is granted."

That was a tremendous victory for me, but then the judge shocked me by turning to my lawyer and saying, "Ms. Sharkey, when can I expect your change of venue motion for Mr. Spado?"

"I'll submit it within the next ten days, Your Honor."

He smiled. "Your client submitted his own motion to move the trial to Los Angeles that I had to reject because it didn't come from counsel. He did a very good job on it, I might add."

The hearing was adjourned. As the marshals removed me to a holding cell behind the courtroom, I whispered to Kelly to stop there and see me.

She was at my cell a few minutes later. I said, "Kelly, you're a great lawyer and a real fighter in the courtroom, but I'd like you to do me a favor on the change of venue motion. Please read mine over and attach it to the one you prepare. You heard the judge say he liked what I did, so it can't hurt."

A few weeks later we were back in court and the judge denied the motion. In rendering his decision, he explained his reasons in detail.

He began by saying he wanted to remain the judge on my case. If the trial were moved to Los Angeles, a judge there would have to give up his courtroom for a trial that could last several weeks. The prosecutors and Kelly Sharkey also wanted to remain on the case, meaning everyone would have had to travel to California and spend considerable time there.

Due to the inconvenience and expense involved, he had no choice but to deny the motion.

He said that although the crimes I was charged with took place in Los Angeles, because I had lived there for so long, that was where a jury of my peers would be found, so he was confident I would get a fair trial in Brooklyn.

Even with that defeat, I still had a lot of respect for Judge Cogan and felt relatively comfortable with his decision.

* * *

As I thought about my defense, my feelings alternated between positive and negative. When I was down, it was a very scary thought that I might die in prison, away from my children, my grandchildren, and my dog and buddy, Maggie. I didn't want to think about that possibility, but with my health issues—diabetes and heart problems—I had to be realistic. I thank God that Judge Cogan made sure I received the treatment I needed.

I tried to take my mind off my problems by reading and writing. I read every book my kids and others sent me, and I corresponded with them and several of my friends. One of them was John Daly. John was a film producer with movies such as *Platoon* and *The last Emperor* among his credits. He passed away not long after I was incarcerated (October 31, 2008), and I really missed his letters.

The time passed. Sometimes it was bearable and other times not so much.

* * *

Sonny Franzese, Joe Digorga, John Capolino and Chris Curanovic went to trial in June 2010. On Wednesday, July 7, they were all convicted. Chris had been offered a plea, which he refused. As of this writing, he is still in a federal prison in New Jersey. Sonny, then 93, was subsequently sentenced to eight years. After those convictions, I was brought to court where Judge Cogan scheduled my trial to begin the following Tuesday.

While I was in the holding cell waiting to go downstairs, Kelly came to see me. She said the prosecutor had just made another plea offer—ninety-seven to a hundred twenty months for pleading guilty to the conspiracy to commit robbery charge. My initial reaction was to reject it because there had never been a gun involved, and the so called "robbery" had been a setup with the "victim." But my fear of dying in prison, away from family and friends, caused me to reconsider. Kelly and I reviewed the details.

I objected to two specific things. The government wanted to enhance the level of severity on the gun charge, which I certainly didn't feel was right, and they wanted to list me as a boss or manager in the criminal organization. I told Kelly if she could get those things changed, I'd consider accepting the offer.

I was taken down to the main bullpen to await the bus, where I talked with Tico. He said that taking the plea was the right way to go.

The bus hadn't yet arrived, and Kelly was back to tell me the government had agreed to make the change I wanted regarding the gun charge, but not for having a managerial role. I told her get it in writing and come see me at the jail the next day.

After Kelly left I was brought back to the bullpen, I was still thinking about going to trial because I felt I could beat my case. I told my friend Tico, and he said, "Spado, take the deal. You've been here 30 months, and with that deal, you will see daylight. If you go to trial on RICO, they will shut your light out and you will die in prison.

Having known Tico's case, as he went to trial and lost, I knew he was right. So, I decided that with the informants they had, and especially with the tape recordings, I had no shot, so I took the plea deal.

When I went in front of Judge Cogan and accepted the plea of 97 months, he ordered the probation office to have a pre-sentence report finished within 30 days. This became another nightmare, as they actually increased my sentence, but then they did another report and decreased it.

The letters that I had asked my family, friends and other people in the entertainment business to write were all in. Now I was ready, and the rest would all be in Judge Cogan's hands. What would he do?

Go figure.

The Hearing

M y reflections were interrupted when a marshal called, "Spado, it's time. Let's go."

They took me from the bullpen to a holding cell behind the courtroom. After a short wait two marshals brought me into the courtroom and to the defense table, where Kelly was waiting. The prosecution team was at their table a few feet away, and Lorretta Lynch, the US Attorney for the Eastern District, was in the same place every time.

The first several minutes of the hearing involved a conversation between the judge and lawyers clarifying some legal issues and getting everything on the record. When that was finished, and prior to passing his sentence, the judge asked me if I had anything I wanted to say. I did.

"Well, I would like to tell the Court I am deeply sorry, particularly to my children and grandchildren. I am very sorry for the crimes and attempted crimes I pled to.

"In reference to my medical thing, to reiterate what Ms. Sharkey said, I distinctly remember my father passing away and his legs were swollen as mine are, every day. There was nothing they could do.

"To be honest with you, when I made it to sixty-three, I thought I had lived my life and was ready to leave this earth then. Instead I'm here. I can tell the Court it will never see me again if I ever get out."

Following my statement, Judge Cogan continued to explain his thought process and what factors he considered in deciding on the sentence he was about to impose.

He said, "In so many organized crime cases I feel as though I'm sentencing two different individuals. On one side of the coin we have a guy who cares for his family and friends, but on the other side, we have a totally different and violent person. That's exactly the situation with you, Mr. Spado."

Then he went into one of the major considerations that influenced him—my health.

"That brings me to Mr. Spado's health condition. Even if I see him as a heavy complainer, which he may or may not be—I don't know—there is no question that he is infirm. This is apparent, and not just from the catalogue of ailments and the prescriptions he's taking, which themselves are daunting. It's not just that he's had these chronic conditions—he's had two years in custody with them. I have to agree with what Ms. Sharkey said when he pled, that we've kind of watched him deteriorate. He looks like a shadow of the man he was when I first saw him a couple of years ago.

"I'm not blaming MDC for that in any way. It may just be that the fact of his incarceration combined with his illnesses have diminished him. I can see it and recognize that the time he has served and will serve is harder on him than it would be on a healthy defendant."

He continued, "Sometimes you have to put someone in jail for what you recognize is going to be the rest of their lives because they are just a depraved person and there's no prospect of rehabilitation or contribution. I don't think Mr. Spado is in that category. The letters from his family and friends show me that he's not a completely depraved person. He is, as I said, one of those people with two sides, and I have to take them both into account."

When the judge finished his statement, the words came, "Will the defendant please rise."

I got to my feet with Kelly by my side and two marshals standing behind us. It was the moment of truth.

The judge said, "Mr. Spado, after having reviewed your pre-sentence report and amendments, including one that I received just this morning, and letters submitted on your behalf, I sentence you to sixty days for the robbery charge. On the gun charge, the 924C, my hands are tied. That charge carries a minimum mandatory sentence of sixty months, and that is the sentence I am imposing on you. That brings your total term of incarceration to sixty-two months, to be followed by four years of supervised release with special conditions: no firearms, ammunition or destructive devices possession, and no association with anyone involved with organized crime or any criminal enterprise. That will include not going into any place where such people are known by Mr. Spado to attend. Probation will furnish a list of such people and places to him. That list is not the limit of his prohibition. His knowledge is the limit of his prohibition.

"Also, I'm going to require that as a condition of his supervised release, he consent to a search of his person, his residence, any business, and his vehicle, as long as the Probation people believe there is reasonable suspicion that he has contraband or is violating the terms of his probation. That search will have to be done at a reasonable time, place and manner.

"I'm not going to impose a fine because he can't afford it. I will impose the mandatory two-hundred-dollar special assessment."

The prosecutor, Cristina Posa, stood up and argued that I took a plea for 97 to 120 months. Judge Cogan responded, "As far as I'm concerned, you charged Mr. Spado twice for the same crime, and if congress wanted to enact a minimum mandatory on that they would have done so. My sentence stands."

* * *

Back in the holding cell, I felt as though the weight of the world had been lifted from my shoulders. The judge had not just honored my plea agreement, he actually improved upon it. With the time I'd already served and an allowance for good time, I'd be released from prison in mid-2012, having served a total of about five years.

That meant there was a good chance my fear of dying behind bars wouldn't happen. I'd probably be able to spend some time with my family as a free man.

However, there was a downside—I was now flat broke.

By the time I accepted the plea, I was using court-appointed counsel, and the judge didn't bother to fine me because I didn't have the ability to pay—a situation certainly wouldn't improve any while I was locked up.

I realized that kind of thinking was putting the cart before the horse, though. First, I had to get through the rest of my prison time. I could worry about my finances afterward.

* * *

Before I move on, there is one more very important point I want to make about mandatory sentencing.

When I watch the news, I hear Bill O'Reilly, who is a very intelligent man, pushing the idea of giving minimum mandatory five-year sentences to illegal aliens who re-enter the United States after having been deported. I understand there are serious concerns about the violent crimes committed by previously deported illegals. However, I don't think the mandatory sentencing Mr. O'Reilly supports is the solution.

I've got news for you on that one. When I was in prison, I saw with my own eyes the way the inmates from Mexico reacted to being in an American jail. The majority of them thought of it as a great opportunity to get three squares a day, a bed, clothes and showers, along with medical and dental care. I believe many of them would love the chance to do five years here. Rather than serving as a deterrent, they will probably be lining up to get in.

Go figure.

Lompoc

When I was sentenced, Judge Cogan recommended I be sent to a medical facility at Terminal Island in San Pedro. However, the Bureau of Prisons had a different idea and sent me to their facility in Lompoc, California.

I was flown out of Brooklyn on December 16, 2010. After a stopover at the reception center in Oklahoma, other inmates and I landed in Victorville on December 17, my birthday. Instead of leaving immediately for Lompoc, they decided to keep us in Victorville over the holidays, and it wasn't a very nice place.

It was overcrowded, with four men assigned to most cells—two sleeping on mattresses on the floor. I got lucky and only had two guys with me. They were good guys and were being sent to Lompoc to enter the drug program and get some time knocked off their sentences.

We were locked up twenty hours a day, only allowed out for four hours after breakfast to shower and exercise. I met a priest, Father Vitale, from San Francisco, who was in his seventies. He was doing six months for protesting at a nuclear site. It was his third conviction for the same offense, and everybody seemed to know him because of his frequent visits.

On Christmas he held Mass in my cell, sitting next to me on my bunk and using bread leftover from breakfast for Holy Communion.

We were held there until January 3, when fifteen of us were put on a bus for Lompoc.

* * *

When we got off the bus, I was the last one in line. Chained and shackled, we entered the prison in single file, stopping at a booth with bulletproof glass and a guard inside. Through an intercom we gave the guard our names and prison numbers. When I stepped up to the window, the guard made an announcement over the loudspeaker.

He said, "I want all you new arrivals to take a look at the guy at the end of the line. His name is Orlando Spado of the Colombo family in New York. Before he was convicted, he was known as The Mob Boss of Hollywood."

What the fuck?

At that moment I realized this place was different than the MDC in Brooklyn. I made a conscious decision not to talk to the guards unless it was necessary. And I wouldn't get too friendly with the other inmates, either, only a few who I was absolutely sure I could trust.

After being issued bedding and prison clothes, it was time for paperwork. One of the forms had a question asking if you were affiliated with any criminal group or gang. I answered "No" and submitted the form.

A few minutes later a guard took me into a side room. Pointing to the question about crime group and gang affiliations, he said, "You made a mistake here."

"No, that's not a mistake."

"But you're a member of the Colombo family, aren't you?"

The only family I'm a member of is the Spado family, and I'm not even the boss of that."

I walked away.

* * *

I'd hated Brooklyn and I really hated Lompoc. The respect level there was not the same as in Brooklyn, and there were a lot of pedophiles in Lompoc. I have to be honest with you, I do not like them and have my own idea of what should be done with those reptiles who prey on children.

Pedophiles were not allowed in our units in Brooklyn. If one got assigned by mistake, in a short time he'd be visited by someone doing a life sentence with nothing to lose and told exactly what was going to happen to him. In a matter of minutes the pedophile would request to be transferred to the Special Housing Unit for his own protection. That's the way it should be.

In Lompoc the dorms held two hundred and forty inmates, twice the capacity of Brooklyn. The bunks were so close to each other there was virtually no room, and the smells were absolutely horrible. For reasons I can't comprehend, some inmates hated to flush the toilets and loved to piss on the floor. That's a disgusting way for grown men to act, but that is the way it was.

However, I did meet some good men, like Iggy from Brooklyn and Lou, Joe and JP from Los Angeles. We walked the yard several times every day, sharing stories and laughing a lot. They certainly helped me pass the time. However, my best time-passer was reading. I started reading books in Brooklyn and continued in Lompoc. In the five years I was locked up, I read over three hundred books from cover to cover.

I got along okay with the blacks, Mexicans and bikers, too. We respected each other, but I didn't get too close to any of them.

So I did my time, kept my mouth shut and my nose clean. The health care was horrible—worse than in Brooklyn. I got my medical issues under control by eating tuna fish daily and walking between five and seven miles in the yard every day.

Probably the worst non-prison thing that happened while I was at Lompoc was in August 2011, when my dear friend Jimmy Caci passed away from natural causes in Palm Springs, two weeks after he turned eighty-six.

I called him every couple of weeks. One time when he answered the phone, he could only mumble. He'd been having some medical problems and was in and out of the hospital, so I told him to hang up and call someone to get him to the hospital right away.

I called back a few days later and there was no answer. I tried to reach him several more times over the next couple of weeks, and then the phone was disconnected. I was sure he was gone, but didn't get confirmation until

I got in touch with Jimmy's sister in Buffalo.

I thought of the old days when Jimmy would be at my door at seven in the morning to get me up. I remember his cooking and drawings, and it made me sad. I knew what I would miss the most, though, was his friendship. Jimmy was a real man and a true friend. No question about it.

* * *

I was scheduled to be released from prison on June 6, 2012. I had to do another six months in a halfway house in South Central Los Angeles, and then four years of probation. In reality, the easy part was behind me because I still had fifty-four months to go before I'd be a really free man.

When the morning of my release came, I was very excited and got up earlier than usual—there were certain things I had to do. You see, in prison nearly every item is valuable, and when the other inmates know you're getting out, they want your unsoiled mattress, bedding and, believe it or not, your toilet paper—which is hard to come by, making it a hot commodity. I gave my stuff to my closest friends and waited to be called to R&D (Receiving and Discharge). When I heard my name, I walked there alone, just as I'd done when processed in.

I looked for my son Anthony, who, along with his friend since childhood, Chris Muto, was going to pick me up, but didn't see them. It turned out they had arrived a few minutes early, and the prick of a roving guard told them they couldn't wait and to come back in an hour. So after finishing the discharge process, I had to wait inside until Anthony and Chris came back.

As I waited, I started thinking of Sonny Franzese

and how badly things worked out for his second family. Michael, his stepson, had been a disappointment to him. Johnny, his natural son, was a witness against him—the first time in the history of the New York Mob that had happened. His daughter, Gia, died from a drug overdose, and his daughter, Tina, died of cancer. His wife, also named Tina, died of cancer as well. Why all this happened, I don't have an answer, but the children from Sonny's first marriage, they all became normal citizens and never had anything to do with *the life.*

One thing I did know was that I didn't want my family to suffer any more because of me—they'd been through enough already. I made a vow that I would change my life and live my remaining years as a person grateful for the family I have because they are the most important thing in my life.

In the end, probably the most important lesson I learned from knowing Sonny was that living a life like his can destroy you and everyone around you. Because of this, I will do what I need to do according to the strict guidelines of my probation and lead as normal a life as I possibly can. So I must thank my friend Sonny for that, because I learned from his mistakes.

When Anthony and Chris pulled in to get me, we hugged each other with great emotion. Afterwards, we stopped at an In-N-Out Burger where they bought me the first real meal I'd had in sixty months. We then drove back to Los Angeles, my home.

It's time for me to begin a new journey—probably my last—and I plan to make it the best one of my life.

Go figure.

Special Letters

Dear Rosemary,

I want you to know that I still think of you often. I find that I should apologize to you for a few things. First and most importantly—I want to apologize for what happened when we lived in Little Neck. I will not mention what it was, as we both know. I sincerely apologize to you for that. At that time, I was under federal indictment, and I was just divorcing my wife Toni and leaving my children, which was the toughest thing I have ever done in my life. Being the first in the family to get a divorce in an Italian family is not easy.

However, we still got married after that, and I absolutely loved you, as you are also a remarkable lady. We had a lot of good times together. And now, here I am, a man at 75 and single, but I can honestly say I had two of the best women in the world, and I blew it twice. Yes, I blew it, but on the other hand, I do not think I was ever built for marriage. It's just who and what I am. I did not live the kind of life to be married and have a home with the white picket fence. It's not who Ori Spado is. I hope you can understand that, and I'm sure by now you have accepted that.

I also need to apologize for when we drove through that snowstorm from Florida to New York to get to my mother's for Christmas Eve—for both what I said, and for my mother, who did not allow us into her home. I will never forget that, as I knew you were hurt, as I was also. We had to spend Christmas Eve in a motel room in Utica. My mother was a great lady, but she was upset with me for leaving my family. It really had nothing to do with you, so please accept my apology for that.

I happen to know that you know I went to prison, and you also knew when I got released. I think that the FBI must have visited you to see what you knew about me, and that they told you. Maybe this isn't what happened, but somehow you knew. It's not that important, but I thought I would mention it.

I hope you're still happily married, and that you have your daughter, Brianna (a beautiful name), the child you always wanted, and I'm happy you have her. I hope you are well, and that you can accept my apologies. If you or your family ever need me for anything, please do not hesitate to reach out to me, and I will do what I can.

Remember the positive and not the negative things, Rosemary, because you are a good woman. I hope someday you get to see this letter. I only want for your happiness, and that you can accept my apologizes.

Yours always,
Ori

Dear Frank Russo,

I could probably write a whole book just on you. You and I sure had a lot of great times together, especially in New York City at the Warwick, and in all those restaurants with all those people you introduced me to. I became friends with them as well. Well, I've written a book, and almost all the people in my book are people you introduced me to: Frank Costello, Russell Bufalino, Carlo Marcello Sonny Franzese, Ralph Serpe and Dino Delaurentiis. In my book, I write that I think you were grooming me for *the life* and what I became. Thank you, as it really was a good life.

I remember like yesterday you telling me how, on Saturday morning, you'd open the cellar doors for your father, and you told me how my grandfather was one of the few at those meetings every Saturday. This confirmed other things I had heard from my father's sister. So, it was in my blood to become whom I am.

We had so many good times—unfortunately, I cannot write about them, but they were great. I'll never forget the time that I slipped marijuana into your cigarettes, and then you had to run because you had a meeting at the bank, and then you had to play golf. You could not figure why you felt so good and happy. I'm laughing just thinking about it.

I'm close with your son Drew, and I remember when he was in college and you and I flew to Phoenix to visit him. Frank, you were an incredibly special part of my life, and I loved every moment of it.

All my love,
Ori

Dear Sonny,

I remember the first time we met at Eugene's restaurant on Second Avenue when Lou Perry introduced us. You had with you your wife, Christina, and your children, Gia, Johnny and Tina. You and I had to whisper because I had to explain a situation to you. Then we ate dinner, and I was allergic to the fish and got sick—no one ever forgot that.

Our next meet was at the Russian Tea Room on 57th at the sit down, and I felt you weren't understanding the problem, so I tried explaining it in different terms. You stared right through me and told me to keep my mouth shut, and you did not have to say it twice. I understood immediately. But it was after that meeting, outside, as we were all standing, that you grabbed my arm and walked me to the corner. You said, "Kid you got balls. From now on you're with me, and I want you and your family at my home for Christmas." I believe that was in 1979, and we've been friends ever since, though you got violated quite often,

Over the years, we stayed in touch through letters and telephone. It seemed every time you came home, I was in New York, and then I moved to Little Neck. We met every day for breakfast, and on Fridays, we met at the Douglaston Manor for dinner with everyone. After that, I moved to Los Angeles, but we always stayed in touch. I came back to New York on a monthly basis, and it was always you and me, eating breakfast at diners, and lunch and dinner at so many restaurants throughout the five boroughs I could not begin to count. You taught me so many things, then. It was you who taught me that we are always for the underdog, and to this day I still do that, and I believe in it. Thank you.

Then you began staying with me at my suite at the

Warwick. I will never forget all those conversations we had in the maids closet because we didn't trust the room, thinking it was bugged—it most likely was. Then, finally, we all got indicted. We were at MDC together, and when we were in the discovery room. We had arguments, as you seriously believed your son Johnny would not testify. But he did.

The last time we physically saw each other was in the court room. Remember that conversation? Because we worked a bad situation out right there until the judge stopped us from talking. People often ask me how I can like someone who did that, and my answer is always this—we are real men, and real men work out their differences. I did my time, and of course you did your time, and once you were in the nursing home, we spoke on the phone a couple times a week. I wanted to come and see you, so I contacted your parole officer, and they declined me, and I did not want you to get violated because of me. Your parole officer told me I could come in June, but you left us all before that.

Our last conversation was maybe a little over a week before you passed on. My dear friend, you are now in peace—finally after 103 years. You always had my love and respect, and that will never change, as you were a friend and a real man amongst real men in a man's world.

I miss you, Sonny.

Your friend always,
Ori

Dear Jimmy Caci, my dear friend and brother,

I must say, I miss you. We were like brothers, and wherever we went, people thought we were. Roy Schniderman from Buffalo introduced us, and at the time, I was in Palm Desert and needed a favor, which I paid you for. However, the favor never got done and you paid me back, and that's when our friendship really began. From then on, we were together every day doing what we did.

During the week, you would be here on a Monday morning by 7:00 a.m. until Friday, and then I would be in Palm Springs for the weekend. We had a lot of fun together, and we made a lot of money. Yes, you were the boss of Palm Springs and the underboss of Los Angeles. Being with you on the West Coast and with Sonny Franzese on the East Coast sure created some arguments. Sonny would argue that I was with him, and you would argue that I was with you because I lived in Beverly Hills—but we managed. I was finally able to bring you back to New York and introduced you to Sonny. That was at the Park Lane Hotel where Keely Smith was performing. Your brother Charlie was the AKA Bobby Milano, another great friend and singer, and we all went and had dinner with Sonny and a few other guys.

But Jimmy, it was you and me against the world. I love you, my brother. Remember that trip we made around the country, and you would not stop until we got to our first destination, which was Florida and then to New York? Remember the dinner at Joe Dente restaurant with 17 other people? Joe insisted that we not pay, as he owned the restaurant, but you and I did pay. I looked at you like you were crazy, but we had just come off a good score.

From New York city you dropped me off at my daughter's,

where I had Christmas, and you went to Buffalo to spend Christmas with your family. After Christmas, I took the train to Buffalo, where everyone in the city was your cousin, and you introduced me to your childhood friend, Joe Todaro, at his restaurant. Remember we got drunk and the cops knew you and brought us to the police station? They didn't arrest us—they just kept us because neither of us could drive.

What a trip. Remember when we finally got to Chicago where we finished our business? Remember how the FBI knew every place we went, and that they thought that you had *made* me? They thought you were bringing me around the country to introduce to everyone. Remember the day when you had it all set to get me *made* (and a couple others), and I argued with you, as I did not want it? Thank god that incident came up at the Sports Club on Ventura, and you and Stevie Cino went to take care it. Then there were the battles with others over that.

You and I had breakfast, lunch and dinner together, and at every restaurant, you drew cartoons for the kids and made them all happy. That is one of the things you learn in prison. I often try to think of how much time you and Sonny spent in prison, and I think it was something like 80 to 90 years total for the two of you.

Remember all our trips to Las Vegas through the backroads? Too many to count. And all the lunches with Stevie? I could not believe how he ate. Oh well. They did not call him "the whale" for no reason, but he was a great guy.

Remember when you went to see Johnny Mash at the deli he owned? He was steaming and told you that he just hung up with his friend, John Gotti, and he was sending guys from New York to California to take care Ori Spado. You stopped that right, and then Johnny and I became close friends.

It's funny how things work out.

And then, when I was recording the FBI and needed to go on record Back East, Sonny was in prison (as usual), so you went to see Joe Todaro in Buffalo, and the two of you called me. Joe was laughing, but he wanted me to keep doing it, but it had to end, and you were right, as I believe that was the real reason I got arrested and sent to prison.

And from prison, we spoke every week until one time you got back from the hospital and you did not seem well. I told you to call Betty and get back to the hospital, and you did, and that was the last time we ever spoke.

Jimmy, I could write an entire book of our life together, as we did so much. Remember when I would be driving, and we would pass a church and I would make the sign of the cross? You said, "How can you do that while we're on our way to rob someone?" But then you started it, and I would laugh. God bless you my brother Jimmy. All my love and respect to you, my dear brother.

Your true friend,
Ori

Dear Jerry Zimmerman,

How can anyone who ever met you ever forget you, especially me. It took some time, as Sonny kept trying to connect us, but he finally did. And I am happy he did. We met at Jerry's Deli on Ventura Blvd., and from the first moment we began earning money, and that just continued—and I mean good money. But it was not only the money, which neither of us could manage to keep, it was the friendship that we developed. I remember those Saturdays hanging out at your pool after picking up our food from Jerry's, of course.

I will never forget that day we had a bad week and did not bring in a dime. We sat and watched the average citizen going into the banks, and you said, "How come we don't get paid every week?" The reason was really quite obvious, as we were not built for that, normal jobs. Then you told me to write you a check for a thousand, and you cashed it with no funds—we split the money. Yet, somehow (as usual) on Monday we made the check good.

I cannot write all the happy times we spent together, or all the things we did, as there were many. I speak to your son Michael often, and he helps me with my computer all the time, so be proud. I sure miss you my friend.

Yours always,
Ori

Dear Jack Gilardi,

I recall the day we met like it was yesterday. I believe it was at Nicky Blair's on Sunset Blvd. I was already sitting down with a lady, and you came in with a young lady. The lady who I was with knew you, and she introduced us, and it became an immediate friendship right there. We always ran into each other at different hot spots in Hollywood, always with the ladies of course, as we both had that in common.

You were always there when people came to me and needed to cast a film. You never hesitated and always did it immediately. And if you needed anything, I was there for you too. That is what true friends do, and we were true friends. More importantly, you were not only a legendary agent to the stars, you were there for everyone who needed help or guidance with their careers.

Jack, you answered every call you got and returned every call. You knew how to communicate with people, and you treated everyone respectfully. I sure wish other agents had that secret, but they do not, as they think differently. They think they are above others, but that is Hollywood, as we know.

Our last lunch was at Via Alloro—I brought my friend Nick Pileggi. I believe that was the last time we saw each other, but we spoke often, right until you passed on. I'm in contact with your son Jacky, and he is a great kid, just like you, very respectful.

Jack, I wanted you to know that you will never be forgotten, as you are the true legend of Hollywood.

All my love and respect, dear friend.
Ori

Dear Joey Pyle, my best mate,

I remember the first time we spoke on the phone. Danny Sims and you were partners managing Mark Morrison (Return of the Mack). We had a great conversation, and you asked me to look after Mark, as he was coming to Los Angeles to record at Warner Brothers.

My son Anthony did just that, and you and I, for some reason, we became close friends across the pond. We instantly bonded and had trust, respect and loyalty. We will always have that. We had phone calls every day, sometimes several, as you would call me from a pub and then introduce me to everyone in the pub.

We finally met when I made my first of several trips to London, and it seemed like we knew each other all our lives. Maybe this is because we thought the same—that we could accomplish more with our brains than with a gun, but we knew if we had to go that way, we would. We became closer than real brothers. I think of all the wonderful time we spent together at pubs drinking, listening to your favorite Irish songs and singing.

It seemed like there were always fights at Caesars, of which your son Joey, became a promoter, but the fight that I remember was on my last visit. I was with my son, Anthony, and John Daly—we four were sitting together and then Joey came out to fight. I remember watching you more than the fight—seeing you smile with joy as you watched your son pulverize his opponent. You were and have every reason to be a proud father of Joey, as he is just like you.

Joey and I speak often, not like you and I, but he checks up on me, and he has become my third son. I check on him too, and just like you, I know that if needed, he would be here for me in a second, and I would be there for him. He and Anthony are like brothers. He came to visit me upon my release from prison and was there for me.

I will never forget your wedding in Las Vegas. I was doing the Wyclef Jean concert at the Aladdin. You came in with the whole crew—everyone had money in their money belts, and then you collected it all and came to my room with it for the work in Seattle. I remember me and Anthony going to all the cages and converting it all to U.S. dollars. Your wedding was great and without any hitches, but then Dave Courtney wanted to get married. Well, as the pastor said, this will go down in the books, and it did.

Joey, it's amazing how we became so close and you became my best mate ever. When you needed something on this side of the pond, or I needed something on that side, as well as in other countries, neither of us ever hesitated and we took care of it immediately. You and I had a bond that no one could ever shake, and we know some have tried. It was shortly after that last trip to London that you had to be back in the hospital, and I remember your son Joey calling me and putting us on the phone together. I wasn't thinking it would be our last conversation, but shortly after that, Joey called and told me you had left us.

I miss you, dear mate, and always you have my love, respect and honor.

From across the pond,
Ori

My dear friend John Daly,

I want you to know that I think of you often. When I look out my kitchen window, I see your office building every day. I will never forget the first time you called me at three in the afternoon, as everyone who knew me knew not to call then because I was napping. But, your intentions were good, as always. You wanted to help my mate, Joey Pyle, as you heard he was ill.

We became remarkably close friends after that, meeting every evening for dinner and cocktails either on Sunset Blvd. or The Four Seasons. You were one of the best independent producers/directors in Hollywood, having won back-to-back Best Picture of the Year awards with *Platoon* and *The Last Emperor*. I was incredibly happy to have been your friend for the rest of your journey. Hollywood needs more people like you. You personally gave or resurrected so many careers.

I still have no idea why that organization called me that year to ask who they should give the Lifetime Achievement Award to—I said John Daly. As you were in the hospital when the announcement was made, they had to film you from your bed. I was standing right there while they filmed you tell about your life of films and the people you've met and helped. Unfortunately, soon after that I was arrested on RICO charges and brought to the Brooklyn MDC, but you never flinched. With all you were going through with your cancer, you wrote, and we spoke on the phone often until that day on October 31, 2008, when you departed.

I remember the day when you called and asked if you could speak to my son, Anthony. There was a young lady you had auditioned and remembered from years earlier—you met her at an amateur acting contest where you were a judge.

You flew her out to give her a leading part, but because the part had a scene that she did not want to begin her career with, she declined. But you asked Anthony to look after her, and he sure did, as they are soulmates and been together ever since, all because of you. We speak of you often and they love you.

I remember the day you departed, as it felt you were telling me it was time to go. I woke up at 6:00 a.m. from my bunk and laid there, and I just knew. Once I got to the phone, I called Tim Shiner and he told me. Rest assured you will never be forgotten and always loved.

I'm out of prison and I have written a book, and I know if you were here the movie would have already been made. I think of you on holidays like Christmas and Thanksgiving, and how you and I would meet at the Beverly Hills Hotel and have dinner together. You were and still are a true friend. I promise that someday soon I will come visit you where you rest with a bottle of wine and glasses so we can talk. God bless you my friend.

All my love,
Ori

Hi Michael Franseze,

I hope all is well with you and your family. I must say, a lot of people are very disappointed that we ended up with a feud between us. And as I've said, I will no longer be saying anything about you. However, there are a few things that I feel it necessary to say to you.

Going back to 1978 or 1979, you and I first laid eyes on each other at the Russian Tea Room. That we know. And yes, you are correct. After that, you and I had no interaction at all until after your release from prison, and you asked your brother John to set a meet with meat the Rangoon Racquet club on Santa Monica Blvd. in Beverly Hills. You and I had a conversation in the ally.

After the meeting at the Russian Tea Room, your father and I became close friends, right up to the day he died. And yes, you are correct. When I was with your father, you never were around, as you were quite busy in those days.

However, in later days I became close friends with Jerry Zimmerman. Jerry was a great guy and a good friend, and he and I made a lot of money together. Jerry always went after the short, quick dollar, but with me, he learned how to go for the bigger dollars. Until the day Jerry passed away, he always had a box of papers in his car about you, things that happened with you, and a lot of documentation pertaining to many things. I wonder what happened to that box after he passed?

I became friends with Billy Ferrante when he lived out here and in Florida as well. Bob Barich and I are still friends to this day. And when I lived in Little Neck, I did go to your dealership in Hempstead a few times and met with your father; however, you were not there at the time.

Michael, there is one thing you did say that still bothers me—that I got your brother Johnny on drugs, which you and I both know is not the truth. I am sure we can agree on that for sure. I spent a lot of time with your mother, but there is no need to repeat what she and your father told me, as I do not think it means anything at this point.

Michael, as I said, there was something you wrote in your first book that was true, and I remembered that, which is the reason that I never took my button. It was not easy for me to talk my way out of it, but I did. And I thank you for that.

I sincerely meant what I said about not saying anything against you or putting you down, or anyone else for that matter; however, if you want, you can continue to say things to keep the feud going, but I will not give a response either way.

I wish you all the best,
Ori

Letters to My Children

By now you know, or maybe you always knew, who and what your father is. I made the wisest choice marrying your mother, although I should never have been married to anyone—it's not who or what I am about. Yes, I wish I could have been there when you woke up and made you breakfast, and yes, I wish I could have been there when you came home from school, but again, that is just not who I am.

I am so happy for the bond that the three of you have. Do not ever lose that for anything, as you well know, it is not that way with me and my siblings, or mainly two of my siblings. Do not allow that to happen with you three, as that would destroy me. Yes, your father is different, but remember I did it my way.

All my love and respect to you and to my grandchildren,
Dad

To my daughter, Princess Gina

I am sitting here looking at a letter you wrote me some time ago. I have it framed. Thank God you are the girl in the family, otherwise it might have been you who followed in my footsteps, which I never wanted for any of my children. Yes, we all had our fair share of differences, and yes, you are tough, stubborn and very independent. But you agreed I was right, and yes, I kept this note, so I have it in writing from you that you acknowledged I was right. Always rest assured that I have your back and only want your happiness, and I'm extremely proud of you, as I am of all three of my children.

I never will forget your graduation. I sat there hearing the name *Gina Spado* so many times for all the scholarships you won that I sat in the audience and cried. I was so proud of you. Well, you are an amazing daughter, and I'm so happy that you're now happy with Pat and your work—you have no idea how happy this makes me.

I certainly remember that after graduating you came to visit me here in Los Angeles. I was living in a high rise on the Wilshire Corridor. You wanted to get married, and your mom and I just wanted you to go to college. Your mom always got me in trouble with you kids, especially you and Ori, so I had your mother on the phone telling me to convince you to go to college in Miami, or here at UCLA, because you could have gone to any college you wanted. We argued, and the next thing I saw was you driving down Wilshire Blvd. in my car, which was a convertible I was renting at the time. But you did as you said you would. You got married and you got your degree, and now look at you.

Yes, you were correct. I did not like the holidays, as I felt they were too long and took away from business. Since being in prison, that has changed, and I have honestly loved the last few Christmases that we've all got together in Florida, so even I can change sometimes.

I remember the day you came to court in Brooklyn with my grandson, Marty, and I saw you both. The marshals would not even allow me to hug you. While I was away, you sent me all those books, and the letter you wrote to the judge stood out from over 50 letters people had written; however, he did not agree that Sonny and I were only friends. Oh well—we tried.

You are an amazing daughter, and you have no idea how happy I am that you're now happy with Pat and your work. I love you always, my Princess Gina, as you will always be daddy's little girl.

Love, Dad

To my son, Ori

You talk like me and you look and act like me. That's scary in a way, but you are a much better businessman than I was, and I'm very proud of that. You know what to do with the money you earn, and I never had that ability, but I think in some way you learned a lot from your old man.

Remember that time I had the whole family in New York for the Thanksgiving parade, and I had a guy who owed some money on Broadway? I knew it would not be a problem, so I brought you with me. Remember when we walked into his office, and I just took over his desk and had him sit in front of me? I was actually teaching you a big selling lesson, that you need to be in control, and you learned it well.

I remember when I was living in Florida, and Ralphie and I were working at what we were doing in the middle of the night. We made a good score, and you woke up to go to school, walked right into my bedroom, and my bed was full of jewelry. You just shook your head, took a shower and went to school. One thing you can always say is that I never hid anything from you kids. I also remember the hotel I was staying at in Royal Palm Beach, and you brought your first girlfriend—remember that my son?

Now I know you are still hurt for two things. Remember I spanked you when we left? I think it was at the zoo in Miami. I forget why I spanked you, but you should be happy and proud, as you hold that honor of being the only one of my children I have ever spanked.

Then, do you remember when you wanted to quit school, and your mother wanted you to talk to a shrink? Once again, she asked me to talk to you, and I agreed with her. You see, your mother made me do it—LOL. Well I always thought she was smarter than me, so I did it. I apologize for that.

Remember when we flew to New York and Sonny picked us up and we went to eat, and I almost had a heart attack when Sonny actually paid for the dinner? I can't remember this exactly, but you and Sonny had a few words about something, and you stood up to him. Later, when we went to his home, he told me you were a great kid, and he loved the way you stood up to him.

Ori, you are a remarkable young man in so many ways that I cannot count them. You are now starting a new chapter in your life, and I just want your happiness and continuing success in the business you have built entirely on your own. Just keep at it, keep it moving, and be positive and happy. I love and respect you, Ori.

Love, Dad

To my dear son, Anthony

Let us start at the beginning, as your mom and I knew when you were being born exactly. It was on a Friday at 1:00 p.m., as you were a caesarean birth, so obviously, I went out the night before and got drunk and passed out cigars. You were born calm, cool and collected, and that is exactly how I feel you live your life.

In school you did very well, and you were an honor student until you went to Florida and went to Wellington. Your grades began to slip, so your mom sent you back to Frankfort to live with your sister, and you did well there. Then you went on to Herkimer College where you played soccer, as you have been playing since you were very young. At Herkimer you did well, and your soccer team was number one in the nation, and then you went on to the University of Central Florida. I remember you called me and asked me what courses you should take, but then you settled on your courses.

At college, you thought about becoming an actor, and you took a part as an extra on *Waterboy*. Well, you quickly decided you didn't want to be on that side of the screen! Then your finals came, and you called me and said:

"Pops, I went to take my finals and my professors didn't know me."

"Is that *because you did not go* to classes? I asked.

"Yeah, that must be it," you said.

So I suggested that you come to Los Angeles and stay here and see how you like it. That was in 1999. I must say, for someone who has always lived by himself, I really enjoyed living with you. Although you're a grouch when you wake up, we had a lot of fun, and then Chris moved in with us, and we

371

all had a great time. Now this is your home. You made it kid. And yes, you did it on your own.

I will never forget the day I got arrested, as I'm sure you won't either. However, in a way it worked out really well for you, as you had no choice but to become more independent and do things on your own. So, as crazy as this might sound, me doing five years in prison worked out well for you, as you had no choice, and I need to say, I'm extremely proud of what and who you've become. If me doing five years did that, then it was well worth it.

When I got released, you were right there with Chris Muto to pick me up, and you have been there for me every step of the way without hesitation. You are still here for me, helping with other things. As I wrote my book, it occurred to me how you were always there with me, in London, Las Vegas and New York too. All my friends love you and respect you.

I will never forget that day when John Daly called and asked to speak with you, and he asked you to look after *a young lady while she* was in town. Giulini is that lady, and I now call her my funny girl—that had to be in 2006, and now look at the two of you: happy, positive and doing good things. I'm proud of you, and I'm proud of Giulini. I only want for you both to always be happy and live an incredibly successful life together, which makes me happy as well. I love you and highly respect you, my son. You know that I'm here for both you at any time.

Love, Dad

A Letter to The U.S. House of Representatives

Allow me to introduce myself.

My name is Orlando Carl Spado; however I, am known as Ori Spado, *The Accidental Gangster*. Yes, I was a gangster, but I am now reformed, doing what I can to help young men and women stay out of *the life* (or gangs).

I have one simple question for all of you. Why do you make promises when you run for office and then change once you are elected?

From 1963-1966, I served my country proudly. Upon my release, when I got home, the very first thing my father did was take me to register to vote as a Democrat. When I asked him why, he said that the Democrats will do things for the little man. That was in 1966—what has changed? Everything has changed.

When I moved to Los Angeles, I registered as a Republican. And now, since my released from prison, I changed to *no party affiliation*, along with millions of others. When I joined the Army, the first thing we were told was not to discuss politics or religion, and now it seems that is all everyone talks about in pure disgust. All the hatred going on in this country is unnecessary, and who is to fault? It begins right there in Washington D.C., from all of you.

You manufacture and pass laws not to help out the people, but for your own good. Yes, both parties do this. The moment you get into office, the first thing you do is raise money for your next election and make up more lies to get our votes—that's what you do instead of getting down and discuss how and what you can do to make this a better country.

Everyone keeps saying that the constitution says this and that. Take a look at it—those men—yes, men. No women were involved in writing it. Those authors did not know what a light bulb was, a phone, a car, or computer, and who were those guys? They were landowners with slaves. Is it not time to get up-to-date? Oh no, you cannot do that, because then the people would have too much of a voice, and god forbid that should happen.

I look at our neighboring countries, and I see happy people. I see governments honestly trying to help their citizens, but why not here in America—the greatest country in the world.

The scales of justice are so lopsided, it's disgusting. The laws of this country, the lengthy prison sentences that do not fit the crime, and minimum mandatory sentencing— these are deplorable and need to change. Why is it that the greatest country on earth incarcerates more people than the rest of the world combined? Why is it the recidivism rate is so high? You know why. Admit it. What are you going to do about it?

The only one who benefits from these laws are the prosecutors, and let's be honest. Being a prosecutor is a stepping-stone into office. In the legal system, prosecutors and law enforcement are given the right to lie and get away with it, and these very same liars run for office and the people vote for them. Yes, both parties do this. I could continue describing all the problems in this country and all the hatred, but remember, water runs downhill. The top is where all this hatred begins and filters down to the people. In my next book, *My Journey Through the Judicial System*, I will discuss more about these laws and the constitution, as Ori Spado interprets it.

So, I ask you all once again, what are you elected officials honestly going to do to help build this country and not tear it apart?

Ori Spado, The Accidental Gangster
Beverly, Hills, California

EPILOGUE

Have I changed? People often ask me this question since the pre-launch of my book, *The Accidental Gangster*. Personally, I am the same guy I always have been—always a gentleman, and only telling the truth. This will never change. This is who I am and always will be.

However, some things have changed. I have always been a man living in the shadows and in the background here in Hollywood and other places around the world. I'm now well-known, and when I walk down the street, people recognize me from my social media, podcast and radio interviews, of which there are many, and there will be many more to come. I have met so many nice people through this journey. It is really a pleasure, and I do enjoy it. I enjoy making people happy.

I'm blessed to still be here to tell my story, and I will continue to do so. I will never stop being for the underdog, and I will continue to do so because it is in my blood. That is who Ori Spado is.

Since my initial release, I have lost three more people very dear to me—my brother, Joe Spado, my friend and legendary agent to the stars, Jack Gilardi, and of course, my friend John Sonny Franzese. I miss the conversations I had with all of them. I remember the other dear friends I have lost. There have been so many—my best mate from London, Joey Pyle, Jimmy Caci, and my very close friend, producer and director John Daly, who, along with Oliver Stone, made *Platoon, Salvador, The Terminator, Hoosiers*, and many more.

John helped and gave careers to actors such as Dennis Hopper, Denzel Washington, Julia Roberts and Keanu Reeves, and directors like James Cameron, Oliver Stone, and many others. John was the last big Hollywood legend I worked with. I have many fond memories of my life in Hollywood, but my fondest by far is when I was called and asked who I would give the Lifetime Achievement Award to, and I said John Daly. I was always there for John, and he was always there for me, even after I was arrested and locked up.

Truthfully, there are not many honorable people in Hollywood. Agents do not return calls, but Jack Gilardi returned every call he got, and he was loyal to the end, as was John, Sonny and a few others.

A legend who is close to my age, still with us, and I had the pleasure of speaking with recently, is Oliver Stone. Oliver is by far is one of the most masterful writers, directors and producers that Hollywood has ever had. Oliver's memoir is coming out very soon, so please purchase this book. I assure you, you will not be able to put it down. And read who he has dedicated it to—I'm not telling. Buy the book and see for yourself.

Yes, my life has changed, and all for the better, since my initial launch I have kept two young men from getting into *the life* or a gang. That in itself is worth me writing this book and makes me incredibly happy. I only hope more young men and women do the same. I get calls from a lot of my friends in prison to this day. I still have a lot of respect for my friends, as they do for me, even though I am no longer in *the life*. Trust me, doing time is just that, doing time, and it's a waste of time.

I handle all my own social media, and I answer almost all of the messages I get, which are countless. I do this because I'm up normally by 4:00 a.m. make coffee, and then I begin my work. Of course, I get some nasty ones, which do not bother me, as I learned long ago that not everyone will love me. I answer them nicely and say, "Thank you, I appreciate that. Did you read my book?"

Since the first release of my book in November 2019, my life has changed, but all for the better. I only hope and pray I can continue to do good for many more people around the world. I will try to make this world a better place any way I can. I believe we are all brothers and sisters, and we can do it. So, let us all join hands, and we can do it together.

I'd like to personally thank the production team of *The Accidental Gangster*. Writers and producers, David Steenhoek and my son Anthony Spado. Directors and producers, George Gallo and Nick Vallelonga.

A very special thank you to my dear friend and the best entertainment lawyer in Hollywood George Hayum for being there every step of the way. From the bottom of my heart I can't begin to say how thankful I am.

God bless everyone and all my love and respect.

Ori Spado
Beverly Hills, California

APPENDIX

All documents and pictures in this book can also be viewed at *www.theaccidentalgangster.com*

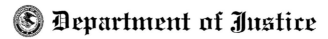

Department of Justice

U.S. Department of Justice
United States Attorney
Eastern District of New York

271 Cadman Plaza East
Brooklyn, New York 11201
Wednesday, June 4, 2008

FOR IMMEDIATE RELEASE
Contact:
Robert Nardoza
United States Attorney's Office
(718) 254-6323

PRESS RELEASE

COLOMBO ORGANIZED CRIME FAMILY ACTING BOSS, UNDERBOSS, AND TEN OTHER MEMBERS AND ASSOCIATES INDICTED

Charges Include Racketeering, Conspiracy, Robbery, Extortion, Narcotics Trafficking and Loansharking

BROOKLYN, NY – A seventeen-count superseding indictment charging twelve defendants – including Thomas Gioeli, the acting boss of the Colombo organized crime family of La Cosa Nostra (the "Colombo family"), John "Sonny" Franzese, the Colombo family underboss, and ten additional Colombo family members and associates – was unsealed today in federal court in Brooklyn. The indictment charges racketeering conspiracy, robbery, extortion, narcotics trafficking, and loansharking. The charged racketeering predicate acts include, among others, four acts of murder, murder conspiracy, and felony murder.

The charges were announced by Benton J. Campbell, United States Attorney for the Eastern District of New York, Kathleen M. Rice, Nassau County District Attorney, and Mark J. Mershon, Assistant Director-in-Charge, Federal Bureau of Investigation, New York Field Division.

The defendants arrested in New York today are scheduled to be arraigned later today before United States Magistrate Judge Cheryl L. Pollak at the U.S. Courthouse in Brooklyn. Colombo family underboss John "Sonny" Franzese is currently incarcerated based on a violation of supervised release following his prior conviction in the Eastern District of New York. Colombo family associate Nicholas Bova is currently incarcerated based on a New York State conviction, and Colombo family associate Christopher Curanovic is currently incarcerated pending trial on the underlying indictment in the Eastern District of New York. The case has been assigned to United States District Judge Nina Gershon.

According to the indictment and a detention memorandum filed by the government today, the charges are the product of a three-year investigation into the illegal activities of the Colombo family. The broad scope of the investigation includes historical acts of murder by the Colombo family as well as more recent criminal activity. The evidence relating to many of the charged crimes consists of hundreds of hours of recorded conversations secured by multiple cooperating witnesses who infiltrated the Colombo family. Those indicted today include Thomas Gioeli, 55; John "Sonny" Franzese, 89; Dino Calabro, 41; Michael Catapano, 42; Frank Campione, 65; Joseph " Joey Caves" Competiello; 36; Joseph Digorga, 67; Orlando Spado, 63; Angelo Giangrande, 55; John Capolino, 39; Nicholas Bova, 31; and Christopher Curanovic, 26.

The indictment and detention memorandum document the Colombo family's brazen use of violence – including murder – to earn money, seek revenge, and obstruct justice, including:

The Felony Murder of Carlos Pagan. Colombo family captain Dino Calabro is charged with the January 9, 1992, armed robbery and felony murder of Carlos Pagan. Pagan, an armored truck guard, was shot and killed during a botched effort by Calabro and others to rob Pagan as he and a co-worker were delivering money to a check-cashing store in Brooklyn.
The Murders of John Minerva and Michael Imbergamo. Colombo family acting boss Thomas Gioeli and captain Dino Calabro are charged with the March 25, 1992, double murder of Colombo family soldier John Minerva and Minerva's friend, Michael Imbergamo. Minerva was murdered as part of the bloody Colombo family war, which pitted two factions of the Colombo family against each other in a violent struggle for control of the family. Imbergamo was not a target of the murder, but was killed because he was with Minerva at the time of the attack. Colombo captains Joseph "JoJo" Russo and Anthony "Chucky" Russo and soldier Joseph Monteleone were previously convicted in the Eastern District of New York for their participation in this double

murder.

The Murder of Frank Marasa. Acting Colombo family boss Thomas Gioeli, captain Dino Calabro, and soldier Joseph " Joey Caves" Competiello are charged with the 1991 murder of Frank Marasa. On June 12, 1991, Marasa was shot multiple times outside his home in Brooklyn in retaliation for his perceived involvement in the murder of a Colombo family associate.

"The charges announced today are part of our Office's relentless campaign to prosecute and convict the highest echelons of the Colombo family, and La Cosa Nostra as a whole, including the late 2007 conviction after trial of former Colombo acting boss Alphonse Persico, Jr., and former Colombo acting underboss John DeRoss, on murder and witness tampering charges," stated United States Attorney Campbell. "The message could not be any clearer – we will not rest until the violent scourge of organized crime is eliminated." Mr. Campbell thanked the Nassau County Police Department, the New York City Police Department, the Drug Enforcement Administration, and the Department of Labor for their cooperation and assistance in the investigation.

"We will continue to root out organized crime and sever its tentacles on Long Island," said Nassau County District Attorney Rice. "We need multi-jurisdictional effort when it comes to taking on the hierarchy of these operations. These characters live and work in New York City and on Long Island so we have to be willing to cross borders to bring them to justice."

FBI Assistant Director-in-Charge Mershon stated, "Our most powerful strategy in countering organized crime families is to effect a vertical takedown of the organization. The very serious charges announced today hold accountable the leadership, mid-management, soldiers, and associates who constitute a key component of the Colombo family."

If convicted, defendants Thomas Gioeli, Dino Calabro, Joseph " Joey Caves" Competiello, Orlando Spado, and Christopher Curanovic face life imprisonment. Defendant Michael Catapano faces 40 years' imprisonment, and defendants John "Sonny" Franzese, Frank Campione, Joseph DiGorga, Angelo Giangrande, and John Capolino face 20 years' imprisonment. Defendant Nicholas Bova faces five years' imprisonment.

The government's case is being prosecuted by Assistant United States Attorneys Elizabeth Geddes and James Gatta, and by Special Assistant United States Attorney Doug Leff. The original underlying indictment charged Colombo family associate Christopher Curanovic with robbery and firearms possession. The charges in the original indictment and the superseding indictment are merely allegations, and the defendants are presumed innocent unless and until proven guilty.

APPENDIX

Greetings Clerk of Courts

Enclosed please find copies of my motion/affidavit to be filed in my case. U.S. V Spado. CRIMINAL ACTION #1:08-CR-00240

I have enclosed an additional copy requesting to be stamped as well as a copy of the docket sheet reflecting the enclosed filing.

Thank you
Respectfully Yours
Orlando "Ori" Spado

I want this on my record to preserve my rights + would also like to become part of the court record.

4/15/10

IN CLERK'S OFFICE
U.S. DISTRICT COURT E.D.N.Y
★ APR 20 2010 ★
BROOKLYN OFFICE

HON. BRIAN M. C___
APR 21 2010

ADDENDUM TO MOTION

AUGUST 9th 2006 - CD # 84

AT 48:35
FATATO - "I'M GOING TO PUT A PISTOL IN HIS MOUTH WHEN HE COMES IN"
HE'S GOTTA GO

FILED
IN CLERK'S OFFICE
U.S. DISTRICT COURT E.D.N.Y
★ APR 20 2010 ★
BROOKLYN OFFICE

381

1

FILED
IN CLERK'S OFFICE
U.S. DISTRICT COURT E.D.N.Y

★ APR 2 0 2010 ★

BROOKLYN OFFICE

2

3

4   UNITED STATES DISTRICT COURT

5   EASTERN DISTRICT OF NEW YORK

6   BROOKLYN, NEW YORK

7

UNITED STATES OF AMERICA,)	CRIMINAL ACTION I408-CR-0024
Plaintiff,)	**AFFIDAVIT IN SUPPORT OF MOTION TO DISMISS**
v.)	
)	Date:
ORLANDO SPADO,)	Time:
Defendant/Petitioner.)	Court: Hon. Brian M. Cogan
)	USDJ/EDNY

8

9

10

11

12

13

14   DEFENDANT SPADO'S AFFIDAVIT IN SUPPORT OF HIS MOTION TO DISMISS

15 BECAUSE OF EGREGIOUS, GROSS GOVERNMENTAL MISCONDUCT REQUESTING THAT

16 THIS HONORABLE COURT INVOKE ITS INHERENT SUPERVISORY POWERS TO DISMISS

17 THIS CASE.

18   Comes now, defendant ORLANDO SPADO, hereinafter referred to as "Spado" via Pro Per

19 in Propia Persona Proceeding Sui Juris in the above captioned case and Titled Motion Claim

20 Affidavit

21   AFFIDAVIT OF SPADO VIA FRCP RULE 56(F)

22   1.   On April 14, 2006 according to government witnesses, informants and others

23   instigated and fomented violence and conspired to murder defendant Spado. (Note:

24   Defendant Spado was not warned by the FBI or AUSA Elizabeth Geddes, James

25   Gatta, Rachel Nash, all representatives of the Department of Justice including FBI

26   Agents D'Agostino and Liwicke.)

27

28   2.   Moreover, additional governmental tapes as follows supports that the government

1

1 and its prized informants both known and unknown did instigate and foment
2 violence, more specifically the plan to murder defendant Spado and extort defendant
3 Spado. (See 05/04/06 CD#67, 06/03/06 CD#75, 06/24/06 CD#81, 08/09/06 CD#84.)

4

5 08/09/06: Guy Fatato, "I will crack him when he comes in." Referring to Spado.
6 Catapano, "If the drug deal don't happen then Ori (Spado) has to go." He also says,
7 "If his uncle (Sonny Franzese) dies, then Ori (Spado) will die."

8

9 Please note that the above FBI/AUSA?Department of Justice tapes also supports that
10 FBI informants and others both known and unknown did in fact try and or plan to
11 extort, kidnap and kill defendant Spado. See US v. Salemme 91F Supp 2d 141
12 (D.Mass.1999). Chief Judge Mark L. Wolf USDJ D.Mass Boston Quintessence
13 governmental misconduct.

14

15 3. Defendant Spado also requests an order of this Honorable Court to order the
16 government to hand over ALL exculpatory material Brady Evidence Discovery which
17 supports the above egregious quintessence misconduct, including all FBI FD 302's
18 and FBI FD 209's, longs, files, tapes, emails and notes. See Brady v. Maryland 373
19 US83,87 (1963) Fed.R.Crim.P Rule 16 and via the local rules of the US District
20 Court, Eastern District of New York.

21 4. Note: Another government witness who appears to be handled by FBI agents
22 D'Agostino and Liwicke, Kenny Kanecko, AKA Kenny Gallo, facilitated an
23 international website depicted under HOLLYWOODMAFIA.COM and YOUTUBE
24 which he states that Spado is a rat for the FBI, he also mailed tapes to friends of
25 mine, showed pictures of my residence and its address, not only putting Spado's life
26 in danger, but also his family's. In addition, he wrote a book of lies about Spado and
27 others. As a result of this negative writing he damaged many of Spado's business
28 opportunities and connections. Kanecko/Gallo absolutely attempted violence while

2

1 under FBI supervision to instigate and foment violence, in the form of unlawful cyber
2 internet communications. All this discovery is also requested. Attachments
3 forthcoming or to to YOUTUBE or HOLLYWOODMAFIA.COM.

4
5   CONCLUSION
6   Wherefore, for all the above stated reasons, Spado requests an evidentiary hearing concerning
7 all the above outrageous misconduct.
8   I declare under penalty of perjury that the foregoing is true and correct, except as to those
9 matters stated on information and belief, and as to those matters I believe them to be true.
10 Dated: 4/15/10   Respectfully Submitted,
11
12
13
14   ORLANDO SPADO,
                                   Defendant/Petitioner/Affiant
15   Pro Per in Propia Persona Proceeding Sui Juris
                                   00989-052 MDC-BROOKLYN
16   PO BOX 329002
                                   BROOKLYN, NY 11232
17
18
19
20
21
22
23
24
25
26
27
28

                                3

APPENDIX

CERTIFICATE OF SERVICE

2   I, defendant Orlando Spado, hereby certify that this AFFIDAVIT/MOTION/CLAIM was sent

3 via United States mail, postage prepaid on this ___15___ day of April 2010 to the following:

4

5 Clerk of Court   AUSA Rachel Nash
    Clerks Office   James Gatta
6 US District Court   US Attorney's Office
    E.D. of New York   E.D. of New York
7 225 Cadman Plaza East   271 Cadman Plaza East
    Brooklyn, NY 11201   Brooklyn, NY 11201
8

9   Signed under penalties of perjury.

10

11   ORLANDO SPADO,
                              Defendant/Petitioner/Affiant
12   Pro Per in Propia Persona Proceeding Sui Juris
                              00989-052 MDC-BROOKLYN
13   PO BOX 329002
                              BROOKLYN, NY 11232

14

15

16

17

18

19

20

21

22

23

24

25

26

27

28

4

1

```
 1                    UNITED STATES DISTRICT COURT
                     EASTERN DISTRICT OF NEW YORK
 2
     - - - - - - - - - - - - - - - - - X
 3
     UNITED STATES OF AMERICA,      :        08-CR-240
 4
                   v.               :        U.S. Courthouse
 5                                            Brooklyn, New York
     ORLANDO SPADO,                 :
 6                                            September 7, 2010
                        Defendant. :         9:45 o'clock a.m.
 7
     - - - - - - - - - - - - - - - - - X
 8
 9                      TRANSCRIPT OF SENTENCE
                     BEFORE THE HONORABLE BRIAN M. COGAN
10                   UNITED STATES DISTRICT JUDGE

11
     APPEARANCES:
12
     For the Government:            LORETTA E. LYNCH
13                                  United States Attorney
                                    By:  CRISTINA POSA
14                                  Assistant U.S. Attorney
                                    225 Cadman Plaza East
15                                  Brooklyn, New York 11201

16   For the Defendant:            KELLEY SHARKEY, ESQ.

17

18   Court Reporter:               Anthony M. Mancuso
                                    225 Cadman Plaza East
19                                  Brooklyn, New York 11201
                                    (718) 613-2419
20

21

22

23   Proceedings recorded by mechanical stenography, transcript
     produced by CAT.
24

25
```

18

1 straight there's a high risk that people they don't intend to
2 get shot get shot. It was purely fortuitous that no one got
3 hurt in this attempted robbery. When you bring in somebody
4 like Mr. Curanovic, it's just a wild card. There's no telling
5 what's going to happen. I think Mr. Spado is clearly a pretty
6 intelligent guy. I think he understood those risks. He just
7 really didn't care about those risks. He just wanted to get
8 the money at the expense of all else.
9   The second fact that stands out for me is
10 Mr. Spado's history and characteristics. There's really a lot
11 in this that cuts both ways. First, forgetting about the
12 racketeering conspiracy or the cocaine conspiracy, it comes
13 through pretty clearly that he does not have a lot of respect
14 for the law. That's illustrated by a lot of the life that
15 he's led. It's also shown by his association with Sonny
16 Franzese. I know his daughter Gina thought that was just a
17 social relationship. But I don't know if Sonny Franzese had
18 many, if any, pure social relationships. I don't think this
19 was one of them.
20   I think the letters from his family and friends make
21 it clear that Mr. Spado is one of these people I see from time
22 to time in organized crime cases where they have both a
23 terrible criminal side and yet a lot of redeeming value. His
24 friends and his family clearly really love him. That comes
25 through very inescapably from the letters. The letters I

ANTHONY M. MANCUSO, CSR OFFICIAL COURT REPORTER

19

thought were quite useful in showing me the character of the man. It's kind of like have having to sentence two different people.

But for sentencing purposes I have to focus on the criminal side because that's what has pervasive social consequences. I will temper that sentence in recognition that this is not a person who has never made any contribution to society. His family relationships prevent me from seeing him entirely that way.

APPENDIX

AB:RJN
F. #2005R00248

UNITED STATES DISTRICT COURT
EASTERN DISTRICT OF NEW YORK

- - - - - - - - - - - - - - - X

UNITED STATES OF AMERICA

   - against -

ORLANDO SPADO,

           Defendant.

- - - - - - - - - - - - - - - X

<u>PLEA AGREEMENT</u>

08 CR 240 (S-5)(BMC)

       Pursuant to Rule 11 of the Federal Rules of Criminal Procedure, the United States Attorney's Office for the Eastern District of New York (the "Office") and Orlando Spado (the "defendant") agree to the following:

       1.   The defendant will plead guilty to Counts Eight and Nine of the above-captioned indictment, charging violations of 18 U.S.C. §§ 1951(a) and 924(c).

These counts carry the following statutory penalties:

<u>Count Eight: Hobbs Act Conspiracy</u>

        a.   Maximum term of imprisonment: 20 years (18 U.S.C. § 1951(a)).

        b.   Minimum term of imprisonment: 0 years (18 U.S.C. § 1951(a)).

        c.   Maximum supervised release term: 3 years, to follow any term of imprisonment; if a condition of release is violated, the defendant may be sentenced to up to 2 years without credit for pre-release imprisonment or time previously served on post-release supervision (18 U.S.C. § 3583(b), (e)).

389

d. Maximum fine: the greater of $250,000, twice the pecuniary gain or twice the pecuniary loss (18 U.S.C. §§ 3571(b)(3), (d)).

e. Restitution: to be determined by the Court (18 U.S.C. §§ 3663, 3663A).

f. $100 special assessment (18 U.S.C. § 3013).

Count Nine: Use of a Firearm in a Crime of Violence

a. Maximum term of imprisonment: Life (18 U.S.C. § 924(c)(1)(C)(i)).

b. Minimum term of imprisonment: 5 years (18 U.S.C. § 924(c)(1)(C)(i))._____

c. Maximum supervised release term: 5 years, to follow any term of imprisonment; if a condition of release is violated, the defendant may be sentenced to up to 5 years without credit for pre-release imprisonment or time previously served on post-release supervision. (18 U.S.C. § 3583(b), (e)).

d. Maximum fine: $250,000 (18 U.S.C. § 3571(b)(3)).

e. Restitution: N/A (18 U.S.C. § 3663).

f. $100 special assessment (18 U.S.C. § 3013).

The sentence imposed on Count Nine must run consecutively to the sentence imposed on Count Eight.

2. The defendant understands that although imposition of a sentence in accordance with the United States Sentencing Guidelines (the "Guidelines") is not mandatory, the Guidelines are advisory and the Court is required to consider any applicable

APPENDIX

Guidelines provisions as well as other factors enumerated in 18 U.S.C. § 3553(a) to arrive at an appropriate sentence in this case. The Office will advise the Court and the Probation Department of information relevant to sentencing, including criminal activity engaged in by the defendant, and such information may be used by the Court in determining the defendant's sentence. The Office estimates the likely adjusted offense level under the Guidelines to be level 20, which is predicated on the following Guidelines calculation:

Count Eight - Hobbs Act Robbery Conspiracy

Base Offense Level (§2B3.1(a))	20
Plus: Managerial Role (§3B1.1(c))	+2
Less: Acceptance of responsibility (§3E1.1(a))	-2
Total:	20

This level carries a range of imprisonment of 33 to 41 months, assuming that the defendant falls in Criminal History Category One. The statutory minimum term of imprisonment on Count Nine is five years (60 months). Therefore, the effective Guidelines range is 93 to 101 months' imprisonment. If the defendant pleads guilty on or before July 20, 2010, the government will move the Court, pursuant to U.S.S.G. § 3E1.1(b), for an additional one-level reduction, resulting in an adjusted offense level of 19. This level carries a range of imprisonment of 30 to 37 months, assuming that the defendant falls in Criminal History Category One. The resulting Guidelines range is 90 to 97 months' imprisonment.

3. The Guidelines estimate set forth in paragraph 2 is not binding on the Office, the Probation Department or the Court. If the Guidelines offense level advocated by the Office, or determined by the Probation Department or the Court, is, for any reason, including an error in the estimate, different from the estimate, the defendant will not be entitled to withdraw the plea and the government will not be deemed to have breached this agreement.

4. The defendant agrees not to file an appeal or otherwise challenge, by petition pursuant to 28 U.S.C. § 2255 or any other provision, the conviction or sentence in the event that the Court imposes a term of imprisonment of 101 months or below. This waiver is binding without regard to the sentencing analysis used by the Court. The defendant waives all defenses based on the statute of limitations and venue with respect to any prosecution that is not time-barred on the date that this agreement is signed in the event that (a) the defendant's conviction is later vacated for any reason, (b) the defendant violates this agreement, or (c) the defendant's plea is later withdrawn. The defendant waives any right to additional disclosure from the government in connection with the guilty plea. The defendant agrees that with respect to all charges referred to in paragraphs 1 and 5(a) he is not a

"prevailing party" within the meaning of the "Hyde Amendment," 18

U.S.C. § 3006A note, and will not file any claim under that law.

The defendant agrees to pay the special assessment by check payable

to the Clerk of the Court at or before sentencing.

     5.   The Office agrees that:

          a. no further criminal charges will be brought against the defendant for his participation in (i) the conspiracy to rob an individual in Los Angeles, California between January 2006 and May 2006, as charged in Count Eight; (ii) the use, carrying and possession of a firearm in connection with the robbery conspiracy in May 2006, as charged in Count Nine; and (iii) the conspiracy to distribute and to possess with intent to distribute cocaine between May 2006 and June 2006, as charged in Count Ten, it being understood that this agreement does not bar the use of such conduct as a predicate act or as the basis for a sentencing enhancement in a subsequent prosecution including, but not limited to, a prosecution pursuant to 18 U.S.C. §§ 1961 et seq., and at the time of sentence, it will move to dismiss the remaining counts of the indictment and the underlying indictments with prejudice;

and, based upon information now known to the Office, it will

          b. take no position concerning where within the Guidelines range determined by the Court the sentence should fall; and

          c. make no motion for an upward departure under the Sentencing Guidelines.

If information relevant to sentencing, as determined by the Office,

becomes known to the Office after the date of this agreement, the

Office will not be bound by paragraphs 5(b) and 5(c). Should it be

judged by the Office that the defendant has violated any provision

6

of this agreement, the defendant will not be released from his plea of guilty but this Office will be released from its obligations under this agreement, including but not limited to: (a) moving for the additional one-level downward adjustment for timely acceptance of responsibility described in paragraph 2 above; and (b) the provisions of paragraph 5 (a)-(c).

6. This agreement does not bind any federal, state, or local prosecuting authority other than the Office, and does not prohibit the Office from initiating or prosecuting any civil or administrative proceedings directly or indirectly involving the defendant.

7. No promises, agreements or conditions have been entered into by the parties other than those set forth in this agreement and none will be entered into unless memorialized in writing and signed by all parties. This agreement supersedes all prior promises, agreements or conditions between the parties. To

APPENDIX

become effective, this agreement must be signed by all signatories listed below.

Dated: Brooklyn, New York
           July __, 2010

                              LORETTA E. LYNCH
                              United States Attorney
                              Eastern District of New York

                    By: _____
                              Rachel J. Nash
                              Assistant United States Attorney

                    Approved by:

_____   _____
                              Amy Busa
                              Supervising Assistant U.S. Attorney

I have read the entire agreement and discussed it with my attorney. I understand all of its terms and am entering into it knowingly and voluntarily.

_____
Orlando Spado
Defendant

Approved by:

_____
Kelley Sharkey, Esq.
Counsel to Defendant

UNITED STATES DISTRICT COURT
CENTRAL DISTRICT OF CALIFORNIA PROBATION OFFICE
November 30, 2016

Michelle A. Carey   Douglas B. Bys
Chief U.S. Probation Officer   Deputy Chief U.S. Probation Officer

<u>CLOSING LETTER</u>

Orlando Spado
317 South Rexford Drive. #307
Beverly Hills. CA 90212

Dear Mr. Spado:

Effective **11/29/2016,** your term of supervised release was terminated. As such, your obligations with the United States Probation Office have terminated.

I wish good fortune for you and your family in future endeavors. Feel free to contact me if you have any questions.

Respectfully,

FOR

JEANIE BLODGETT
U.S. Probation Officer
Telephone No. (213) 894-3628

INDEX

C
Courtney, Dave, 277, 361
Crabbe, Red, 78
Curanovic, Chris, 310, 316, 329, 335

D
Dacquino, Joey, 126, 127, 128
Daly, John, 183, 334, 360, 362, 372, 377, 378
Damone, Vic, 56
De Laurentiis, Dino, 58, 62, 88, 178, 181
DeMare, Jim "Jimmy", 44, 48, 62, 69
DeMare, Tom "Tommy", 80, 209
Dente, Joe, 161, 209, 300, 355
DePalma, Greg, 223, 226, 228
Digorga, Joseph, 316, 335
Dion, Celine, 156

E
Egger, Bob, 51, 57

F
Falk, Peter, 59
Fatato, Gaetano "Guy", xvi, 294 - 297, 310, 327, 332
Fiveson, Walter, 54, 61, 75, 112, 115, 222, 225, 265
Flansburg, Scott, 172
Florio, Danny, 281
Foreman, Freddie "Brown Bread Fred", 277
Fortini, Orlando, 45, 48
Franzese, Johnny, xvi, 249, 271, 294, 297
Franzese, Michael, 99, 262
Franzese, Sonny, xiii, 75, 78, 89, 93, 135, 179, 206, 316, 326, 332, 335, 347, 352, 355, 377
Franzese, Tina, 78, 79, 100, 157, 210, 211, 271, 272, 273, 275, 348, 353

G
Gambino, Carlo, 484
Gambino, Tommy, 48
Garcia, Jack, 229
Gardner, Eddie, 142
Gasperini, Bill, 224, 226, 227
Generilli, Jim, 85, 86, 89, 93
Giangrande, Angelo, 316
Ginsberg, Seth, 325, 330

INDEX